Faulkner and Wome

FAULKNER AND YOKNAPATAWPHA
1985

Faulkner and Women

FAULKNER AND YOKNAPATAWPHA, 1985

EDITED BY
DOREEN FOWLER
AND
ANN J. ABADIE

UNIVERSITY PRESS OF MISSISSIPPI
Jackson and London

*This book has been sponsored by the University of Mississippi's
Center for the Study of Southern Culture*

*The paper in this book meets the guidelines for permanence and durability of
the Committee on Production Guidelines for Book Longevity of the Council
on Library Resources.*

Library of Congress Cataloging-in-Publication Data

Faulkner and Yoknapatawpha Conference (12th : 1985 :
    University of Mississippi)
    Faulkner and women.

    Papers presented at the 12th annual Faulkner and
Yoknapatawpha Conference at the Oxford campus of the
University of Mississippi, 1985.
    Bibliography: p.
    Includes index.
    1. Faulkner, William, 1897–1962—Characters—Women—
Congresses.   2. Women in literature—Congresses.
I. Fowler, Doreen.   II. Abadie, Ann J.   III. Title.
PS3511.A86Z7832113   1985   813'.52   86-11054
ISBN 0-87805-311-5 (alk. paper)
ISBN 0-87805-312-3 (pbk. : alk. paper)

Contents

Introduction

This much is certain: "Faulkner and Women" is a provocative topic, which over the past decades has generated considerable and lively critical debate. Two full-length studies focus solely on the theme—Sally Page's groundbreaking work, *Faulkner's Women: Characterization and Meaning* (1972), and David Williams's mythic approach, *Faulkner's Women: The Myth and the Muse* (1977); and a recently published bibliography, Patricia Sweeney's *William Faulkner's Women Characters: An Annotated Bibliography of the Criticism, 1930–1983* (1985), cites some 500 relevant books and essays. Widespread interest in the conjunctive subject is also substantiated by two events which took place in 1985: in March, in response to a call for papers on the topic "Faulkner and Women," the annual Faulkner and Yoknapatawpha Conference received eighty-four submissions—almost double the number of essays submitted the previous year, and in December the annual meeting of the Modern Language Association included a special session, "Gender and Sexuality in Faulkner's Fiction."

While the subject of Faulkner in relation to women has elicited a welcome outpouring of critical enthusiasm, so complex and problematic is this field of inquiry that as yet there has been little consensus on the most fundamental questions. Even the issue of Faulkner's attitude toward women is heatedly contested by critics. For example, while some scholars, among them Linda Wagner and Cleanth Brooks, praise Faulkner's sympathetic portrayals of women characters, others, like Leslie Fiedler, Albert Guerard, and Irving Howe, locate a deep-seated strain of misogyny in Faulkner's fiction.

The allegation of misogyny, which was first levelled in the 1940s by Maxwell Geismar and which has been echoed repeatedly since then, is particularly troubling because it is apparently so difficult to dismiss completely. If we turn to Faulkner's own public statements about women to refute the claim, we find as much evidence to support as to deny misogyny. For example, in an unpublished class conference at the University of Virginia in 1957, Faulkner stated "I think women are wonderful. They're stronger than men." (It is interesting to note parenthetically here that in *Go Down, Moses* Ike McCaslin uses a similar phrase to praise blacks: "[They're] stronger than we are" [Modern Library, 294], Ike says.) But, throughout his life, Faulkner was also as likely to assert, as he did in a 1926 letter to Anita Loos, that "I am still rather Victorian in my prejudices regarding the intelligence of women."

When we examine the fiction to assess the charge of misogyny, there too the evidence appears to be contradictory. On the one hand, it is true that Faulkner presents a variety of distinctive women (as Linda Wagner argues),[1] and that often Faulkner's women embody the endurance and indomitability which he extolled in the Nobel Prize address (as Mimi Gladstein contends in her essay in this volume). On the other hand, however, many of Faulkner's women characters—most notably, Lena Grove, Eula Varner, and the unnamed woman in "Old Man"—seem to lack the intellectual awareness that typically characterizes Faulkner's male characters. There are, of course, exceptions to this rule of female dullness, but the exceptions seem to fall into one of two categories. Introspective women in Faulkner's fiction either strikingly resemble their male counterparts, thus reinforcing the equation of cerebration with masculinity (examples are Addie Bundren, Joanna Burden, Drusilla Hawk, and Charlotte Rittenmeyer) or, like Aunt Jenny Du Pre and Miss Rosa Millard, they are elderly ladies safely past the age of sexual desire and desirability. Where in Faulkner's fiction do we find a woman who is young, sexual, unashamedly feminine, and also capable of ratiocination? Possibly Linda Snopes Kohl embodies these qualities, and Linda may embody as well Faulkner's last thoughts on the subject of women.

These and other knotty problems are taken up in the essays in this volume which were originally delivered in the summer of 1985 on the Oxford campus of the University of Mississippi at the Twelfth Annual Faulkner and Yoknapatawpha Conference. The essays have been arranged in this volume in five groups: the first group of three papers introduces some of the diverse and wide-ranging areas of inquiry (e.g., feminism, sexism) which the subject "Faulkner and Women" invites; there follow three examinations of the narrative strategies Faulkner typically applies to women characters; next are five studies which explicate the conference theme in a specific novel, followed by three essays which consider woman-related issues in the short fiction; finally, the volume concludes with companion pieces—a discussion of "Faulkner and Women Writers" which is paired with Toni Morrison's remarks on William Faulkner.

In the first of three introductory essays, Joseph Blotner, Faulkner's friend and biographer, approaches the conference theme by way of Faulkner's life and attempts to locate "real life models for some of Faulkner's fictional women." While cautioning that Faulkner imitated other fiction as often as he imitated life, Blotner observes intriguing correspondences between Estelle Faulkner and characters like Cecily Saunders, Belle Mitchell, and Temple Drake; between Helen Baird and Charlotte Rittenmeyer; and between Joan Williams and Linda Snopes Kohl. These biographical speculations are followed by a discussion of feminism and its application to Faulkner's work. In "The Mutual Relevance of Faulkner Studies and Women's Studies," Ilse Lind argues that Faulkner and feminism are not, as has been sometimes thought, mutually exclusive categories, but instead mutually interactive. To illustrate her thesis, Lind cites three recent, important works in women's studies, Myra Jehlen's "Archimedes and the Paradox of Feminist Criticism," Anne Goodwyn Jones's *Tomorrow Is Another Day*, and Nancy Chodorow's *The Reproduction of Mothering*, and demonstrates how these works productively interrelate with Faulkner's fiction. Closely related to Lind's subject, feminism, is the issue of sexism, which John Duvall broaches in his paper, "Faulkner's Critics and Women: The Voice of the Community." After carefully analyzing the interpretive discourse of Faulkner's critics, Duvall asserts that scholars often "appropriate the voice of the Southern community" in Faulkner's fiction, leaving themselves liable to the charge of sexism.

The three subsequent studies all focus on the narrative strategies Faulkner typically employs to render women. For example, Soviet scholar Sergei Chakovsky observes the persistent presence of the epicene woman as well as the repeated pairing of male and female characters in the fiction and attributes these narratives practices to Faulkner's recognition of androgyny—humanity's lost, but never forgotten, state of oneness. Another essay which considers the narrative deployment of women in Faulkner's texts is Philip Weinstein's "Meditations on the Other: Faulkner's Rendering of Women." Taking examples from a broad spectrum of novels including *The Sound and the Fury, Light in August, Absalom, Absalom!*, and *Go Down, Moses*, Weinstein compares the way women are narratively presented with the way men are and finds that "women exist in a significantly different relation to the narrative voice" than do men. Whereas men are perceived as understandable phenomena, women are "marvels to be wondered at." The third essay in this grouping analyzes a particular technique that Faulkner repeatedly uses to portray women—the mythic method. In "Mothers and Daughters in Endless Procession: Faulkner's Use of the Demeter/Persephone Myth," Mimi Gladstein finds three pairs of mothers and daughters in the fiction who conform to the classical archetype of grieving mother and ravaged daughter: Caddy and Quentin Compson, Addie and Dewey Dell Bundren, and Eula and Linda Snopes. Concluding her remarks, Gladstein proposes that through his use of this mythic paradigm Faulkner communicates his most optimistic message: "the endless renewal of the Eternal Feminine" as well as "his sense of female strength and endurance."

Each of the five subsequent essayists confines his/her remarks to the exposition of the theme "Faulkner and Women" in a single text. For example, in "Desire and Despair: Temple Drake's Self-Victimization," Robert Moore focuses on *Sanctuary* and Temple Drake's rapid transition from Ole Miss coed to "fallen woman," a transformation which has often been singled out by critics as a characteristic manifestation of Faulkner's misogynistic vision. Moore counters this interpretation with his premise that Temple's corruption is not meant to signal innate female depravity but rather is intended to suggest "the process by which evil begets evil" and "victim becomes victimizer." "Temple's unexpected perjury at Lee Goodwin's trial," Moore contends, "is the key to understanding Faulkner's vision of evil." Like *Sanctuary*, *Light in August* is another novel which often has been identified as exemplifying Faulkner's woman-hatred. Two critics, André Bleikasten and Doreen Fowler, address some of the woman-related issues raised by this text. In his paper, "In Praise of Helen," Bleikasten considers the characterization of Lena Grove, who has often been cited as one of Faulkner's "bovine," "mindless" females.[2] Bleikasten offers another interpretation: Lena is a mythic figure, "a new avatar of the primal mother, an earth goddess." But like nature itself, this mother-god has two sides: she embodies both a "lost world of innocence and wholeness" as well as "the dark chaos from which all life springs and to which all life returns." While the focus of Bleikasten's discussion is Lena Grove, the subject of Doreen Fowler's study is Joe Christmas, one of Faulkner's fiercest misogynists. In "Joe Christmas and 'Womanshenegro,'" Fowler explores the causes of Christmas's misogyny and finds that his hatred of women is closely linked to his hatred of blacks and that both derive from the same source: a fear and rejection of the mild qualities in his own nature that ally him with women and blacks—a fear of his own identification with "womanshenegro." Another text which poses perplexing questions about women is *The Unvanquished*, Faulkner's novel about war and women. In "Faulkner and Womankind—'No Bloody Moon,'" Winifred Frazer explicates a single phrase, Aunt Jenny's cryptic expression, "No bloody moon," which seems to turn Bayard away from a cycle of vengeance. Frazer's explication leads to a general discussion of the significance for Faulkner of the feminine element of blood. The last text treated in a full-length study is *A Fable*, the novel which Faulkner labored over for almost a decade and which he sometimes referred to as his "magnum o." Concluding a close textual analysis of the religious allegory, Noel Polk opines that *A Fable* depicts "a military world which not only seeks to escape the feminine but also actively fights back, if not at the feminine itself, then at least at certain symbols of femininity which linger around the battlefield."

In the following three essays woman-related issues are examined in Faulkner's most frequently overlooked texts—the short fiction. In "Woman and the Making of the New World: Faulkner's Short Stories," Soviet scholar Alexandre Vashchenko analyzes three stories, "A Courtship," "Mountain Victory," and "Delta Autumn," which deal with critical turning points in American history. In each of these texts, Vashchenko contends, Faulkner investigates an important national development through the conflict between an individual man and woman. In a closely related essay, "Double Murder: The Women of Faulkner's 'Elly,'" Alice Hall Petry detects a similar pattern of meaning at work in an enigmatic story, "Elly." According to Petry, "Elly" should be read allegorically: the conflict between Elly and her grandmother represents the clash between the New South and the Old. Like Vashchenko, Petry shows how women function in Faulkner's texts as symbols of social change. The last essay to contribute a reading of the short fiction is Myriam Díaz-Diocaretz's "Faulkner's Hen-House: Woman as Bounded Text." Whereas Vashchenko's and Petry's concern is the relationship between women and history in the short stories, the Chilean poet, translator, and scholar, Díaz-Diocaretz, looks closely at Faulkner's semantics to see what structures are associated with women and finds that "women exist, in Faulkner's discourse, as hens, protected, surrounded by boundaries that act as fence and restrictions, creating confinement and shelter."

The collection closes with companion pieces: first, in "Faulkner and Women Writers," Judith Bryant Wittenberg attempts to assess the literary influence that women writers who preceded him may have had on Faulkner; then, in the course of answering questions from the audience, Toni Morrison discusses, among other subjects, the literary influence exerted upon her writing by William Faulkner.

While the papers collected in this volume comprise the substance of the Twelfth Annual Faulkner and Yoknapatawpha Conference, a word also should be said about the numerous special events which took place in conjunction with the conference. These events included a reading by Toni Morrison of her work-in-progress, "Beloved"; a presentation of *Voices from Yoknapatawpha;* a musical interpretation of Faulkner's work presented by composer David McKay; a slide show, "Knowing William Faulkner," narrated by Faulkner's nephew, J. M. Faulkner; a workshop, "Black Women in the Works of William Faulkner," conducted by Sister Thea Bowman; a discussion session led by Oxford residents who knew William Faulkner; guided tours of North Mississippi; exhibits of the University's Faulkner holdings, of art works portraying Southern women, and of books published by the University Press of Mississippi and other presses; a picnic served on the grounds of Rowan Oak, Faulkner's antebellum home; a buffet supper served on the grounds of Faulkner's childhood residence in Oxford; and a series of Faulkner films presented by the University's Communication and Resource Center.

In conclusion, the editors of this volume would like to thank all the individuals whose generous support makes possible the annual Faulkner and Yoknapatawpha Conference.

Doreen Fowler
The University of Mississippi
Oxford, Mississippi

NOTES

1. Linda Welshimer Wagner, "Faulkner and (Southern) Women," *The South and Faulkner's Yoknapatawpha,* ed. Evans Harrington and Ann J. Abadie (Jackson: University Press of Mississippi, 1977).

2. Leslie A. Fiedler, *Love and Death in the American Novel* (New York: Dell, 1969), 320.

Faulkner and Women
FAULKNER AND YOKNAPATAWPHA
1985

William Faulkner: Life and Art

Joseph Blotner

"I think women are wonderful. They're stronger than men."
WILLIAM FAULKNER
Unpublished class conference
The University of Virginia, 1957

In undertaking a study of Faulkner and women, this conference addresses a subject which is not only timely but one which has become a central concern in Faulkner studies. The first two doctoral dissertations I have been able to find on this subject were completed in 1969, and one of them, by Sally R. Page, was published in book form three years later.[1] A perusal of *Dissertation Abstracts International* reveals that there have been at least five more since then, and the most recent one listed, completed by Patricia E. Sweeney in 1983 and published in January of 1985, further suggests the extent to which studies in this area have proliferated; it is called *William Faulkner's Women Characters: An Annotated Bibliography of Criticism, 1930–1983*.[2] Thinking back to his remark which I quoted a moment ago, these bibliographical data may be both an affirmation and a portent. Women scholars have made distinguished contributions to Faulkner studies in increasing numbers in recent years, and I trust that the affinity of many of them for Faulkner will remain as they continue with the reshaping of the "canon" in American literature.

I would like to pursue the subject of Faulkner criticism by women just a bit further before I turn to the central focus of my talk: the relationship between women in Faulkner's life and in his art. I think, for instance, of women who have addressed various

3

facets of our topic, here, at previous Faulkner conferences. Ten years ago Elizabeth Kerr spoke on "The Women of Yoknapatawpha,"[3] and she continued her work in this area in subsequent books. I am fascinated by the quite natural diversity in the approaches of female critics. Ellen Douglas, concluding her talk entitled "Faulkner's Women," presented here in 1980, said "Quentin [Compson], of course, does hate the South that he loves and hates, just as Faulkner hates the South that he loves and hates, *as symbol,* the women who universally symbolize the South. Faulkner says to us that man is filled with fear and outrage and bafflement by women, that he blames them for his predicament, that he yearns for a world in which they are sinless and he is nobled, that his heart is filled both with the need for love and the aspiration toward perfection, with guilt and hatred for his own failures and the need to blame somebody else for his own predicament. In this sense, woman is wilderness, is South, is lost innocence, is failed and sinful humanity. Of course, Faulkner hates women. Of course, Quentin hates the South."[4]

In 1976 Linda Welshimer Wagner, concluding her talk entitled "Faulkner and (Southern) Women," argued that "if there is a pattern in Faulkner's characterization of women, it is that women are never to be stereotyped. Faulkner's women are uniformly unpredictable." And she concluded with this assertion: "I term Faulkner a feminist because he neither denied or disapproved that variety. Instead, he celebrated it, immortalizing it in some of his greatest fiction, and giving Western literature some of its most memorable women since Shakespeare."[5] A year later, with a similar title, "Faulkner's Women," but a different analysis, Ilse Dusoir Lind made a striking claim: *"Faulkner is the only major American fiction writer of the twenties and thirties who incorporates into his depiction of women the functioning of the organs of reproduction."* But she went beyond biology. She concluded, "What a probing of two of his medical sources here shows is that he was far more modern than we have allowed, far more audacious than we have perceived, far more reverential of human life as it manifests itself in woman than we have credited."[6]

Lest I be accused of female chauvinism in trying to demonstrate the range of this particular body of criticism, let me quote from one of the single most fascinating essays I know in this area, delivered here two years ago by Noel Polk, and entitled, "'The Dungeon Was Mother Herself': William Faulkner: 1927–1931." He focused on a female character who, he said, "is something of an epicenter in Faulkner's work of this period. If she is not in fact at the center of every rumble in the fictional soil of Yoknapatawpha, she is nevertheless at the point just above the disturbance, the point from which the disturbance emanates. She is one, but she is also many: she is often seen framed in windows looking out at the world passing by or at children playing in the yard; she is frequently bedridden, frequently invalid, and she is often seen juxtaposed against the pillow, her hair splayed out, Medusa-like, in grotesque parody of the sexuality she abhors, fears, and represses in herself and in others."[7] (Parenthetically, this analysis makes me think of one of those seven dissertations, a study that employs Jungian archetypes,[8] a partial demonstration of the range of method as well as the range of opinion to be encountered.)

We will have to be cautious in moving back and forth between the life and the work, in what we infer about each from the other. Meditating on the figure Professor Polk sees as so pervasive in Faulkner's work of those years, I think again about the quotation with which I began, or rather, about the question which elicited it. The questioner had asked William Faulkner if, as had been alleged, he was a misogynist. The answer he gave then makes me think of another, to a question about the genesis of *Light in August*. He replied, "that story began with Lena Grove, the idea of the young girl with nothing, pregnant, determined to find her sweetheart. It was—that was out of my admiration for women, for the courage and endurance of women. As I told that story I had to get more and more into it, but that was mainly the story of Lena Grove."[9]

As you have perhaps inferred, I would like to believe that Faulkner's overall view is as he stated it, that he admired women, and that the worst one could say of him in this context is that if he created some women who are detestable, he created some others who are admirable, just as Shakespeare did. But I suppose that as we move from the life to the art, we should remember D. H. Lawrence's famous aphorism, "Don't trust the teller, trust the tale." Having made these preliminary observations, I'll paraphrase Philip Roth's analyst who says, at the end of *Portnoy's Complaint,* "Now we can begin."

Like Joyce, Mann, Proust, and Lawrence, Faulkner was a writer who employed modernist techniques but also drew extensively upon his family, his extended family, and background in a very traditional way for the material upon which he employed these techniques. One need only compare the four generations of Sartorises with the four generations of Fa(u)lkners to see how well he used fact as a basis for the workings of imagination. I am going to try to avoid repeating the commonplace and rehearsing the obvious in this exploration, but it seems to me that we have no option but to take testimony from William Faulkner's family, especially from the women of the family, on our particular subject. His mother's devotion to him and his work is well known, but she said nothing that I know of on the subject of his general attitude toward women. (I can, however, cite parenthetically one remark attributed to her whose tenor will not sound strange to any woman here whose relationship with her mother-in-law has ever been less warm than she would wish: "I don't know why," Maud Falkner was said to have said, "my sons marry the women they do.")

So we must move to the next generation, the one Maud Falkner was referring to. After Estelle Faulkner told a reporter for *The Cavalier Daily,* the University of Virginia student newspaper, that her favorites among her husband's work were *The Sound and the Fury* and then *As I Lay Dying,* she added, "Some people think Mr. Faulkner hated women by the way he wrote about them. When someone asked me why he dislikes them so, I said that I wasn't aware that he did. I was scared he liked women a little too much."[10] No doubt some of you are thinking ahead at this moment, to the direction in which Estelle Faulkner's comment points, and in due course we shall have to pursue it, both with and without testimony such as I am citing here.

The next generation, represented by Jill Faulkner Summers, William and Estelle Faulkner's daughter, also provides explicit evidence. Jill told an interviewer, "Pappy liked ladies, liked women, you know, plain and simple." She went on immediately to refer to Joan Williams, novelist and short story writer-to-be, who was an important part of Faulkner's life intermittently for five years. (At this point we begin to move from the general to the specific, the way, as a matter of fact, in which my thoughts moved when I was writing the paragraph above, when Estelle Faulkner's recalling her anxiety about other women made me think of Meta Carpenter, who was an important part of Faulkner's life intermittently over a period of seventeen years.) Continuing her responses on this subject, Jill said, "I think that probably Pappy's idea of women—ladies—always revolved a great deal around Granny. She was just a very determined, tiny old lady that Pappy adored. Pappy admired that so much in Granny and he didn't find it in my mother and I don't think he ever found it in anybody. I think that maybe all of these including my mother were, just second place. It's difficult to say."[11]

There is yet another generation to quote from, the one after Jill's, in the person of Victoria Johnson, not far from Jill in age, but the granddaughter of Estelle Faulkner, the daughter of Victoria "Cho-Cho" Fielden, Estelle's child by her first husband, Cornell Franklin. In a panel discussion here at the conference nine years ago, Victoria Johnson said, "I could see a change over the years in his attitude toward women. The older women in the family—and that would include my mother—were thought of as fragile but indomitable types and they were on a pedestal in a way and yet they were not considered to think very much or do very much except in the home and they were not really given credit for having much of a brain. Then when Jill and Dean and I came along somehow there seemed to be a new respect, perhaps it was only because we went to college. But he seemed to value our thoughts and ideas more and expected us to speak—and he seemed to listen to us." (The Dean whom Victoria refers to is Dean Faulkner Wells, the daughter of William Faulkner's youngest brother, Dean Swift Faulkner, upon whose death Faulkner became a kind of surrogate father to the as yet unborn child. A member of the same panel, Dean did not speak explicitly to this subject, but I take it that she was generally in accord with the analysis Victoria gave.) Professor Evans Harrington had elicited the comment from Victoria which I quoted a moment ago. His next question elicited a response which might have given comfort to Ellen Douglas. Professor Harrington asked Victoria to recount an experience she had with her step-grandfather when she was in New York. "This goes back," Victoria said, "to his rather strong distrust of women. He was very concerned that we not get into any trouble with men." Visiting New York when Victoria had left her apartment to spend the weekend visiting friends of her parents, Faulkner tried on a Friday night to reach her, Victoria said. "When I got back to the apartment Sunday there was a telegram stuck under the door. I opened it and read, 'I have tried to get you *all night long*. You know what I will have to tell your mother and father.'"[12]

At this point I am going to use, for transitional purposes, a comment from another Faulkner, and for a bit of balance, perhaps, a male one. Closest to William Faulkner in age was his brother, Murry C. "Jack" Falkner. All the brothers seem to have shared not only the devotion to their mother but also to their maternal aunt, Holland Falkner Wilkins. "Dear Auntee," Jack wrote in his memoir, *The Falkners of Mississippi*, "what Falkner privileged to know her could ever forget her. Surely no more fiercely loyal member of the clan ever lived. She it was who became an unmistakable character in a number of Bill's stories: the one whose steadfast devotion never wavered, whose lasting love never lessened, and whose pride of family was so intense that she sustained and supported the other members no matter what misfortunes they brought upon themselves as a result of their uncontrolled impulses, lack of judgment, or just plain orneriness."[13] We can look ahead now, from Auntee to Aunt Jenny Du Pre and Granny Millard, and to all the other indomitable women who resemble them in the Faulkner canon.

As we prepare to do this, let us look at the fixed points in the world of William Faulkner as he was growing up. The male presence was, of course, powerful, even if present only in memory and legend. When the children were asked in grade school what they wanted to be when they grew up, William Falkner, his brother Jack knew, would always say, "I want to be a writer like my great-grand-daddy." The figure of Colonel William C. Falkner was implanted in the child's imagination from very early. A dominating force in the lives of his family was "The Young Colonel," John Wesley Thompson Falkner, the grandfather who sold the railroad and moved his eldest son and his family to Oxford, thus changing inevitably the lives of all of them and opening out for young William possibilities which could never have existed for him in Ripley, New Albany, Pontotoc, or any stop along the line of the Gulf & Chicago Railroad Company. Maternal grandfather John Young Murry—Confederate soldier, physician, and pious Presbyterian—also left his impress upon the lives and memories of his clan, but in the next generation the male influence waned, as William Falkner could find little, it seems, to emulate in his gruff, inarticulate, and well-meaning father, Murry C. Falkner.

The female constellation was more numerous and in the long run more powerful. Paternal grandmother Sallie Murry Falkner was the matriarch in Oxford. Her equivalent in Memphis was Alabama Leroy Falkner McLean, "The Colonel's baby," of whom the family said, when she dies and goes to Heaven, either she or God is going to have to move out. Faulkner once inscribed a book to a kinsman with a reference to Aunt 'Bama, "who owns both of us." Strong-minded women, one sees, ran in the family. There at home, with the tiny, iron-willed mother of four sons, was another powerful female force who readily accepted the authority delegated to her: Caroline Barr, "born in slavery,"

Faulkner would say in dedicating *Go Down, Moses* to her, recalling in his eulogy of her how she had been "one of my earliest recollections, not only as a person, but as a fount of authority over my conduct and of security for my physical welfare, and of active and constant affection and love. She was an active and constant precept for decent behavior. From her I learned to tell the truth, to refrain from waste, to be considerate of the weak and respectful to age. I saw fidelity to a family which was not hers, devotion and love for people she had not borne."[14] I can't refrain from mentioning what many of you are thinking: Here is Mammy Callie of Oxford, and Molly Beauchamp of Yoknapatawpha. There is yet one more to be mentioned in this constellation, smaller than the others and even younger by two years than William Falkner himself: Sallie Murry Wilkins, Auntee's daughter and favorite playmate of her cousins, of whom Murry Falkner said to Auntee, "Huldy, I'll give you any two of my boys for your girl."

Moving beyond Faulkner's family and forward in time, one thinks of other women who were important to him: Estelle Oldham, his first real love, and then the women of his youth in the years after Estelle married another man. In his teens and even later William Faulkner could demonstrate excruciating shyness. One sees in him the shy lover and sometimes the bold one—in verse, certainly, and perhaps in action as well; at least one hopes so. These two styles call to mind two very different women. In the early 1920s when Faulkner labored in the post office on the University of Mississippi campus, he would sometimes seek respite with a weekend visit to his friend, Phil Stone, working in a branch of the family law firm in Charleston. Faulkner developed an attachment for a stenographer in the office named Gertrude Stegbauer. He would ask her out, but according to Stone he was so shy that he would ask Stone to accompany them. Visiting Stone's elder brother at the family cottage on the beach at Pascagoula, he was not that shy, however, with a vigorous and forthright young artist named Helen Baird.

Years later she told me that there was never anything serious between them. "He was one of my screwballs," she said. However that may be, Faulkner's feelings for her were very different. The verbal evidence is to be found in the often erotic and specific poems he wrote for her, which he lettered and bound under the title *Helen: A Courtship*,[15] and in a letter of longing, however, which he never sent. Whether his courting was only verbal and vocal, one can only guess. In the years of his late thirties and afterwards, one thinks of Meta Carpenter, a Mississippian like himself with something of his feeling of nostalgia for home in the alien world of Hollywood. Then later came the younger women who figured in his life: Joan Williams, when he had entered his fifties, and then, later in that decade, Jean Stein, whose youth and admiration for his genius supplied elements in his life that he apparently strongly needed. Perhaps I have mentioned enough women in the life of William Faulkner for present purposes, and we can certainly think of other friends as we move through the work.

I would suggest that there are at least five major kinds of female figures in Faulkner's work: the admirable little girl (e.g., Caddy Compson as a child), the slim and virginal young woman (Pat Robyn in *Mosquitoes*), the voluptuous young woman (Eula Varner), the mature temptress (Belle Mitchell in *Sartoris*), the matron (respectable: Maggie Mallison [Gavin Stevens's sister], and disreputable: Reba Rivers in *Sanctuary*), and the venerable matriarch (Granny Millard). There are doubtless variations of these types and possibly major additions to them. Faulkner used most of them throughout his career as a fictionist.

In the verse that he wrote as a young man, both published and unpublished, the figure of the slim and virginal young woman predominates, as in the nymphs in "L'Après-Midi d'un Faune," *The Marble Faun*, and quintessentially, in "On Seeing the Winged Victory for the First Time." In treating Faulkner's verse and to some extent his prose fiction, one has to be aware of the possibility that in any given instance he may have been working from a literary type instead of, or as well as, from an actual model. (And here one should remember the triad he cited so often as the source of the artist's material: observation, imagination, and experience—not forgetting how avid a reader he was.) I would suggest that something of his perception of Estelle Oldham—a slim, dainty, fastidious girl—as well as his reading in pastoral poetry got into these early poems. If some of these creatures flee, some of them are also seductive and threatful (I think here of the title figure in the sketch "Nympholepsy"), finally reaching their apotheosis in figures such as that of Eula Varner. If Pat Robyn and others like her can be subsumed under what we might call the Diana archetype, surely Eula Varner and others like her (though none approaches her in power) can be subsumed under what we might call the Venus archetype. Do I have a nomination for a Venus-model? No, just a guess, apart from the speculation that any Mississippi town could produce a nubile beauty to dazzle the senses of a young poet. My guess would be the young woman who may have served unwittingly as the model for Jenny in *Mosquitoes*, the apparently delectable stenographer, Gertrude Stegbauer. (Compare the name and the figure: what better demonstration of the transmutational power of art?)

How did the alternately shy and bold lover see himself vis-à-vis these nymphs? Perhaps wishfully, like most young men. I think here of the reference in the unfinished novel *Elmer* to the painter Adolphe William Bougereau. One of his pictures which Faulkner may have seen in Paris in 1925 is suggestive: *Nymphes et satyre*, which shows "a dreamy but virile satyr being dragged into the water of a marsh by no fewer than four naked beauties."[16] (Jumping decades, one may here perhaps be permitted to recall the erotic drawings Meta Carpenter described which he made to commemorate their weekends in their rented Malibu cottage.[17])

By the mid-twenties the Venus-figure appears in his prose and with her, in his verse, that of the mature temptress. I am referring, of course, to Eula Varner in the until recently unpublished *Father Abraham* (the germ of *The Hamlet*) and to the visualization of New Orleans as a dead courtesan in a Petrarchan sonnet by that same name, a poem Faulkner liked well enough to collect in *A Green Bough* eight years later.[18]

But what of the novels, especially the one that Faulkner worked on in New Orleans in 1925, which appeared in the following year as *Soldiers' Pay?* In it he showed his capacity for creating a wide range of female characters, both white and black. Estelle Faulkner said that her husband-to-be used her as a model for one of the characters. She did not say which one it was, but she did say that it "hurt my feelings terribly."[19] Which one could it have been? There are only two candidates: Cecily Saunders, the hero's pretty, vain, and heartless fiancée, or Margaret Powers, the world-weary war widow with a bad conscience over the husband she had not loved enough. Given Faulkner's proclivity for empathizing with wounded and even moribund heroes such as Donald Mahon, Cecily seems to me the more likely choice. When Estelle Faulkner told me once that she saw something of herself in *Sanctuary,* I concluded that Temple Drake's popularity as a coed may have suggested to Estelle something of her own. It was not until the posthumous publication of *Count No 'Count,* the memoir by Faulkner's friend and sometime agent, Ben Wasson, that a more direct borrowing, for another book, suggested itself. There Ben recalled standing by the piano at the Oldhams' one day on the occasion of one of Estelle's visits home before her divorce from Cornell Franklin. He turned the sheet-music pages, and when she finished playing and rose they spontaneously kissed. Then Ben saw that Estelle's daughter had entered the room. Later, when Ben would read the scene in *Sartoris* in which Horace Benbow and Belle Mitchell, embracing in the music room, are interrupted by Little Belle, he would remember that afternoon at the Oldhams'.[20] But if pages such as these gave Estelle pain, there were others which did not.

In the summer of 1921 he had presented her with a sequence of fourteen love poems called *Vision in Spring*. Six years later, for Cho-Cho's eighth birthday Faulkner typed and bound for her a forty-seven-page gift book called *The Wishing-Tree*. It recounted the adventures of a little girl named Dulcie on her birthday. Cho-Cho was clearly meant to identify with Dulcie, and one page from the end Faulkner wrote, "Dulcie's mother was beautiful, so slim and tall, with her grave unhappy eyes changeable as seawater and her slender hands that came so softly about you when you were sick."[21]

We have already glanced at Faulkner's first three novels, and perhaps this is the place to mention the third of them again, *Sartoris*, if only to recall the presence there of the matriarch figure, who will recur in various avatars in *The Unvanquished*, *Intruder in the Dust*, *The Reivers*, and a number of short stories.

The links between life and art are more conjectural after *Sartoris*. The novel published later that same year, *The Sound and the Fury*, is particularly tantalizing. Faulkner would say that, fated to lose his first child in infancy, he decided to create for himself "a beautiful and tragic little girl."[22] Even recalling this, I cannot help thinking of Sallie Murry Wilkins, as close to her three male cousins as if they were siblings, and almost with them a paradigm for the Compson children in age and distribution. Phil Stone was convinced that the model for Mrs. Compson was his mother, "Miss Rosie" Stone, hypochondriac and connoisseur of disasters. This may well be true, but it does relatively little for us in explaining the poignant power of that novel. More useful to me, I think, is André Bleikasten's image of its central figure, Caddy, as "a dream of beauty wasted and destroyed."[23]

Both John Cullen and Phil Stone could recall country women they thought of as models for characters in *As I Lay Dying*, even to a shared name: Dewey Dell. But once again these antecedents, if in fact they came into play in the artist's imagination, were but—as he so often put it—materials from the "lumber room," which he shaped to build his artifice.

The same thing is true of *Sanctuary*, whether one thinks of Faulkner's account of hearing a horrific tale of violation from a young woman in a Memphis-area speakeasy combined with an outrage endured by an Ole Miss coed, or whether one remembers his well-documented accounts of spending social evenings in Clarksdale and Memphis bordellos, recalling too his admiration for the model for Miss Reba, a woman who, with a face like that of a battered professional athlete, had somehow survived the rigors of her tragic and degrading profession. But no matter how many stories, rumors, and whispered accounts he had drawn upon, the power of the novel ultimately derives from a private vision of evil and corruption.

When we come to novels such as *Light in August*, and I think now particularly of Gail Hightower's mother, we may perhaps invoke the archetypical figure in Noel Polk's essay which I referred to earlier. (And though his paper here deals more with France than Yoknaptawpha County, perhaps he may develop that figure further for us.) Again local lore is not lacking. Years ago I was told that significant correspondences existed between the lives of Rev. Gail Hightower's wife and that of an Oxford clergyman's wife. As for Lena Grove, I have often thought that Faulkner may have speculated about what would have happened to Dewey Dell Bundren if, undeterred by her abortive efforts in the basement of the drug store in Mottson, she had gone on to try to find her lover, Lafe, even after she had been bilked of the ten dollars he had given her to free him of his obligation and her of her burden. But what does this tell us of Faulkner and women? He knew there were women like Addie and her daughter, Dewey Dell, like the insufferable and priceless Cora Tull too, and he did his best to portray them as they were, dealing as best they could with their difficult lives.

Novels such as *Pylon* give us more to work with. We know about Faulkner's fascination with the world of tramp aviators, the way he immersed himself in it, how he knew about the extraordinary careers of friends such as Vernon Omlie and his wife, Phoebe, whose career probably suggests a number of the events in the life of Laverne Shumann. Beyond that Faulkner was there to do what he could as his brother Dean, and Dean's wife, Louise, struggled to make a living under conditions not much better than those of Roger and Laverne Shumann. There is an observation one can make here though that looks back to Faulkner's remarks about the strength and courage of women. He saw this in Louise Faulkner and doubtless knew of it in Phoebe Omlie. Laverne Shumann had it in full measure, and Faulkner must have felt this courage and capacity for sacrifice every bit as keenly as did the nameless reporter obsessed with it in his novel.

As I am convinced that Laverne resembles Phoebe in her appearance and her career, so I am convinced that Charlotte Rittenmeyer in *The Wild Palms* is modeled on Helen Baird: the stature, the complexion, the hair, the burn scars, and the papier-maché figures. But what are we to make of the fact that Charlotte, arrant romantic that she is, sweeps the unsophisticated Harry Wilbourne off his feet, whereas Helen Baird dismissed William Faulkner, she said, as "one of my screwballs" and married a promising lawyer (as had Estelle Oldham) instead? What should we call it? Wish-fulfillment? The "what if?" proposition? Perhaps we should here recall not only Harry's "between grief and nothing I'll take grief," but also Meta Carpenter's recollection of her anguish and Faulkner's in Hollywood, when they were deeply involved with each other but Faulkner's ties to his child, his homeland, and his wife too, were too strong to be broken to free the two lovers. There is a good deal in *The Wild Palms* about women's capacity for belief in the things they want to be true, for commitment to romance and to sacrifice which is ultimately as destructive as that of Horace Benbow or any of Faulkner's men. Faulkner told his publisher that to him this novel "was written just as if I had sat on the one side of a wall and the paper was on the other and my hand with the pen thrust through the wall and writing not only on invisible paper but in pitch darkness too, so that I could not even know if the pen still wrote on paper or not."[24] Much of the misery came from a painful burn on his back, but much of it came too from pain in his heart.

The Snopes trilogy gave Faulkner an opportunity to employ both the Venus type and the Diana type. When a questioner observed that Eula Varner, in *The Hamlet*, seemed larger than life, Faulkner quickly agreed, adding that "she was an anachronism, she had no place there, that that little hamlet couldn't have held her, and when she moved on to Jefferson, that couldn't hold her either. But then that'll be in the next book."[25] It was not simply her premature voluptuousness; it was a quality clearly mythic: "her entire appearance suggested some symbology out of the old Dionysic times—honey in sunlight and bursting grapes, the writhen bleeding of the crushed fecundated vine beneath the hard rapacious trampling goat-hoof."[26] I am not aware of any woman in Faulkner's life at this time who could have stood for the portrait of this extraordinary creature. Here again, I suppose, one invokes imagination, observation, and experience. But in Faulkner's completion of the trilogy with *The Town* and *The Mansion*, his Diana figure does suggest a real-life analogue, and one only a little less potent, at least in her effect on Gavin Stevens, than the other one. I am referring, of course, to Linda Snopes. Stevens's sister, Margaret Mallison, speaks wryly of Gavin's "forming her mind" as he brings her books of poetry to read, and Margaret knows that his motivation is not just educational. I think it is obvious that Faulkner was drawing on his complex feelings for Joan Williams, whom he referred to once as his protégé. This is, I think, what she wanted to be, but he clearly wanted her to be more than that to him. In the fiction this mix is also clear. Joan Williams's own novel, *The Wintering*, deals with the same sort of relationship.[27]

There are obviously volumes more to be said on this subject about the works I haven't discussed and those I have. So perhaps it is best for me to refer to just one more: his last, *The Reivers*. What a picture of male innocence and female experience it presents: the initiation of eleven-year-old Lucius Priest, presided over by that Venus-figure, Corinthia Everbe, who also, despite her profession, has something in her character that would not shame a Diana. And if Miss Reba does not play the role of the mature temptress here, there seems little doubt that despite her toughness and outspokenness, she would be equal to any occasion that arose in the pursuit of her profession, even though her function now seems to be managerial. And in the background are those familiar figures of Mother, Grandmother, and Aunt Callie.

Lest I be thought to make too positive a case, to emphasize too much Faulkner's admiration of women and his attraction to them, I suppose I should cite his famous remark to Jean Stein. "If a writer has to rob his mother," he said, "he will not hesitate; the *Ode on a Grecian Urn* is worth any number of old ladies."[28] I think that even though Faulkner was saying what he thought about the artist's potential ruthlessness (something his daughter saw in him), there was also operative here a certain kind of tough-guy bravado he sometimes liked to affect. His chivalry to women was very real; like others who knew him I saw it on many occasions, but at the same time I can't help remembering something he once said to me—though there was in it something of the kind of humor that gets expressed in male camaraderie. "It's wrong to think about women as if they were dishonest men," he said. "They ain't. They're just women." I suppose I could try to pretty that up without something about the Ancient Eve in his poetry, but I won't.

Years ago when I interviewed Myrtle Ramey Demarest, a childhood friend and later a young woman he liked enough to give her a sampling of his poems,[29] she said to me, of *The Reivers*, "I wish my father were alive. He could tell you who everybody in that book is." This assumption—that the artist primarily transcribes life—is one that annoyed Faulkner and his fellow townsman, Stark Young, and many another writer. One of the reasons why I have not instanced more models is that Faulkner did his work so well. When asked by a Virginian, "Can we expect to find ourselves perhaps in one of your later books?," Faulkner answered, "you needn't be surprised to find anything that I've seen in Virginia in what I write next. But also remember that I'm convinced I can improve on the Lord and so you won't quite recognize yourself if you do. You'll be changed."[30]

One last footnote on Life and Art and Faulkner and Women. In an early essay, he wrote, "I read and employed verse, firstly, for the purpose of furthering various philanderings in which I was engaged."[31] He continued the practice in later years, though "philanderings" is not the right word for some of those relationships, as we see in *Helen: A Courtship, Mississippi Poems,* and *Vision in Spring.* Last summer, on the morning of the day we were to leave for a month in Italy, I received a long distance phone call from a man who had read some comments I had made about *Vision in Spring* and who perhaps knew something of my Faulkner work. He said that many years ago William Faulkner had given his aunt, now deceased, such a collection of love poems. Another aunt had them in her possession, and he wondered if I would be interested in seeing them. I said that I certainly would. I took down the information that he gave me and said that I would be in touch with him or his aunt upon our return from Italy. When we returned, I went to my desk but could find the notes nowhere. I ransacked my filing cabinets with the same result. To make matters worse, I could not remember the man's name; all I remembered was that he was a Louisiana opthalmologist and, from his accent, a Cajun. Since then I have enlisted the aid of William Faulkner's doctor and Phil Stone's nephew; I have searched through medical society membership lists, and even invoked the aid of one medical journal— all so far without success. There is one thing about the conversation which I remember very clearly, however: the man's aunt was named Gertrude Stegbauer. So somewhere today, perhaps in southernmost Louisiana, there exists a cache of Faulkner poems—a further testimonial to William Faulkner's feeling for women.

NOTES

1. Sally R. Page, *Faulkner's Women: Characterization and Meaning* (Deland, Fla.: Everett/Edwards, 1972).

2. Patricia Elizabeth Sweeney, *William Faulkner's Women Characters: An Annotated Bibliography of Criticism, 1930–1983* (Santa Barbara, Calif.: ABC-Clio Information Services, 1985).

3. Elizabeth M. Kerr, "The Women of Yoknapatawpha," in *The University of Mississippi Studies in English*, 15 (1978), 83–100.

4. Ellen Douglas, "Faulkner's Women," in *A Cosmos of My Own": Faulkner and Yoknapatawpha, 1980*, ed. Doreen Fowler and Ann J. Abadie (Jackson: University Press of Mississippi, 1981), 166.

5. Linda Welshimer Wagner, "Faulkner and (Southern) Women," in *The South and Faulkner's Yoknapatawpha: The Actual and the Apocryphal*, ed. Evans Harrington and Ann J. Abadie (Jackson: University Press of Mississippi, 1978), 131, 146.

6. Ilse Dusoir Lind, "Faulkner's Women," in *The Maker and the Myth: Faulkner and Yoknapatawpha, 1977*, ed. Evans Harrington and Ann J. Abadie (Jackson: University Press of Mississippi, 1978), 92, 104.

7. Noel Polk, " 'The Dungeon was Mother Herself': William Faulkner: 1927–1931," in *New Directions in Faulkner Studies: Faulkner and Yoknapatawpha, 1983*, ed. Doreen Fowler and Ann J. Abadie (Jackson: University Press of Mississippi, 1984), 65–66.

8. Kae Irene Parks, *Faulkner's Women: Archetype and Metaphor* (Ann Arbor, Mich.: University Microfilms Incorporated, 1980).

9. *Faulkner in the University*, ed. Frederick L. Gwynn and Joseph L. Blotner (Charlottesville: University of Virginia Press, 1959), 74.

10. Barbara Hand, "Faulkner's Widow Recounts Memories of College Weekends in Charlottesville," *The Cavalier Daily* (Charlottesville, Va.), 20 April 1972, 1.

11. A. I. Bezzerides, *William Faulkner: A Life on Paper* (Jackson: University Press of Mississippi, 1980), 104–5.

12. "Faulkner and Women," in *The South and Faulkner's Yoknapatawpha*, 150.

13. Murry C. Falkner, *The Falkners of Mississippi: A Memoir* (Baton Rouge: Louisiana State University Press, 1967), 8.

14. William Faulkner, *Essays, Speeches, and Public Letters*, ed. James B. Meriwether (New York: Random House, 1965), 117.

15. William Faulkner, *Helen: A Courtship* and *Mississippi Poems*, intro. Carvel Collins and Joseph Blotner (Oxford, Miss., and New Orleans, La.: Tulane University and Yoknapatawpha Press, 1981).

16. Joseph Blotner, *Faulkner: A Biography* (New York: Random House, 1974), 162–63.

17. Meta Carpenter Wilde and Orin Borsten, *A Loving Gentleman: The Love Story of William Faulkner and Meta Carpenter* (New York: Simon and Schuster, 1976).

18. William Faulkner, *The Marble Faun* and *A Green Bough* (New York: Random House, 1965), 58.

19. Barbara Hand, *The Cavalier Daily*, 4.

20. Ben Wasson, *Count No 'Count: Flashbacks to Faulkner*, intro. Carvel Collins (Jackson: University Press of Mississippi, 1983), 81.

21. William Faulkner, *Vision in Spring*, intro. Judith L. Sensibar (Austin: University of Texas Press, 1984) and *The Wishing Tree* (New York, Random House, 1966), 81.

22. James B. Meriwether, "Faulkner Lost and Found," *New York Times Book Review*, 5 November 1972, 7.

23. André Bleikasten, *The Most Splendid Failure: Faulkner's "The Sound and the Fury"* (Bloomington: Indiana University Press,1976), 66.

24. *Selected Letters of William Faulkner*, ed. Joseph Blotner (New York: Random House, 1977), 106.

25. *Faulkner in the University*, 31.

26. William Faulkner, *The Hamlet* (New York: Random House, 1940), 95.

27. Joan Williams, *The Wintering* (New York: Harcourt Brace Jovanovich, 1971).

28. *Lion in the Garden: Interviews with William Faulkner, 1926–1962*, ed. James B. Meriwether and Michael Millgate (New York: Random House, 1968), 239.

29. William Faulkner, *Mississippi Poems*, intro. Joseph Blotner (Oxford, Miss.: Yoknapatawpha Press, 1979).

30. *Faulkner in the University*, 123.

31. *William Faulkner: Early Prose and Poetry*, intro. Carvel Collins (Boston: Little, Brown and Company, 1962), 115.

The Mutual Relevance of Faulkner Studies and Women's Studies: An Interdisciplinary Inquiry

ILSE DUSOIR LIND

When women's studies began in the late 1960s, Faulkner studies were already in their third decade. Initially, the two fields seemed opposed, for the women's movement arose concomitantly with the civil rights movement, employing some of the same political strategies. At the time, therefore, it had an anti-Southern aura—or so it seemed to me, for I found that as a woman who was known as a Faulkner scholar in the 1960s, I was often challenged to justify my interest in an author associated with a region that was historically racist and sexist. Nevertheless, my interest in Faulkner study held, and I also found myself drawn into the women's movement. When the Modern Language Association issued its call to develop programs to expose and combat the widespread negative stereotyping of women in literature, for example, I developed a course, "The Image of Woman in American Literature," focusing on literature written by American women authors. The topic of this conference, "Faulkner and Women," consequently brings two of my long-standing—even lifelong—interests together.

The relevance of women, as a topic, to study of Faulkner has been amply demonstrated throughout this conference. When I promise by the title of my paper to deal with the *mutual* relevance of Faulkner studies and women's studies, I merely carry it one step further. The feminist criticism which was begun in the late '60s has come to full maturity in the intervening years, and Faulkner studies, too, have been transformed since Blotner's

21

biography in 1974 provided the substantial base upon which various new interpretations could be mounted. In addition, there have been volcanic upheavals in the critical realm, deriving from new knowledge about the nature of language. Whenever knowledge explosions occur in contiguous fields, the number of points or places at which they can intersect increases at a geometric ratio. This means that today there are numerous ways in which women's studies and Faulkner studies can be brought into meaningful relationship. In this paper, I propose to discuss three such interrelationships as they can be discovered to exist in three different areas.

1

The first involves exchanges between Faulkner study and feminist theory in recent critical writings by the distinguished French Faulkner critic, André Bleikasten, and the noted American feminist, Myra Jehlen, who—as it happens—is also a Faulkner scholar. Bleikasten, in "Fathers in Faulkner," an essay collected in *The Fictional Father: Lacanian Readings of the Text,* demonstrates that Faulkner in his work was incessantly preoccupied with the symbolic role of the father.[1] He calls attention to the way Faulkner dwelt on his male ancestors and how his imagination was obsessed by the ghosts of such ancestors. He shows how in Faulkner's fiction the identification of the son with the father (or the failure of such identification) is crucial in more than one work, how fathers—or father surrogates—teach (or fail to teach) the son how to play the appropriate roles in outdoor nature and in society. He points out that paternity is the key issue in the problem of the white father and the black son. He notes how often Faulkner stresses the unimportance of the biological father in comparison to the legal father. By force of cumulative example and by the use of other critical strategies, he reveals Faulkner to be quintessentially patriarchal, a supreme exemplar of the patriarchal attitudes. Such a finding, which until now we have not been able to formulate with such definitiveness, is of immense value for feminist study of literature. It shows in a direct and obvious way how Faulkner scholarship can be of use to feminists who wish to demonstrate the pervasive structure of male bias in literature.

When we consider "Fathers in Faulkner" in relation to Myra Jehlen's essay, "Archimedes and the Paradox of Feminist Criticism," anthologized in *Feminist Theory: A Critique of Ideology*, we see the reciprocity of Faulkner study and feminism illustrated in yet another way.[2] Jehlen, in her essay, addresses a crucial problem in feminist theory; namely, that feminist literary critics find themselves in a paradoxical position when they attempt to make judgments that apply exclusively to women, because women are situated in a man's world. This means that there is no place where feminists can set down an instrument that will give them measurements that can be accepted as standard.

One way of approching this dilemma, Jehlen suggests, is the development of a comparative method to measure the relativity of gender definitions. As a model she suggests juxtaposing novels written by male authors against novels writen by female authors when both deal with essentially the same subject, as for example, comparing Henry James's *Portrait of a Lady* to Edith Wharton's *The House of Mirth*, since both deal with late nineteenth-century upperclass life as confronted by a female protagonist. Such comparisons, Jehlen maintains, should be radical in the sense of going to the roots—of taking into account the special circumstances affecting writing by women, including such recently understood factors as the cultural preconditions that exert an influence on women authors and the constraints imposed by the conventions which are inherent in genres themselves, as, for instance, the expectation of marriage as a happy ending in nineteenth-century fiction. Such comparisons, Jehlen believes, will eventually provide increased understanding of women's interests and outlook as compared to those of men, and help bring about a better "meshing of a definition of women and a definition of the world."[3]

Turning again to Bleikasten's "Fathers in Faulkner," but this time giving attention to the structure of his essay, we see that he has employed the kind of comparative strategy Jehlen recommends, although he has employed two male writers in his comparison. For his method in his essay is to expose Faulkner's patriarchal bias by evolving an extended comparison between Faulkner and Freud. Extrapolating Freud's ideas about the father as they appear in his psychological writings and juxtaposing these to Faulkner's as they are implied in his fiction, Bleikasten presents the two as "differential versions of common concerns" which reveal Freud and Faulkner to share a striking number of assumptions.[4] The persuasiveness of his conclusion—that Faulkner is as patriarchal as Freud—is greatly enhanced by this use of the comparative method, which enables him to approach Faulkner's fiction not as one who wants to impose an ideology or prejudice of his own upon it, but as one who permits the meaning of Faulkner's fiction to reveal itself when it is placed next to the texts of Freud—Freud as restructured by a Lacanian linguistic focus, it should perhaps be added.

The comparisons that Jehlen urges are similarly aimed at showing how two viewpoints, when placed side by side, will reveal significant similarities or differences. Bleikasten's success in exposing Faulkner's patriarchal leaning means that Faulkner's work can be used by feminist critics in executing comparisons of works by Faulkner and Southern women authors when they write on essentially the same historical subjects, such as plantation culture, the Civil War, Reconstruction, the New South, and others. Many novels by Southern women qualify for use in such comparisons. To cite only a single example, Evelyn Scott's *The Wave*, which deals with the Civil War, might be analyzed in comparison to Faulkner's rendering of the Civil War in *The Unvanquished* or *Absalom, Absalom!*, with a view to showing how authorial gender exerts an influence in two writers who are both from the South and who are both essentially modernist in their literary orientation.

To return to a broader consideration of the way feminist criticism and Faulkner criticism intersect, Bleikasten and Jehlen also reveal complementary thinking in two other pieces, Bleikasten's "For/Against an Ideological Reading of Faulkner's Novels" and Jehlen's *Class and Character in Faulkner's South*.[5]

The gist of Bleikasten's essay on ideological reading is that Faulkner's novels embody the values of his society. In and of itself, this is not an original idea, but in Bleikasten's handling it reverberates with new meanings, for he approaches it from a dual point of view, showing not merely how Faulkner embodies the values of his culture in his writing but also how he as a man stood in tangential relation to his society personally, as a member of his community who was also a writer. The main purpose of Bleikasten's essay, however, is to argue *for* the development of consciously ideological readings of Faulkner's work, to encourage increased awareness of the extent to which all criticism is infused by ideology of one sort or another. He points out that the old New Criticism is not really objective or detached but is infused with ideological assumptions of its own, of which the critic is often unaware. He takes pains to define "ideology" in the poststructural sense here, seeing all meaning as being culturally determined. He points out as well that all cultural activity is under some kind of ideological pressure and that the approach of an established Faulkner critic like Cleanth Brooks is not innocently traditional but is ideological in its own terms. In short, Bleikasten in this essay tries to bring Faulkner study into line with other academic fields where the new knowledges that underlie the poststructural approaches are currently being assimilated at a faster rate.

Significantly, Myra Jehlen, in her *Class and Character in Faulkner's South*, a book that was mistakenly judged, when it first appeared, to be a work of historical interpretation which fell short of its aims, is a forerunner of Bleikasten in this attempt to modernize Faulkner criticism along poststructural lines. Bleikasten, in a footnote to his essay, praises Jehlen's book, which had appeared six years earlier, as exceptional among recent Faulkner studies for the pertinent questions it raises about Faulkner's ideology, even though he finds these insufficiently developed.[6] When we examine Jehlen's stated purposes more closely, we find that she begins her study by defining the term "ideology" in the same post-Sausserian way he does, stating that she aims to show not how Faulkner's work *mirrors* his society but how his very language *embodies* it, language being not a mirror but in and of itself constituent. For her, Faulkner's work does not describe Southern culture; rather, the history of Mississippi and the fiction of Faulkner are analogous embodiments of the same culture. This may seem like the splitting of hairs, but it actually involves a key difference in critical orientation. Because she and Bleikasten share a common outlook about ideology, reciprocities of the kind I have been describing flow easily back and forth between them, illustrating the increasing tendency at present to make use of semiotic theory—in deconstructivism, reader-response approaches, Lacanian analysis, ideological criticism, and others. At this conference, we have seen how useful such methods are in exploring Faulkner's attitudes towards women. Examining the interactions between Jehlen and Bleikasten, we see how they can be applied fruitfully in both Faulkner study and women's studies, in ways that can benefit both fields.[7]

2

In criticism grounded in a more traditionally historical approach, the mutual relevance of Faulkner studies and women's studies can be illustrated through consideration of Anne Goodwyn Jones's *Tomorrow Is Another Day* in relation to Faulkner's early literary career.[8] Jones is here concerned primarily with white Southern women authors, but in a lengthy introductory essay she generalizes her findings, discussing literature and sexuality in traditional Southern culture as these interrelate and exert an influence on the lives and writings of both male and female authors. Hers is the first such examination of the dynamics of sex roles in the traditional culture of the South as they bear on writers.[9] As such, it is of potential use in Faulkner study because Faulkner scholars are still struggling with the problem of forming an image of Faulkner as a beginning writer that is compatible with the clearly defined image of Faulkner as an established author. Extremely difficult to interpret has been his habit of dressing according to his mood during late adolescence and early manhood, when he often appeared in town or on campus wearing a variety of different outfits, sometimes dressed as a Royal Air Force officer, sometimes as a dandy, sometimes as a young man of fashion, or sometimes, again, as a careless bohemian. The undergraduates on campus made sport of his clothes-consciousness by referring to him as "quair" and as the "bea—u—tiful young man with the cane,"[10] and this suggests that he may have been effeminate. However, the early poems express heterosexual, rather than homoerotic desires, suggesting that a fundamental uncertainty about his sexual identity was not the chief motivating factor. Judith Sensibar, in exploring this early period while ordering the early poetic sequences, concludes that his public masquerading during this period was symptomatic of a profound psychological disturbance. Noting that in his early poetry as well, he frequently disguised himself by employing various personae, often identifying with Pierrot, the supreme masquerader of literary convention, she argues that he displayed the distinguishing features of an imposter, a psychotic personality lacking a central identity.[11]

But Jones's study, with its strong historical emphasis, reduces the need to resort to psychopathological explanation and makes it possible to view such odd behavior as far more comprehensible within its cultural context. Following are a few of Jones's observations that bear on the issue of Faulkner's male identity at this period.

First, she sees the Southern white man as being threatened in his sense of sexual identity by a variety of historical factors which exerted a negative influence from the time of the establishment of plantation culture. As an American, the upper-class Southern white man was psychically torn from the beginning by his conflicting faith in Jeffersonian democracy and his rationalized defense of slavery as an institution. Jones finds the less authoritative tone of early Southern literature, as compared to that of New England, to reflect the lesser assurance of Southern males. She views the Southern male ego following the Civil War as again sustaining a major assault when the South was defeated in military combat despite the courage of her fighting men. Still later, extending even into the early twentieth century, she sees the failure of the South to share in the vigorous industrial development of the North and East as undermining the Southern male psyche, for it forced many of them to accept a degree of economic dependency which placed them in a passive position, one resembling the traditional role of women in Western society more than it did that of the patriarch. Those who wanted to pursue careers in literature or the arts naturally found such dependency intensified, since their families were rarely in a position to provide financial assistance.

As applied to Faulkner, such observations render his need to engage in masculine role-playing considerably less bizarre, especially since all of his masquerading involved symbolic assertions of male identity. Also, within a small community like the one in which he came to manhood—where everyone knew everyone's social status and life history—the message conveyed by such psychological acting-out was all too plain, and eccentricities of this sort were readily tolerated. In addition, Faulkner's personal economic circumstances during his unusually long apprenticeship must be borne in mind. For despite the fact that his grandfather was president of a local bank, his own parents' financial reserves were chronically meager. During the early 1960s, when I was spending my summers in the Oxford vicinity trying to learn more about Faulkner in relation to his world, I recall speaking with a druggist in Charleston, Mississippi, who claimed to have been a member of the fraternity to which Faulkner belonged while attending Ole Miss. He told me that he knew Faulkner then, but that he had never heard of his being called "Count No 'Count" for the reason that he was thought to be a dandy or effeminate. "We gave him this name in the fraternity," he said, "because whenever we would ask him if he wanted to go in on the price of a bottle, he would say, 'No, count me out.'"[12] Faulkner's ability to survive on a subminimal personal allowance for more than a decade in order to develop himself as a writer is probably as extraordinary a feat as any other aspect of his achievement. However, as any woman knows, such a personal style is not conducive to romance, and in an era when escorting a girl of one's own to a major dance of the season meant hiring a hansom in which to transport her and her chaperone, it is not surprising that he mostly watched from the sidelines or that he was not considered seriously as a suitor by the families of the belles with whom he fell in love.

Another of Jones's observations that illuminates the complexities of this phase concerns the importance of the cult of Southern womanhood, which was still central to the region's conception of itself. Constituting a mix of strongly felt convictions about class, race, and patriotic identification with the Old South, the idealization of women exerted a powerful influence on Southern white women, but it affected the Southern men who were their social counterparts as well. The Southern white woman was expected to be the incarnation of personal beauty, chastity, and social grace. In order to live up to this impossible standard, she had to cultivate the art of role-playing, always properly attired for her part, always controlling her libidinous urges and always being gracious.

In Jones's opinion, the demands of the cult caused the Southern woman to become alienated from herself because the ideals to which she was expected to conform did not come from within herself; rather, they were socially imposed from without, evolved within the society to serve its special needs as a racist culture. As a consequence, the Southern woman tended to experience a psychic split. On the one hand, she often felt hypocritical while fulfilling her role. On the other, because she internalized these role expectations at deep levels, she often felt ashamed of herself as a natural woman. Aspiring to be as pure as

the marble statue to which she was often compared, she still
knew that her innermost thoughts and desires showed her to be
merely human. Citing a recent study of diaries kept by Southern
women, Jones shows how they repeatedly accused themselves of
being dishonest when they acted as their culture demanded and
also guilty about their "animal" nature, often likening the mind
of a woman to "a cage of unclean beasts."[13]

The conflicted attitude toward female sexuality which appears
in Faulkner's work, in other words, is analogous to that which
prevailed in the culture, and Faulkner reflects the male obverse
of the dichotomous attitudes held by females. In *The Marble
Faun*, for example, besides dealing with themes that concern
nature and art, he incorporates a sexual motif which reflects
this.[14] In the poem, the faun contemplates the nymphs around
him with erotic longing and constantly pursues them but always
lets them get away. Decorous restraint governs him, keeping his
passions in check, and he indulges in a sweet-sad nympholeptic
revery of which he is consciously aware. He would like to
"break" his "marble bonds," but his sense of what is expected of
him is too deeply ingrained. When he finally dares to imagine
himself surrendering to his impulses and becoming one with the
natural world, he fears being overwhelmed by disgust at "this
unclean heated thing" that is at the center of life's renewal.[15] By
the poem's end, therefore, he is again a marble statue in a formal
Southern garden. Thus, when in later fiction he expresses revulsion against female biological functioning by permitting his male
characters to describe so natural a function as menstruation as
filthy and vile, he is giving voice to the paradoxes that are
inherent in his culture's veneration of white women.

Even more useful to an understanding of Faulkner's approach
to women in his fiction are Jones's observations about the impact
of the flapper era on traditional mores in the South. Despite the
new sexual styles of the gay teens and twenties, she maintains
that the flapper did not modify the image of the Southern lady in
a fundamental way because she did not challenge the patriarchal
structure directly. Jones points out that some of the most famous

flappers, like Zelda Fitzgerald, came from the South. Estelle
Oldham, as Ben Wasson's recent memoir reveals, was an even
more famous flapper in Mississippi than Zelda was in Alabama,
no less daring in her behavior within her own milieu.[16] But such
playfulness proved deeply troubling to the men who were drawn
to these new daring young women. In *The Marionettes*, where
the female protagonist, Marietta, is modeled on Estelle (as
Sensibar has demonstrated irrefutably), Marietta's erotic sophis-
tication is depicted as being decadent, rather than merely play-
ful.[17] Pierrot in that play refuses to believe that Marietta has
become sexually initiated through her own free will; he can only
think of her loss of virginity as leading to her death. Such a grim
approach to female erotic expression becomes a pervasive theme
in Faulkner's fiction—as we have seen—especially during his
first decade as a novelist, when it is elaborated with many
variations in female protagonists like Caddy, Temple, and Elly.

Also highly illuminating is Jones's analysis of the effect of the
literary careers of Southern women writers on Southern male
authors. Quite to her surprise she found that the careers of
Southern literary women did not show them to have suffered the
anxieties about authorship which Gilbert and Gubar found
characteristic of New England female authors, as described in
The Madwoman in the Attic.[18] On the contrary, Southern
women were praised for writing, the idealization of Southern
womanhood including the view that Southern ladies were custo-
dians of culture, besides being incarnations of chastity and
beauty. Their response to such an expectation, needless to say,
was to be prolific. However, as Jones goes on to explain, their
creative expressions, emanating as they did from personalities
that had suffered the constraints of living up to an impossible
ideal, were often parochial and sentimental, and they also reflected their failure to receive the necessary intellectual development—for the schooling they received at women's colleges was
far from adequate. The general standard they set as writers was
thus not very high, and a Southern male poet who was seriously
contemplating a literary career like that of Yeats or Conrad Aiken

during the early teens of the century could not take pride in identifying with the Southern women authors who for so many decades had dominated the literary marketplace.

In light of all this, is it to be wondered that Faulkner's early work conveys a sense of masculinity strongly embattled? Or that he should have been driven to protect his emerging manhood in his first literary endeavors by the use of irony, Prufrockian irresolution, poetic indirection, and the assumption of mask after mask? That he should have felt compelled to state, in writing about Poe in one of his early reviews, that certain of Poe's literary qualities were distinctly *masculine* [emphasis mine]?[19] Or that he should have thought it necessary to say to Anita Loos that he still harbored the old Victorian prejudices against "the intelligence of women"?[20] Jones's feminist-oriented study of Southern women writers, as we can see, intersects with Faulkner study at many points in a consideration of Faulkner's first literary phase. And Faulkner scholarship and criticism, reciprocally, provide a means whereby Jones's insights receive further testing and validation.

3

Finally, in psychological theory applied to literature, Nancy Chodorow's *The Reproduction of Mothering: Psychoanalysis and the Sociology of Gender* merits consideration as an adjunct to existing psychological approaches in Faulkner criticism.[21] Chodorow's work has not yet been employed in literary study, to my knowledge, and is offered here for speculative consideration. As a Freudian revisionist, Chodorow brings a feminist perspective to the study of early child development, placing less stress on the Oedipal conflict and more upon what she calls object-relations, the interactions taking place between a child and its primary caretaker from the time of birth. She does not reject the Oedipal phase as a source of potential psychic conflict, but sees the development of boys and girls to be asymmetrical with respect to the Oedipal conflict, as well as to other aspects of

development. In general, she tends to approach the mother-
child relationship more as a totality than Freud does, giving
attention to a wider range of interactions taking place between a
child and its primary caretaker from the time of birth. She
emphasizes that the first relationship between a child and another human being, who is usually the mother, is crucial in the
formation of personality structure and in determining a child's
later attitudes towards mothers and women. Rather than assuming that the human female is innately endowed with a capacity to
mother that is wholly instinctual, she maintains that mothering
is also a learned ability, one that every human being—male and
female—possesses in some degree as a consequence of having
been mothered. In girls, she argues, this knowledge receives
reinforcement through immediate identification with the mother
as a female person and through the socialization process, which
acculturates the girl as a person who will become a wife and
mother. In male children the tender or nurturing emotions are
suppressed in preparation for the boy's assumption of a male
social role. Chodorow's many keen insights derive—as the sub-
title of her book indicates—from her ability to synthesize findings from more than one intellectual discipline. Following are a
few observations—I shall limit them to three—which are inspired by a reading of *The Reproduction of Mothering* with an
eye to its possible application in Faulkner study.

The first concerns the negative images of older women in
Faulkner's work. Among Faulkner scholars, Noel Polk has done
the most to make us aware of the way that nightmarish images of
older women, particularly mothers, haunt Faulkner's fiction during the years surrounding the writing of *Sanctuary*—from approximately 1927 to 1931.[22] Medusa-figures and harshly judg-
mental women appear repeatedly, and there are also intimations
of women who imprison or engulf, in dungeons, caves, and
bottomless morasses. The mother-child theme appears repeatedly during these years, to a point where it is obsessive, mothers
often being depicted with emphasis on their emotional un-
availability to their young, even to those who have a desperate

need of maternal love, like Quentin Compson and Darl Bundren.

Polk urges that further exploration of these negative mother-images and of the sources underlying them be undertaken. A first thought is that Faulkner himself may have failed to receive sufficient maternal nurture, and this idea has, in fact, been put forward, on more than one occasion.[23] However, Chodorow is useful here in cautioning that negative images of the mother must not be construed as realistic interpretations of her or as rational commentary on the quality of her care, since they derive from the prelogical phase of development. They express inner stresses which may derive from other factors besides the specific quality of a given mother's care. As the pioneering studies of early child development upon which Chodorow draws make clear, even children whose nurture is adequate when judged by the common standard may experience what they feel to be an insufficiency of mothering, since infants vary markedly in the degree and quantity of maternal closeness they require.[24]

Some constitutionally hypersensitive infants, as one may readily imagine Faulkner to have been, are overwhelmed by external stimuli unless the mother provides more than average protective shielding during the first six weeks, as they progress from symbiotic union with the mother to beginning individuation. Emotional disturbance in psychotic infants is sometimes traceable to such a lack, and disturbed infants of this type often manifest fabulous memory of the smallest details of certain affect-laden situations. This is highly suggestive in its application to Faulkner, whose work sometimes seems a tissue of affect-laden memories. Infant stress can also occur in relation to the mother during the first year if the child attempts to develop its resources before it is fully ready to do so, and again during the second year, when an enterprising child begins practicing small separations which the mother may interpret as a sign that it is now quite grown up, without knowing that its ego-capacities are still very limited. In such circumstances, a normal child adapts, but usually at great psychic cost, internalizing the stresses it experiences and absorbing them into the fundamental personality structure. Such early traumas greatly increase the difficulty the child has in blending its good and bad images of the mother during the third year.

An anecdote suggesting that Faulkner may have suffered separation anxiety in excess of average is provided by Faulkner's needing, at around the age of three, to be returned home from an overnight visit to relatives because his distress could not be allayed.[25] Also pointing to intrapsychic factors indicating a need for more than average protective shielding is Maud Falkner's report of never having been able to get a night's rest during his entire first year. From the second year onward, as we know, he had to compete with subsequently born siblings for maternal attention. Meanwhile Murry Falkner, a manly man of conventional stereotype, did not participate actively in the duties of the nursery and soon also proved to be constitutionally incapable of relating to young children in a flexible and accepting way. Thus, the work of rearing the first three boys fell heavily upon Maud, who—besides nursing the children, running the household, and educating her young children before they attended school—also maintained domestic discipline. Her role as mother was obviously complex and conducted under strain at times. What links the images of older women in Faulkner's fiction to the bad-mother images of the pre-Oedipal period is that they emphasize the mature female's autonomy and authority in negative terms, with desire for closeness to the mother linked to fears of regressive merger. The seductiveness and sensuous appeal of the mother which characterizes the Oedipal conflict is present far less often.

A second way that Chodorow is useful is in her ability to bring us to a clearer awareness of Faulkner's unusual preoccupation with the physical mother—with woman as genetrix, the one who conceives, carries, gives birth, and breast-feeds. Faulkner's unusual concern with this aspect of woman finds its expression more in the textual detail of his work than in the forefront action of his fiction; nevertheless, its persistent presence marks it as a theme which is deliberately incorporated, and as one which adds an important dimension to his artistic vision.

For example, when, in one of his many references to the womb, he speaks of "the dark and velvet silence" of life within it, he invites contemplation of prenatal experience.[26] When he compares the sound of the Pyreanean cicada to "the purring sound . . . made by the unsleeping untoothed mouth . . . around the sleeping nipple,"[27] he brings suckling within imaginative compass. When he shows Lena at the opening of *Light in August* responding to the heaving of the foetus after she has ingested a can of sardines, he shows his interest in the advanced stages of pregnancy. Physical birth receives his attention in the same work when Hightower bloodies his hands while assisting as midwife in Lena's delivery, and again in "Old Man," when the convict cuts an umbilical cord with a tin can. In *The Hamlet* he depicts Eula Varner, whom he calls "the supreme uterus," as always clutching a sweet potato, a tuber which bears a striking resemblance to the uterus in anatomical illustration. In *As I Lay Dying* he depicts Addie as thinking about the space where she "used to be a virgin," representing it in the text as a blank which is rectilinear in shape, with unbounded sides, by the omission of a few letters.[28] I assume he is referring to the vagina, which also serves as the birth canal. In the text of the novel, this space balances with the drawing of the coffin to complete a pattern of sex and death, a major theme in that work. Faulkner's Duchampian humor here is breathtaking, and we are surprised to find, in making use of the concordance to the novel, that "Addie's space" does not appear anywhere in this otherwise meticulous scholarly work, perhaps because a space is not a word and cannot be alphabetized. But the coffin as a drawing is included, even though it is not a word. When we inspect the volume as a whole to find an explanation for the omission, we discover that none is provided, and we see also that no women scholars are listed as members of the advisory board.

The final way that Chodorow's work serves Faulkner study is in helping us to gain a clearer perception of how Faulkner's own experience of having been mothered reflects itself in his work through his tender concern for people and the world. Whereas his preoccupation with the father revolves chiefly around issues concerning male roles, his identification with the mother expresses itself more in terms of a caring attitude toward human beings. This nurturing orientation is perhaps best illustrated in the poignant short story, "Tomorrow," where a Mississippi countryman, unassisted, mothers an infant from birth. Ironically, after he has succeeded in raising a splendid boy, he finds that the orphan is now wanted by his dead mother's male relatives and that he has no basis in law to claim the boy as his own.

Similarly suffused by the caring emotions are Faulkner's empathetic renderings of children. Chodorow states that fathers tend, in general, to relate to their children more in terms of what their offspring will become when they grow up, as compared to mothers, whose relation to their young starts with the meeting of preverbal needs, which accustoms them more to accepting children as they are at a given moment. Faulkner's approach to children is maternal in this Chodorowian sense, and his fictions show his affections to always be enlisted on their behalf. He is always implicitly on the side of whatever promotes the development and growth of the young and opposed to whatever might harm or stultify. The emotional appeal of his characterization of children derives from this protective interest in their well being. It reveals itself repeatedly in his concern with formative influences, as in his depictions of the Compsons and Bundrens as children, his attention to Joe Christmas's years in the orphanage, and in his account of Miss Rosa's and Hightower's traumatic childhoods.[29] His tendency to be emotionally allied with the young explains as well his contempt for men who flee the responsibilities of parenthood, like Lucas Burch in *Light in August,* and his moral disapproval of males who deny their own children, like Thomas Sutpen. It also figures in his compassion for the beaten wives of rural Yoknapatawpha whose maternal impulses are thwarted by their domineering or reckless men.

Faulkner's solicitude for young life and for those who nurture it expands to a broader concern for the world itself in stories like "Delta Autumn," where Roth Edmonds gives no more thought to shooting a doe when he hunts than he does to abandoning the woman upon whom he has fathered a son. Such male disrespect for women, for the creatures of the earth, and for the earth itself is always condemned by Faulkner. The earth is always imaged by him as female, as mother. One of the most pervasive notes which sounds throughout his ouevre is love of the earth and lamentation for what man has done to it, denuding it of its forests, souring its soil with cordite, and converting the native wilderness into "a howling waste."[30]

This environmental concern, linked to his delicate sensitivity to human vulnerability, establishes what might be described as a maternal underlay in his work which is present even when he is obsessively preoccupied with the role of the father. In his own life, as we know, he was far closer to his mother than to his father. His interaction with his mother exerted a far more powerful influence. The pull in both directions—toward identification with the mother *and* with the father—endows his work with its highly charged dynamic tension. The two impulses are not mutually exclusive. Rather, they are simultaneously present.[31] Awareness of this duality in his work does much to soften the impact of its misogyny.[32]

Given the many insights that *The Reproduction of Motherhood* offers, this psychological work seems indispensible to any consideration of the topic of Faulkner and women in 1985. Like the writings by Jehlen and Jones examined earlier in this essay, it is of value to Faulkner study, not because it is feminist as such, but because its insistence upon bringing a deliberately formulated point of view to the contemplation of its subject matter renders it more intellectually precise. In approaching its subject with the determination to include women's experience and outlook, rather than to exclude it, it is more self-consciously ideological and hence more able to bring what it examines into sharper focus. This is why, when the insights provided by such outstanding feminist studies as these are brought to bear upon unresolved problems in the Faulkner field, they manifest so surprising a capacity to correct. Used in conjunction with existing Faulkner scholarship, they show not only how Faulkner's work rewards inquiry from more than one perspective but how a dual-gender approach brings certain oft-seen yet still unseen aspects of his texts into clearer view.

NOTES

1. Ed. Robert Con Davis (Amherst: University of Massachusetts Press, 1981), 115–45.

2. Ed. Nannerl O. Keohane, Michelle Z. Rosaldo, and Barbara Gelpi (Chicago: University of Chicago Press, 1982), 189–215.

3. Jehlen, 200.

4. Bleikasten, 120.

5. New York: Columbia University, 1976. Bleikasten's essay appears in *Faulkner and Idealism: Perspectives from Paris* (Jackson: University of Mississippi Press, 1983), 27–50.

6. Bleikasten, "For/Against an Ideological Reading of Faulkner's Novels," 49.

7. Elaine Showalter in *The New Feminist Criticism: Essays on Women, Literature, and Theory* (New York: Pantheon Books, 1985). Such reciprocities give evidence of being first steps toward a literary history and criticism in which the experiences of both men and women as represented in literature are included.

8. Baton Rouge: Louisiana State University Press, 1981.

9. Ibid., 8 and 12.

10. Joseph Blotner, *Faulkner: A Biography* (New York: Random House, 1974), 180–256. In the interests of space, material drawn from these pages will not be footnoted separately with each use of Blotner as a source.

11. Judith L. Sensibar, *The Origins of Faulkner's Art* (Austin: University of Texas Press, 1984), 50–51, 233, 234 nn.

12. I wish once again to express my thanks to the American Philosophical Society for the Fellowships in 1963 and 1964 which enabled me to explore Faulkner's background for the purpose of accruing insights about Faulkner's life and career, and to the New York University Graduate Arts and Science Fund for the travel grant awarded me in 1962.

13. Jones, 23.

14. *The Marble Faun* (Boston: Four Seas Company, 1924).

15. Ibid., 46.

16. *Count No 'Count* (Jackson: University Press of Mississippi, 1983), 76–78.

17. I wish to thank Jill Faulkner Summers and the Alderman Library of the University of Virginia for permission to examine the handlettered copy of *The Marionettes* with its illustrations by Faulkner. The undeniable resemblances between Faulkner's drawing of Marietta and Estelle Oldham are established by Sensibar in the new photograph of Estelle which appears in *The Origins of Faulkner's Art*, 27.

18. New Haven: Yale University Press, 1979.

19. *William Faulkner: Early Prose and Poetry*, ed. Carvel Collins (Boston: Atlantic Monthly Press Book, 1962), 101.

20. *Selected Letters of William Faulkner*, ed. Joseph Blotner (New York: Random House, 1977), 32.

21. Berkeley: University of California Press, 1978. Among the most recent, I have in mind especially the brilliant Freudian/Lacanian interpretation by John T. Irwin (*Doubling and Incest* [Baltimore: Johns Hopkins University Press, 1975]) and André

Bleikasten's *The Most Splendid Failure* (Bloomington: Indiana University Press, 1976) on the interpretation of Quentin.

22. " 'The Dungeon Was Mother Herself': William Faulkner: 1927–1931," *New Directions in Faulkner Studies*, ed. Doreen Fowler and Ann J. Abadie (Jackson: University Press of Mississippi, 1984), 61–93.

23. The neuropsychiatrist, Dr. S. Bernard Wortis, who saw Faulkner for nine sessions in 1953, suggested to Faulkner that he "might not have received enough love from his mother" (Blotner, *Faulkner: A Biography*, II, 1454). Judith Wittenberg in *The Transfiguration of Biography* (Lincoln: University of Nebraska Press, 1979) also hypothesizes that Maud Falkner was excessively detached as a mother. In the course of preparing this paper for publication, I came upon new information about Wortis's psychoanalytical orientation, which showed him to be not a Freudian, but an eclectic. In view of this, I have removed the speculations about how Wortis's Freudian analytical approach might have affected Faulkner, since they now seemed frivolous. Without departing from the summary of my paper as submitted, I have instead offered further textual support for the three main points made in this section.

24. Elizabeth Mahler, *On Human Symbiosis and the Vicissitudes of Individuation* (New York: International Universities Press, 1968), 44–47, 87, and passim..

25. *Faulkner: A Biography*, I, 66. For further references to this period, see chapters 8–11, pp. 51–114. Blotner's rendering of Maud Falkner conforms in essentials to the impression of her that I formed through many conversations with Mrs. Rose Rowland and Mrs. Calvin Brown, her near-contemporaries, who did not find her to have been overbearing, emotionally detached, or unsupportive of the males of her family. However, Cho-Cho, Estelle's daughter by her first marriage, was reported to me as having complained that her mother "was not there" for her, that she seemed more like a movie star than a mother, by her sixth-grade teacher, of whom she had made a confidante about this.

26. *Absalom, Absalom!* (New York: Random House, 1936), 234.

27. *A Fable* (New York: Random House, 1954), 42.

28. New York: Random House, Vintage Books, 1964, 165. This is not Faulkner's first representation of "woman's space" by a blank space on the page. Guerard notes that in *Flags in the Dust*, the word "unchaste" is followed by a blank, which is in turn followed by a question mark, when Horace Benbow wonders about Little Belle's virginity (111); *Flags in the Dust*, ed. Douglas Day (New York: Random House, Vintage Books, 1974), 203.

29. David Minter is sensitive to this aspect in his *William Faulkner: His Life and Work* (Baltimore: Johns Hopkins University Press, 1980).

30. *Requiem for a Nun* (New York: Random House, 1966), 102.

31. For example, André Bleikasten, in his preface to the concordance of *The Sound and the Fury* (ed. Noel Polk and Kenneth L. Privratsky), observes that, despite the prominence of Faulkner's attention to the father, the frequency table shows that the word "mother" appears 246 times, whereas the word "father" occurs only 170 times.

32. This pervasive sympathy toward women is doubtless a factor that explains why many women scholars of Faulkner defend his rendering of women, maintaining that he portrays a wide range of female characters in ways that reflect his admiration and sympathy for them. For further information on individual female scholars commenting on individual women characters in Faulkner's fiction, see the more than two thousand entries in Patricia Sweeney's *William Faulkner's Women Characters: An Annotated Bibliography of Criticism, 1930–1983* (Santa Barbara, Calif.: ABC-Clio Information Services, 1985).

Faulkner's Critics and Women: The Voice of the Community

JOHN N. DUVALL

I find myself in a strange position, seeking a beginning. As a man speaking about women in the novels of William Faulkner, I wonder what empowers me to speculate on female subjectivity in the Faulknerian universe. I am further discomforted by something Cleanth Brooks once wrote about people who object to the cohesive Southern community; the only ones who might find fault, suggests Brooks, are social scientists, young literary rebels, and neurotics.[1] Since I am neither a social scientist nor a literary rebel, I am left only the position of neurotic from which to speak. And so I reluctantly embrace that position in order to examine another community, the interpretive community—that collection of individuals who write or speak on a particular topic (say, for example, the novels of William Faulkner) and whose behavior is significantly governed by institutionally specific practices (say, for example, a conference on William Faulkner with all its attendant ritual).

To begin arbitrarily, then, let me assume two voices. Here is the first:

> Nearly every woman in Faulkner's novels has violated the existing moral code: Candace Compton [sic] indulged in premarital sex relations, became pregnant, married a man other than the father of her child, divorced, and ended up as a prostitute. Dewey Dell, Lena Grove, and Milly Jones also became pregnant prior to being married, and were abandoned by the men who misled them. Eula Varner and Temple Drake . . . lived lives of social and sexual immorality. Hightower's wife abandoned her husband to live the shameful

life of a prostitute in Memphis, Tennessee; Addie Bundren had an illegitimate son by a priest. Charlotte Rittenmeyer abandoned her two young daughters and her husband for carnality and lechery; these are the most outstanding of the many corrupt women in the famed but barren Yoknapatawpha county.[2]

And now another voice:

> Woman is the source and sustainer of virtue and also a prime source of evil. She can be either, because she is, as man is not, always a little beyond good and evil. With her powerful natural drives and her instinct for the concrete and personal, she does not need to agonize over her decisions. There is no code for her to master—no initiation for her to undergo. For this reason she has access to a wisdom which is veiled from man; and man's codes, good or bad, are always, in their formal abstraction, a little absurd in her eyes. Women are closer to nature; the feminine principle is closely related to the instinctive and natural.[3]

From the perspective of 1985 the first statement seems overtly misogynistic, criticism in the Doc Hines school, as it were. The second voice, however, that of Cleanth Brooks, represents a commonsense assessment within Faulkner studies. Both voices, I would like to argue, illustrate how Faulkner critics often appropriate the voices of the Southern community (as represented in Faulkner's novels and short stories) for their own writing practices. What does it mean for a critic to participate in the systems of labels used by the characters within a story or novel?

What, for example, is happening when a critic can speak of one of the themes of "Hair" as "the innate badness of women," a judgment that repeats an assessment of the story's narrator?[4] In his role as interpreter of Susan Reed, a young woman rumored to have had an abortion, the Ratliff-like itinerant salesman who narrates "Hair" gives voice to communal ideology on women:

> It's not that she was bad. There's not any such thing as a woman born bad, because they are all born bad, born with the badness in them. The thing is, to get them married before the badness comes to a natural head. But we try to make them conform to a system that says

a woman can't be married until she reaches a certain age. And nature
don't pay any attention to systems, let alone women paying attention
to them, or to anything. She just grew up too fast. She reached the
point where the badness came to a head before the system said it
was time for her to. I think they can't help it. I have a daughter of my
own, and I say that.[5]

Despite the paternal sympathy the narrator expresses for Susan
(after all, he's a father himself and would prefer these truths
about female nature not to be so), a male fear of female sexuality
underlies his comments. The badness the narrator speaks of is
feminine desire, specifically sexual desire beyond the control of
men. Women for this narrator are close to and driven by nature.
Opposed to nature are "systems" or culture. The resulting binary is woman-chaos-nature/man-order-culture. The narrator's so-
lution is to contain the problem by getting the offending female
married as quickly as possible so that her sexuality can be
legitimized; in other words, place female sexuality under male
control. If interpreters outside the text (such as the critic cited
above) employ the same words and language as those interpreters within the text, then the outside interpreters are implicated in the same ideology as the inner interpreters. In short,
the interpretive community of Faulkner critics, on matters of
sexual politics, frequently sounds very much like the good people of Jefferson.

But we needn't stay in Yoknapatawpha County to hear the
disapproval of women. The interpretive community's condemnation of Charlotte Rittenmeyer, for example, with its implicit judgment of female sexuality, all too frequently sounds like
the voice of "They," the forces of respectability and con-
ventionality in "Wild Palms." And the condemnations of her
come whether she is seen as an amoral flapper, as M. E. Bradford would have her, or as an amoral earthmother, as David M.
Miller types her.[6] "Charlotte," Michael Millgate decides, "is to
be criticized for demanding the abortion"; moreover, her "desire
not to have [additional] children is . . . the outward sign of
something lacking in her make-up, in her capacity for life."[7] For

Sally R. Page, when Charlotte "attempts to use sexuality as a means of escaping the reality of life's limitations rather than as a means of reproducing life, she aligns herself with the forces which destroy life."[8]

The sexism of the interpretive discourse, however, is not always so visible. In the title of Cleanth Brooks's chapter on *The Wild Palms*, "A Tale of Two Innocents," there is a subtle ideological charge operative in the word "innocent." Brooks speaks of "man's innocence" as a theme that "obviously fascinated Faulkner."[9] Innocence, as Brooks defines it, is "a quality of stubborn idealism and ingrained romanticism that continues to leave its human possessor puzzled, shocked, or even 'outraged.'"[10] Ostensibly Brooks uses at this moment "man" in the generic sense of men and women, yet in the next paragraph it becomes clear that Brooks's "man" is strictly male. Pointing to Horace Benbow, Gavin Stevens, Thomas Sutpen, and Quentin Compson, Brooks concludes that "for understanding women, most of the male sex in Faulkner's novels display incorrigible innocence"; by Brooks's next sentence "innocence" means simply that one "has never slept with a woman."[11] What results in Brooks's argument then is a dubious binary caused by a conflation of two meanings of innocence, the one we contrast with experience and the one we contrast with guilt: male innocence is opposed to (guilty) female (sexual) experience.

One should recognize that when Brooks asserts that "Faulkner sees the role of man as active" because "man makes choices and lives up to the choices," and the "role of women as characteristically fostering and sustaining . . . upholding the family and community mores," Brooks is writing from his commitment to a particular conception of society derived largely from his affiliation with Vanderbilt's self-proclaimed reactionaries of the late 1920s and early 1930s, the Southern Agrarians.[12] Brooks attended Vanderbilt between 1924 and 1928 at a time when the Fugitive Poets were attempting to become the more political Agrarians. The Southern Agrarians strongly critiqued modernity and Northern industrial society, while praising Southern culture as the last repository of the best of the European tradition. Their jumping-off point, a condemnation of the alienation caused by the consumer society of industrialism, is similar to Marxist critiques of modernity, yet the Agrarians were staunchly anticommunist. Accusing the Marxists of an idealism and utopianism, the Agrarians themselves posited a Golden Age in the Southern past which they sought to reestablish before it entirely disappeared. "The answer" to the problems of modernity, as Andrew Lytle puts it, "lies in a return to a society where agriculture is practiced by most of the people."[13] One can certainly begin to hear the extent to which Agrarian discourse speaks through Brooks's commentary on Faulkner in an essay such as Lyle Lanier's "A Critique of the Philosophy of Progress." Commenting on the "decline of the family," Lanier asserts that "the family is the natural biological group, the normal milieu of shared experiences, community of interests, integration of personality"; one nearly wonders, when encountering a phrase like "the unified manner of living inherent in the agrarian family and community," whether one is holding *The Yoknapatawpha Country* or *I'll Take My Stand*.[14] Brooks's (male) subject/(female) object dichotomy is necessary for his claim that "Faulkner is a conservative writer who sees the family as the basic unit of the community."[15] What then poses as innocent, apolitical, aesthetic criticism is actually a defense of the family, insisting upon the maintenance of sharply divided gender roles.

Nowhere is Brooks's position clearer than the "Preface" to Sally Page's *Faulkner's Women*, where he asserts that Faulkner "believes it a mistake for either sex to try to adopt the special values of the other. The sexes must maintain their roles."[16] This belief in a male/female dichotomy in which man as an acting subject is opposed to woman as an acted upon object informs not only the corpus of Brooks's commentary but also, to a great extent, the discourse of the Faulkner institution itself. What such a binary position overlooks is the vast array of characters who simply cannot be so dichotomized. Faulkner's soft-spoken, passive men are legion: Ernest Talliaferro and Horace Benbow are comically and tragically ineffectual; Byron Bunch, Henry Stribling, and Stonewall Jackson Fentry are fostering and sustaining; Harry Wilbourne allows life to live itself through him. Conversely, there are numerous strong, decisive women: Margaret Powers, Joanna Burden, Charlotte Rittenmeyer, and Laverne Shumann all make choices and live up to them. Brooks himself recognizes that these two categories are inadequate and supplements them by ascribing deviance to female characters who do not fit his scheme; although male characters (such as the ones named above) do not come under any special censure for crossing the gender line, Brooks dismisses women who desire something more than the limited roles allowed them as "masculinized" and "warped and twisted."[17] A question that needs to be asked is whether it is Faulkner who is "radically old-fashioned" in his conception of women or whether it is his critics who are perhaps medieval.[18]

Brooks's reading of *Sanctuary*, in which he establishes his major concern in speaking about women and men, illustrates why such a question is pertinent:

> In nearly every one of Faulkner's novels, the male's discovery of evil and reality is bound up with his discovery of the *true nature of woman*. Men idealize and romanticize women, but the cream of the jest is that *women have a secret rapport with evil which men do not have*, that they are able to adjust to evil without being shattered by it, being *by nature* flexible and pliable. Women are the *objects of idealism*, but are not in the least idealistic.[19]

Once again the male-subject/female-object dichotomy manifests itself, and the strong implication is that, for a male, to know women is to know evil. Brooks's affiliation with the Southern Agrarians may be read from his confident use of the natural. For Brooks the Agrarian, anatomy is destiny, and he only speaks of female subjectivity from the biological, never the ideological, pole. Brooks takes the male-female relation in *Sanctuary* as the model for understanding such relations in all of Faulkner's novels, but just as Brooks's use of *Light in August* to defend the community can't be justified with other novels, it is equally problematic to make *Sanctuary* the model for understanding Faulkner's women. The problem is that Brooks inserts himself into the novelistic discourse by taking up a position which is Horace Benbow's; that is to say, that if Horace could step outside the novel and write an article about *Sanctuary*, it would be very like Brooks's chapter. While at the old Frenchman place, Horace rambles about why he left home. During his monologue, he asserts that "nature is she; because of that conspiracy between female flesh and female season."[20] He elaborates this belief later in his monologue when he comments on his observing Little Belle's facial expressions reflected in a mirror she doesn't see: "I could see her face, see her watching the back of my head with pure dissimulation. That's why nature is 'she' and Progress is 'he'; nature made the grape arbor, but Progress invented the mirror."[21] Horace's dichotomy is Brooks's exactly. Additionally, both Brooks and Benbow participate in the same kind of binary thinking that the narrator of "Hair" engages in. In both *Sanctuary* and "Hair" this woman-nature/man-culture distinction is spoken by interpreters inside the text. Brooks, the outside interpreter, consistently (if indirectly) identifies Faulkner with the utterances of certain male characters who exhibit benevolent paternalism. Such interpretive moments are a strategy of containment, and rhetorical violence adheres in the deductive leap to formations beginning "For Faulkner . . ." since they are always an appeal to the authority of the author, part of critics' attempts to legitimate their readings.

What the discourse of Faulkner studies so often lacks, as the preceding examples illustrate, is a self-reflectivity that would call into question its assumptions when speaking about gender. In order to suggest a process of self-reflectivity, I will discuss how and what the interpretive community calls Joe Christmas's killing of Joanna Burden. I have chosen this way into *Light in August* in the belief that what is casually taken for granted often betrays deep ideological investments, since "the fact of agreement, rather than being a proof of the stability of objects, is a testimony to the power of an interpretive community to constitute the objects upon which its members (also simultaneously constituted) can then agree."[22]

My understanding of ideology is taken in part from the French philosopher Louis Althusser, whose rethinking of the old Marxist concept of ideology as distorted or false consciousness led to a much less reductive way of speaking about ideology. By taking into account developments in psychoanalysis and linguistics, Althusser was able to suggest that our thinking takes place within categories external to us; therefore, when we give voice to our thoughts, it is unclear whether we speak language or if language speaks us. For Althusser, if I may bring together statements from "Marxism and Humanism" and "Ideology and Ideological State Apparatuses," ideology is a "profoundly *unconscious*" "system (with its own logic and rigour) of representations (images, myths, ideas or concepts)" "of the subject's real conditions of existence."[23] The particular system of representation about which we, as writers writing about writing, should be most concerned is language. Some of the most interesting work on the ways others' words become our words was done by the Bakhtin circle in the 1920s. *Marxism and the Philosophy of Language* was published in 1929 under the name V. N. Vološinov, but Bakhtin now is believed to have extensively collaborated in the project. Bakhtin/Vološinov perceives language as an inescapable zone of ideological representation: "The logic of consciousness is the logic of ideological communication, of the semiotic interaction of a social group."[24] Hence, "the word is the fundamental object of the study of ideologies" because of its constitutive role in consciousness and communication.[25] For Bakhtin/Vološinov, since language is a belief system, every word is ideological and hence the potential site of legitimate political struggle. One particular word that gives us an entry into the ideological unconscious of the discourse of Faulkner studies on *Light in August* is *murder*—"the unlawful killing of a human being with malice aforethought" *(OED)*. Although the sole owner and proprietor of Yoknapatawpha County uses, on his country's map, the less connotatively charged *kills* to describe

Christmas's act, nearly every critic in the political spectrum from Cleanth Brooks to the Marxian Myra Jehlen agrees that Joe *murders* Joanna.[26] I would like to suggest, however, that when we hail Joe Christmas as murderer, we hail ourselves in the moment of our own speaking as members of the textual community (Jefferson) and the extra-textual or interpretive community.[27] Moreover, we involve ourselves in sexist (as well as racist) ideology when we call Joe a murderer.

I use the pronoun "we" in the above paragraph because I too in my teaching and thinking about *Light in August* have made the easy and immediate judgment that Christmas is a murderer. The text pushes one to such a conclusion in a number of ways. We are prepared both before and after the fact to choose "murder" as the word to describe Christmas's act. It is only fitting that Byron Bunch (whether one believes him to be of the community or not) should be the first to speak the word "murder" since he consistently absorbs and reflects the voice(s) of the community. Even before Brown/Burch betrays Christmas "to avoid being accused of the murder itself" Byron tells Hightower that Joanna's death is immediately perceived as murder:[28] "The sheriff found out how somebody had been living in that cabin, and then right off everybody began to tell about Christmas and Brown that had kept [Christmas and Brown's selling whiskey] a secret long enough for one or maybe both of them to murder that lady" (86). Certainly chapter 5 seems to establish "malice aforethought." Two moments are particularly damning: first, there is Christmas's thought while standing over Brown/Burch, *"This is not the right one"* (97), which establishes "the razor with its five inch blade" as a lethal weapon; second, there is his statement seeming to provide a motive: "She ought not to started praying over me. She would have been all right if she hadn't started praying over me" (99).

Yet the repetition of the sentence *"Something is going to happen to me"* (97, 110), with its resonances within the Faulknerian universe, begins to work in another direction; for Temple Drake in *Sanctuary,* the Reporter in *Pylon,* and Harry

Wilbourne in *The Wild Palms*, their use of the same line suggests their victimization rather than their agency. When chapter 12 picks up where chapter 5 leaves off with Joe preparing to mount the stairs to confront Joanna, his thoughts still suggest an intent to kill her: "He believed with calm paradox that he was the volitionless servant of the fatality in which he believed that he did not believe. He was saying to himself *I had to do it* already in the past tense; *I had to do it. She said so herself*" (264). Even the intervening pages in chapters 6–12, generally seen as humanizing the murderer, present us with incidents that prepare us for Joe's "murder" of Joanna. For example, there is Joe's violence against women in his attack on the black girl and later on the prostitute who was unconcerned with his racial background; also we see Joe strike his adoptive father with a chair. This makes Joe a double murderer for some critics, though such critics forget that McEachern was attacking Joe (who has been the victim of child abuse at the hands of his adoptive father) and that McEachern may have survived the blow to the head.

The opening of chapter 13 follows just three pages after the climactic moments leading up to the white space on page 267—that crucial absence in both the text and Joe's memory that withholds the details of Joanna's death—and presents a fuller version of the community's reaction to her death than we get from Byron's second-hand information that he shares with Hightower in chapter 4. We are manipulated again at the manifest level into accepting the community's judgment by the repetition of the word "murder." "*Murdering a white woman the black son of a*" (275), says a disembodied voice in the crowd at the fire. There is the "thousand dollars' reward for the capture of [Joanna's] murderer" offered by her nephew (278). Additionally, Christmas's attack upon the black church, particularly his striking Roz Thompson (which for some critics means that Joe is a three-time murderer), makes it easier to hail Christmas as murderer in his killing of Joanna.

In the scene in which Christmas confronts Joanna on the night she is killed, what do we really know? Yes, Joe's thoughts have been bloody and violent; he thinks in fact of his killing of Joanna as already accomplished. Too we know that both parties have agreed that "there's just one other thing to do" (265). But when he enters her room on that fateful evening, Joanna asks him to light the lamp. He initially responds threateningly: "It won't need any light." (266); but then, leaving his unopened razor on the table, he complies with her request and lights the lamp. His defiance in refusing to pray, which recalls his childhood refusal to learn his catechism, is not violent but merely stubborn.

What is important here is to see what object Joanna as acting subject has in view at this moment. The passage leading up to the white space in which Joanna's death occurs is crucial:

Then he saw her arms unfold and her right hand come forth from beneath the shawl. It held an old style, single action, cap-and-ball revolver almost as long and heavier than a small rifle. But the shadow of it and of her arm and hand on the wall did not waver at all, the shadow of both monstrous, the cocked hammer monstrous, backhooked and viciously poised like the arched head of a snake; it did not waver at all. And her eyes did not waver at all. They were as still as the round black ring of the pistol muzzle. But there was no heat in them, no fury. They were calm and still as all pity and all despair and all conviction. But he was not watching them. He was watching the shadowed pistol on the wall; he was watching when the cocked shadow of the hammer flicked away. (267)

Although Joe is, in a limited way, the cognitive subject ("he saw"), focalizing our perceptions in this passage, Joanna is the pragmatic subject and her object, which has been to get Joe to pray with her, is now to kill him, and but for the failure of the gun to fire, she would have succeeded. Significant too is the realignment of the snake image. In chapter 2 Byron thinks of how Christmas's name ought to have been an "augur" like "a rattlesnake its rattle" (29) and how he works like a man "chopping up a buried snake" (35). In this instance it is Joanna who is linked to the snake through "the cocked hammer . . . poised like the arched head of a snake."

Is Christmas a murderer if he kills his attempted killer? The vast majority of commentators never question Joe's guilt. A few critics do, however, begin to sense some contradiction, and it is interesting to observe the tortuous ways in which they describe this fatal encounter and still manage to label Joe's act a "murder." One critic, for example, suggests that the "final provocation is [Joanna's] *threatening* [Joe] with a pistol" and that she is "*apparently* prepared to kill Joe."[29] But surely pulling the trigger of a gun at point blank range is more than an apparent threat. An even stranger juxtaposition may be seen in the observations of another critic who sees the potential for calling Christmas's act "self-defense" but then concludes that "the de facto explanation may be that Joe retaliated by committing *murder* in his own *defense*."[30] What is odd here, of course, is the pairing of self-defense and murder, appellations which are mutually exclusive. Just as when Christmas strikes McEachern, isn't he acting in what could be called self-defense, not murder? If Joe's intent seems violent and murderous, surely Joanna in her calm religious fervor is equally murderous, if not more so, since she makes the first deadly move.

It is of course a moot point, as there is no trial, whether Christmas's act of killing Joanna could be seen as justifiable homicide, but it is a point that nevertheless bears brief pursuit. A general principle for justifiable homicide in Mississippi law that could have provided a precedent in 1932 was established in 1879 in *Cannon* versus *the State:* "That one has malice against another does not deny him the right to kill that other in self-defense." In fact, "[t]he right of self-defense may arise though one is defending himself against danger which he himself has provoked, so as to make the homicide justifiable" (*Patterson* versus *the State*, 1898). Most telling of all perhaps is the ruling in *Pulpus* versus *the State*, 1903: "The fact that defendant provided himself with a deadly weapon and sought another with a design to kill him, and was the aggressor in the encounter in which he killed deceased, did not deprive him of the right of self-defense, *if the killing was not pursuant to the original purpose to kill*."[31]

And this is precisely what I would argue if I were playing

Gavin Stevens in a trial—that Joe's willingness to reopen communication with Joanna constitutes a suspension of his original
intent to kill her. If Joe had simply walked into Joanna's room and
slit her throat, the word "murder" would undoubtedly be correct. But his decision to light the lamp and his laying aside the
unopened razor are, it seems, signs of a willingness, even at this
late moment, to work towards a reconciliation. The dialogue
fails, however, because Joanna is unwilling to speak as a human
being and becomes instead another avatar of an avenging God: "I
don't ask [that you pray]. It's not I who ask it" (267). Because she
will be the avenger, she pulls out the pistol and with almost no
hesitation tries to kill Joe. As readers we are quite willing to
supply motives for Joe's "murdering" Joanna. We may conclude,
for example, that Joanna has come to represent every tormentor
in Joe's life: she is McEachern praying over him (and Joe refuses
three times in this last meeting to kneel with her as he had
refused three times to learn his catechism); she is Doc Hines in
her religious fanaticism; she is Mrs. McEachern through the
parallel food throwing scenes; she is Bobbie Allen, only now the
surprise is menopause instead of menstruation; she is the dieti-
tian because of her sexual desire, association with food, and
perhaps even because when the gun fails to discharge, she seems
to deny an expected punishment. All these parallels may be
relevant and may have flashed through Joe's mind in the moment
of the pistol hammer's falling, but that doesn't make his killing
Joanna a murder.[32] Joe's tragedy that Faulkner speaks of may be
that Christmas kills the only person he loves, and in his running
away he is only perceived as a "nigger murderer."[33] What the
text suggests is that this communal judgment is doubly twisted,
since Joe, in addition to being nonblack, is nonmurderer. That
the community passes judgment without a trial should immediately call into question its correctness, and we are perhaps
more culpable for accepting this judgment since we are allowed
to see and know so much more than the community.

In the community's eyes Joe is a murderer because Brown/
Burch calls him a nigger, because Joe runs away, and, signifi-

cantly, because Joanna is a white woman. Thadious Davis argues cogently that the town's construction of Joanna as Southern womanhood despoiled by the Negro illustrates the working of racist ideology. But in the interpretive community's acceptance of "murder" into its discourse, there is a corresponding sexist ideology, disturbing in its near invisibility, that replicates the Jeffersonians' "nice believing" (273). When we call her death "murder," we tacitly affirm that woman is victim (and we unknowingly participate in the crowd's hope that she has been raped) and that the death of a woman, keeper of the finer values of society, mother-sister-daughter though spinster, is somehow special, more important than that of a man. (Normally I would refrain from reading contemporary culture off the surface of a historical text, but in this instance the parallel seems worth noting. Recall the television coverage of the crisis at the Libyan embassy in London in April of 1984. The coverage became a contemporary "emotional barbecue, a Roman holiday almost" [273] in the way it stressed the death of an English policewoman, "young and quite attractive," as one CBS commentator on the Sunday morning news put it, "writhing on the ground." Certainly if a *male* police officer had been killed, such comments would never have been made.) We take, it seems, a perverse pleasure, disguised as moral outrage, in the violent death of a woman. To place Joanna on equal ground (as combatant or duelist) with Joe in their final meeting would give her an agency, a subjectivity that would take all the romance out of her death; to see woman as victim is to see woman as passive object. Women, this attitude asserts, are people to whom things happen, not who make things happen, and certainly they can't (or won't) kill anyone. Misogyny and the idealization of women are constituted in the same impulse; they are the two sides to a single sheet of paper.

Perhaps now we have arrived at the beginning this essay searched for at the outset. That beginning lies in a self-reflectivity that one may attain through a critical historicizing of the interpretive context. Historicizing the interpretive context allows the critic who enters the language game of Faulkner studies to avoid an unconscious repetition of an ideology that she would consciously reject. The overvaluation of the paternal voice within the texts of William Faulkner has reduced the scope of Faulkner's message about human interaction to the play of acting males and acted upon females. This interpretive paternalism acts as a conservative buttress for the family, nuclear and extended, which in turn props up a particular conception of community. Originating in the discourse of Southern Agrarianism, this strain in Faulkner studies goes much deeper than the particular criticism of Agrarianism's first and best popularizer, Cleanth Brooks, or of a neo-Agrarian like M. E. Bradford. The very questions asked about Faulkner's texts are constantly framed within a discourse that privileges "community" and "family." Self-reflectivity must accompany reconsiderations of such issues as the characterization of women, male-female relationships, and sexual identity in the texts of William Faulkner. The key attitude is one of radical suspicion, particularly of those ways of summarizing plots or of describing character relations that seem most secure. Consensus does not always signify a movement toward the truth of Faulkner's texts; rather, it often places us squarely in the prison house of masculinist ideology, where we condemn the fully sexual female subject out of our own insecurities and fears.

NOTES

1. Cleanth Brooks, *A Shaping Joy* (New York: Harcourt Brace Jovanovich, 1971), 225.

2. Lewis A. Richards, "Sex Under *The Wild Palms* and a Moral Question," *Arizona Quarterly*, 28, No. 4 (Winter 1972), 329.

3. Cleanth Brooks, *The Hidden God* (New Haven: Yale University Press, 1963), 27.

4 Walter K. Everett, *Faulkner's Art and Characters* (Woodbury, N.Y.: Barron's Educational Series, 1969), 144.

5. William Faulkner, "Hair," *Collected Stories* (New York: Random House, 1950), 133.

6. M. E. Bradford, "Faulkner's 'Elly': An Exposé," *Mississippi Quarterly*, 21, No. 3 (Summer 1968), 186; David M. Miller, "Faulkner's Women," *Modern Fiction Studies*, 13, No. 1 (Spring 1967), 16.

7. *The Achievement of William Faulkner* (New York: Random House, 1963), 171 and 173.

8. *Faulkner's Women* (Deland, Fla.: Everett/Edwards, 1972), 134.

9. *William Faulkner: Toward Yoknapatawpha and Beyond* (New Haven: Yale University Press, 1978), 207.

10. Ibid., 208.

11. Ibid.

12. Brooks, *Hidden God*, 35. In characterizing the Agrarian position as reactionary, I do not mean to be a name caller. The word "reactionary" in fact exists at the very origin of the Agrarian movement. In a letter to Donald Davidson of August 10, 1929, Allen Tate suggested "[t]he formation of a society, or an academy of Southern *positive* reactionaries." See Lewis P. Simpson's "The Southern Republic of Letters and *I'll Take My Stand*," which quotes the Tate letter at length, in *A Band of Prophets*, ed. William C. Havard and Walter Sullivan (Baton Rouge: Louisiana State University Press, 1982), 67–68.

13. "The Hind Tit" in *I'll Take My Stand: The South and the Agrarian Tradition* (New York: Harper & Brothers, 1930), 203.

14. *I'll Take My Stand*, 154.

15. Brooks, "Primitivism," *English Institute Essays: 1952*, ed. Alan S. Downer (New York: Columbia University Press, 1954), 23.

16. Brooks, "Preface" to Sally R. Page's *Faulkner's Women*, xvi. Brooks's argument has directly influenced a number of critics. Page herself often sounds like an extended gloss on Brooks's conception of gender roles: "Faulkner makes it clear that in the face of familial and social decay the only source of moral order and endurance is woman's ability to fulfill the creative and sustaining role of motherhood. Woman's purpose is the bearing of children and in her submission to that process she achieves serenity and virtue" (93). Similarly, Bradford's Faulkner will not tolerate deviance: "Since women are the backbone of the community, the vessels of its perpetuation, some aspects of their place must remain fixed if family and society are to survive. Refusal to address and act the steward of life within the framework of 'given' circumstances is in no other group so serious. With it comes chaos" ("Faulkner's 'Elly,'" 180). To what extent, we need to ask, is this position (which Brooks, Page, and Bradford implicitly claim is Faulkner's intended message) the sociopolitical program or ideological orientation of the critics?

17. Brooks, *Hidden God*, 34.

18. Ibid., 27.

19. Cleanth Brooks, *William Faulkner: The Yoknapatawpha Country* (New Haven: Yale University Press, 1963), 127–28, emphasis added.

20. William Faulkner, *Sanctuary* (New York: Jonathan Cape & Harrison Smith), 13.

21. *Sanctuary*, 15.

22. Stanley Fish, *Is There a Text in This Class? The Authority of Interpretive Communities* (Cambridge: Harvard University Press, 1980), 338. I would agree with Edward Said that we must go beyond Fish to ask "what political interests are concretely entailed by the very existence of interpretive communities" (*The World, the Text, and the Critic* [Cambridge: Harvard University Press, 1983], 26).

23. *For Marx*, trans. Ben Brewster (New York: Pantheon, 1969), 231–36; *Lenin and Philosophy and Other Essays*, trans. Ben Brewster (New York: Monthly Review Press, 1971), 167.

24. V. N. Vološinov, *Marxism and the Philosophy of Language*, trans. Ladislaw Matejka and I. R. Titunik (New York: Seminar Press, 1973), 13.

25. Ibid., 15.

26. Myra Jehlen in *Class and Character in Faulkner's South* (New York: Columbia University Press, 1976) begins promisingly enough in suggesting an ideological study, but in actual analysis her haste in summarizing plots leads her at times into plain errors of fact and with *Light in August* into a replication of the hegemonic verdict. Although Stephen Meats in "Who Killed Joanna Burden?" (*Mississippi Quarterly*, 24, No. 3 [Summer 1971], 271-77) argues that Brown/Burch from the evidence the community has should have been the chief murder suspect, Meats finally agrees that Joe surely must be the murderer; that Joanna's death is a murder is never questioned.

27. The word "hail" here refers to Althusser's concept of the interpolation of the subject in "Ideology and Ideological State Apparatuses." My point is simply that the act of hailing fixes as much she who hails as he who is hailed.

28. William Faulkner, *Light in August* (New York: Harrison Smith and Robert Haas, 1932), 91; all references are to this edition and will hereafter be cited in this essay internally by page numbers.

29. François Pitavy, *Faulkner's "Light in August,"* trans. Gillian E. Cook (Bloomington: Indiana University Press, 1973), 111 and 116, emphasis added.

30. Regina K. Fadiman, *Faulkner's "Light in August": A Description and Interpretation of the Revisions* (Charlottesville: University Press of Virginia, 1975), 167–68, emphasis added.

31. *Mississippi Digest 1818 to Date*, vol. 8 (St. Paul: West Publishing Co., 1936), sec. V, nos. 101–13.

32. For the purposes of this paper, I am reducing the possible ways of viewing a killing to murder or self-defense. In fact there exists a third category, manslaughter, which comes into play in the everyday workings of the judicial system. Manslaughter, an unlawful killing without malice aforethought, mediates the grey area between murder and self-defense. And perhaps it would be metaphorically correct to place Christmas's killing of Joanna in this category, since Joe always stands in a grey middle ground, whether between black and white or masculine and feminine.

33. Asked about Joe Christmas while at the University of Virginia Faulkner responded: "Well, Joe Christmas—I think you really can't say that any man is good or bad. I grant you there are some exceptions, but man is the victim of himself, or his fellows, or his own nature, or his environment, but no man is good or bad either. . . . And I don't think he was bad, I think he was tragic" (*Faulkner in the University*, ed. Frederick L. Gwynn and Joseph L. Blotner [New York: Random House, 1965], 118).

Women in Faulkner's Novels: Author's Attitude and Artistic Function

SERGEI CHAKOVSKY

At the 1982 Faulkner and Yoknapatawpha Conference during a meal break in our daily scholarly labors—appropriately held at the "Busy Bee" eating place—Ann Abadie and Myriam Díaz-Diocaretz were conducting a sort of poll. Among other things they asked was what we would think of devoting a future conference to Faulkner and women. I recall answering something glib and presumably gallant to the effect that I thought very highly of both, though not perhaps in conjunction.

Later as I considered what occasioned that remark, I realized two things. First, the topic seemed to me, well, topical. Wouldn't it veer our audience from the larger social, psychological, aesthetic preoccupations of Faulkner's art to something interesting and important in itself, yet more or less "incidental" to the subject of a literary study? Given the nature of much contemporary criticism, which, confronted with the problem under discussion, much too often has retreated into partisan—male or female—moralizing, makeshift psychoanalysis, or idle speculation about the author's private life, these misgivings may not seem totally ungrounded. But then, I reasoned, the study of such patently "literary" matters as imagery, style, sources of literary influence could be as extraneous to the meaning and value of a work of art and the author's identity as the "trivial" meditation on—to quote René Wellek—"Hamlet in Wittenburg, the slim and young Falstaff, 'the girlhood of Shakespeare's heroines' and the question of how many children had lady Mac-Beth."[1]

Alexander Pushkin once remarked that a writer "ought to be judged by the laws he himself had recognized above him."[2] The obvious, yet ever-relevant implication of this phrase is that novels, plays, poems, and other types of creative writing should be read, understood, and evaluated not as "words" but as works of verbal art, that is, according to their original intention. A striking definition of the latter is Faulkner's description of his "life's work in the agony and sweat of the human spirit" as an attempt "to create out of the materials of the human spirit something which did not exist before,"[3] yet something that would serve as a "kind of keystone in the Universe; that, as small as that keystone is, if it were ever taken away, the universe itself would collapse."[4]

A lot of aesthetic theory is compressed in this "empirical" poetic definition. It points to what I see as a basic ontological problem: how does a literary artifact, made not even of clay (like Gordon's or Charlotte Rittenmeyer's figurines), acquire if not "size," "weight," then the no less objective *presence* in the human universe? how does "another reality" (to use Marx's expression) of a work of art become so compelling as to attain the status of the "keystone" in our perception of the world? These eternal questions have to be borne in mind for at least two reasons. First, to avoid getting the ends and the means of creative writing mixed up, and thus critical misjudgment. Second, to lay proper stress on the writer's active, expressive-transfigurative role in respect to the reality he depicts.

Distorted perspective of analysis looms as a tangible threat with our particular subject precisely because women characters play such an indisputably prominent role in Faulkner's novels. They would not have such a profound impact upon us as they do were it not for the unifying and interpretative presence of Margaret Powers and Miss Jenny Du Pre; the words and moral standpoints of Addie Bundren and Rosa Coldfield; the human authority of Dilsey and Nancy Mannigoe; the existential challenge of Cecily Saunders, Caddy Compson, and Temple Drake; the eternal life symbolism of Lena Grove and the woman of "Old

Man"; the social awareness of Joanna Burden, Charlotte Rittenmeyer, and Linda Snopes. It is equally obvious, despite all
vividness and psychological depth of depiction, that woman did
not constitute for Faulkner a kind of self-sufficient object of
artistic "study"—the way she did, presumably, for writers like
Stendhal, Flaubert, Turgenev, or James. For Faulkner no *one*
thing did. Not even "the South," as he pointed out in a well-
known letter to Malcolm Cowley[5]—an admission which I tend to
see if not as a moment of truth, then as an important correlative
to his ostensibly indisputable Southern allegiance. No one thing
"but" "man's history . . . his anguish, his triumph, his failures,
the whole passion of breathing."[6] And, of course, Faulkner tried
to find a way to "distill" it "to its absolute essence," not only to
make this ephemeral world stand solid and real to the reader but
to "move" according to the author's will.

Striving to create this world he would "recycle" into an artistic
whole such disparate and otherwise self-sufficient matters as
time, history, men, women, woods, dogs, mules—not necessarily in that order—likening himself to "the carpenter building
the fence," "using the quickest tool to hand."[7] He would rightfully disclaim interest in pure "ideas," for not only the patently
"functional" devices of art but many of the seemingly straightfor-
ward ideological propositions are for him means toward one basic
end—"to tell a story, in the most effective . . . the most moving,
the most exhaustive" way.[8] Yet, since the "tools" he uses are not
tools at all but objects of various social interests, the values and
meanings attached to them, such "profane" questions as "did he
love women or did he hate them?" acquire unexpected validity.
Such questions are certainly justified on the part of the general
public whose *life* the author uses as his "material." They are
justified on the part of the more sophisticated readership having
as their target area the author's philosophy of life in one of its
crucial aspects. They are just as unavoidable as they are indispensable for our scholarly purposes. For one thing, they afford
us the view of a "literary fact" as a broader historical, socio-
psychological, and cultural phenomenon. They urge us to look

for and try to understand that integrating philosophy of life which forms the ideological bedrock of a work of art, accounting for what at first sight could pass for "capriciousness" or "inconsistency" of style and characterization. All things aside, those latter allegedly intrinsic properties of Faulkner's fiction put our "specific" question right into the mainstream of Faulkner studies.

I hardly have to remind you that the charge of "inconsistency" has been brought against Faulkner on innumerable occasions, mostly—if not always—stemming from the author's "failure" to conform to our preconceived notions of how his novels should have been written. That Faulkner's artistic vision was "polar" (as Conrad Aiken was the first to notice) and his poetics "contrastive" (as aptly defined by Ivan Kashkin) is certainly true and explains a number of things. What needs stressing, however, is that those "contrasts" were not specifically designed just to shock or puzzle the reader—to produce elaborate "oxymorons" and "moments of unresolved tension," if I may use those key expressions of Walter Slatoff's *Quest for Failure* contrary to their original context. The problem, may I repeat, is to uncover the motivating idea behind those "contradictions," to appreciate their artistic necessity. This, I have to admit, is not always easy.

Two seemingly irreconcilable stances are reflected in contrasting sets of images, the opposing stylistic patterns of Faulkner's novels. The first is the perception of woman as the keeper of "truth, or as near truth as he [man] dare approach,"[9] and reflects admiration for woman, "a profound faith in her,"[10] or rather in "that most sacred thing in life: womanhood."[11] On the other hand are various "misogynistic" elements: in Joe Christmas's actions, in the pronouncements of Eupheus Hines and Simon McEachern, or in the famous—or infamous—coda of *The Wild Palms* ("Woman . . . t" the tall convict said" [*WP*, 238]). The problem is aggravated by the fact that the most approving reference in this sampling (the last one from *Sanctuary*) is voiced by a detestable, corrupt lawyer, Eustace Graham, while the most contemptuous one is the sentiment of a naive and profoundly decent man—the tall convict, who almost lost his life trying to save a woman. Things are likely to get even more complicated if we try to define the author's feminine ideal.

One would rightfully assume, for instance, as most critics do, that Lena Grove represents all those light- and life-bringing virtues of womanhood that Faulkner was deeply fascinated with. But it seems strange to hear the glorification of those virtues from such a confirmed accomplice of "evil" as Clarence Snopes, who takes the idea to its logical extreme: "the church aint got no place in politics, and women aint got no place in neither one. . . . Let them stay at home and they'll find plenty to do" (S, 194). Had "that abounding serenity as of earth" which Narcissa Benbow "seemed to emanate . . . since her marriage and the birth of her child" (S, 60) made her more understanding and compassionate? Isn't Lena Grove's counterpart in "Old Man" a bit *too* simpleminded?

Opposite this type is the "epicene" female, a kind of woman that Faulkner, according to Cleanth Brooks, was "obsessed" with since she was "closely involved with his concept of romantic love and with his concept of the whole realm of romance."[12] I agree with Brooks that "the epicene girl . . . powerfully engaged the imagination of the young Faulkner,"[13] but not just the "girl" and not just the *young* Faulkner—the author of "Elmer," *Mosquitoes*, and *Soldiers' Pay*. Many of the otherwise very different female (and, incidentally, male) characters of his later novels—from Temple Drake through Joanna Burden and Charlotte Rittenmeyer to Linda Snopes of *The Mansion*, as well as their respective male partners—are described in "epicene"—"androgynous"—terms. But there is very little, or rather much more than, "romance" in his treatment even of the earlier "cases"—to say nothing of the later ones.

Trying to bridge these logical gaps, it would hardly suffice to say that, paradoxically perhaps, Faulkner had his emotional "stock" in *all* attitudes expressed in his novels, being subject to considerable affective fluctuations. One has to learn how to overcome those "fluctuations" (more or less typical of sensitive men, as psychologists say) to produce good literature. A more plausible way is to take heed of the fact—and here I rely on the authority of Evans Harrington—that "Faulkner's attitude to women [was] shaped by Mississippi," which some people, not without justification, see as a sort of "gynocentric society"; so, like many of his fellow countrymen and the characters of his books, Faulkner would "be often in awe of [women] if not astonished or outraged by them."[14] All pros and cons weighed, the least we can do, I think, is to use Quentin Compson's "formula" toward the South and say that, like Quentin, certainly Faulkner "[does]n't hate" women. We could then step back and watch the chain reaction of connotations, hopefully, absorb the problem. Yet, it is likely to pop up again, mainly, I think, because the attitude behind the artistic transfigurations of women that we find in Faulkner's novels pertains to another conceptual plane, transgressing the love-hate dichotomy or rendering it irrelevant.

To understand this attitude we have to go beyond the "words" the author says *about* women on to their (the women's and the words') functioning in his artistic system. This entails—to belabor the obvious—a reminder to ourselves that what we are dealing with are mostly reactions of fictional male characters not to women in general or some woman in particular, perhaps not to a woman at all, but to what she comes to represent in a particular figurative context. Thus, the attitude woman commands in Faulkner's novels is inconceivable outside of her *"reflective-yet-rival"* role towards the male protagonist and his existential dilemma. It has to be pointed out that male-female relationships are initially, as it were, "extraneous" to this dilemma since it involves bigger issues: man and his fate; his individual will and the "will" of events; his claims for personal uniqueness and the objective social, historical, natural laws he is subject to. One can say that woman is always "unexpected" yet unavoidable in Faulkner's novels.

The program character of such a type of conjunction of "male" and "female" elements is made obvious by the opening scene of Faulkner's first published novel, *Soldiers' Pay.* "Lowe, Julian, number——, late a Flying Cadet, Umptieth Squadron, Air Ser-

vice, known as 'One Wing' by the other embryonic aces of his
flight, regarded the world with a yellow and disgruntled eye. He
suffered the same jaundice that many a more booted one than he
did, from Flight Commanders through Generals to the am-
brosial single-barred (not to mention that inexplicable beast of
the field which the French so beautifully call an aspiring aviator);
they had stopped the war on him."[15] So, the nonexistent
("number——") member of an equally nonexistent ("umptieth")
squadron regards nothing less than the *world* with "a yellow and
disgruntled eye," since "*they* had stopped the war on *him.*" This
is the first paradoxical introduction to the theme of the novel
which soon "dawns upon" Lowe and his boisterous though also
"nonexistent" fellow traveller—"number no thousand no hundred and naughty naught Private (very private) Joe Gilligan":
"they stood feeling the spring in the cold air, as if they had but
recently come into a new world, feeling their littleness and
believing too that lying in wait for them was something new and
strange" (*SP,* 8, 22). This is where Faulkner's woman comes into
play.

Unlike her "haphazard" male counterparts (who will be constantly "mixed up" in the course of action), Margaret Powers
commands singular presence and strength of character: "Lowe
remarking her pallid distinction, her black hair, the red scar of
her mouth, her slim dark dress, knew an adolescent envy of the
sleeper [Donald Mahon, whom she befriends]. She ignored
Lowe with a brief glance. How impersonal she was, how self-
contained. Ignoring them" (*SP,* 32). Remarkable as her looks are,
she significantly appears in the novel first as a "voice" behind the
scene, thus "heralding"—as even her name would indicate[16]—
that "new and strange" reality with which the male characters
find it increasingly difficult to cope.

She is to serve as a somewhat affectedly demoniac "custodian"
of that reality, challenging men to live on the "mooned land
inevitable with to-morrow and sweat, with sex and death and
damnation" (*SP,* 319). She would also help them do that, setting
an example and lending an explanatory word should the need

arise, thus becoming a sort of "guru," basically the role women are to play to men (for example, Belle Mitchell and Ruby Lamar to Horace Benbow; Joanna Burden to Joe Christmas; or Charlotte Rittenmeyer to Harry Wilbourne). Assigning "roles" to Faulkner's characters—male and especially female—is a hazardous task, since it attempts to refute the part alloted to them by the "Player," "Fate," or the critic that constitutes their psychological pivot. Yet, for the sake of analysis we could point out that Margaret Powers, a "big-city" girl with considerable social pretensions, chiefly represents the intellectual while the "country natural" Emmy (Reverend Mahon's housekeeper, hopelessly in love with his son) represents the sensual or "corporal" element in a woman. Together with Cecily Sanders, occupying the middle ground, in every sense of the word, including her social stature, they form the "collective face" of womanhood, a matrix of sorts for future individual realizations.

As compared with Margaret Powers, Cecily Saunders is more lively and much more paradoxical. Equally "self-contained" or rather "impalpable and dominating," she resembles "a flower," or "a young tree," and is called "the symbol of a delicate, bodyless lust" or an "epicene," "shallow fool" (*SP*, 224, 226). In short, she is as "inevitable" and oxymoronic as life itself—to the cynical and corrupt classical scholar Januarius Jones as well as to the aspiring small-town "Don Juan" George Farr.

The integrating effect a versatile female character hence exercises on her "tunnel-visioned" male counterparts becomes the motivating principle and compositional device in *The Sound and the Fury*. With respect to the character-narrators Caddy acts as a predominant power which to a great extent levels their differences—that is, Benjy's latent suffering finds a more articulate expression in Quentin; their unhappy love for the unknowingly treacherous Caddy (love-hate) turns into an open hostility on the part of Jason who becomes her most evident victim. In relation to the heroine the three characters act more or less as one, their rambling narrative providing a backdrop for the unbendingly logical progression of Caddy's story.[17]

The described function generates the outwardly "incongruous" yet innately consistent spectrum of the male characters' perceptions of women. The psychological link between the extremes of adoration and hate is provided by the recurrent motif of envious admiration for women's ability to "be so impervious to the mire which they reveal and teach us to abhor; [to] wallow without tarnishment in the very stuff in the comparison with which their bright, tragic, fleeting magic lies" (S, 282). Seen as a challenge, it is likely to make man feel "himself like one of those furious and aimless bugs that dart with sporadic and unbelievable speed upon the surface of stagnant water as though in furious escape from the very substance that spawned them" (S, 254). This feeling may result in anxiety, harsh words, or even violence.

Woman's organic, unconstrained (or at least seen as such by the male characters) "oneness" with reality accounts for a truly outstanding feat she is meant to accomplish in Faulkner's novel. Like Dante's Beatrice, in Gordon's interpretation, she is to carry "upon her frail and unbowed shoulders the whole burden of man's history of his impossible heart's desire."[18] Translating this into our vernacular, we could say that woman is also often to carry "the whole burden" of the "impossible" construction of Faulkner's novels. What I mean primarily is that women characters normally form the link between the "poles" of Faulkner's novels—between the metaphysical, highly symbolic and the vividly realistic planes, transferring meaning from one to the other, "endorsing" the otherwise highly improbable sequence of events.

"Foolish" as Cecily Saunders may be, it is she who becomes the "acting" protagonist of Soldiers' Pay—despite all implicit "claims" of the male characters. And it is in the sudden vision of "the wheel of the world, the terrible calm, inevitability of life, turning through the hours of darkness, passing its dead center point and turning faster . . . breaking the slumber of sparrows" (SP, 244) that the symbolic meaning of the novel is revealed. This metaphor is transmuted in one of the rector's closing remarks, the "wheel" becoming the circle of life, enveloping man: "'God is *circum*stance, Joe. God is in this life'" (*SP*, 317, italics mine).

It is not just the action of *Soldiers' Pay* that goes in concentric "circles" round the "dead center point"—the living dead figure of Donald Mahon; or the circular movement of the plot in *The Sound and the Fury*, its four parts anticipating the spirallike logic of the author's whole career. The metaphor and the dictum could be of general significance to Faulkner's mode of artistic thinking. Incidentally, the idea and the corresponding imagery of "a vortex of fury and turmoil" (*WP*, 226) reaching through various planes of Faulkner's work could be seen as a manifestation of its deep poetic nature, the very words "vortex" and "verse" being of the same origin (Latin: *vertere*, to turn, to whirl).[19] What I mean is not just the formal poetic "rudiments" abundant in Faulkner's prose, but Joe Christmas's "entering . . . the street which ran for thirty years. . . . It had made a circle and he is still inside it" (*LA*, 255): the tall convict's realizing "how there was a peculiar quality of repetitiveness about his present fate, how not only the almost seminal crises recurred with a certain monotony, but the very physical circumstances followed a stupidly unimaginative pattern" (*WP*, 193); Quentin Compson's realizing that his tragedy is "second-hand";[20] or his brother Jason's unsuccessfully trying to grasp "the whole rhythm of events" (*SF*, 385) that besiege, "*circumstand*" him.

One could argue that it is not so much (or just as much) poetry as it is philosophy. That is the point I am trying to make: that with Faulkner those are particularly closely knit, so we really have to delve into his poetics to understand his (not the fictional persona's or the characters') philosophy. The results thus obtained contradict some of our well-established reader's notions.

Having placed the "burden" of Faulkner's fictional world, or at least a considerable part of it, on women's shoulders, one would assume that the "male-female" opposition should be the coupled force that sets Faulkner's fictional world into motion. In a way this is right but in another way it's quite wrong. True, this dichotomy is central to the consciousness of Faulkner's self-centered male characters: speculations on what women will do and men won't, shouldn't, or cannot (and vice versa) run from *Soldiers' Pay* to *The Reivers*. On the other hand, the very function ascribed to the woman in Faulkner's novels questions the validity of this fundamental yet often unduly restrictive cultural convention. In fact, this is one of the most sensitive points at issue in the continuous *dialogue* between the author and the protagonist, which is the undercurrent of Faulknerian discourse. Ostensibly adopting the "language" of his hero's consciousness (e.g., the "male-female" opposition), recognizing, as it were, his claims for personal uniqueness, the author would test it by the reality of the plot. And the plot is often dominated by a woman. So trying (typically) to "obstruct" the plot, to alter the pre-destined course of events, the protagonist or the narrator who respresents him will be trying to "neutralize" the woman.

The first appearance of Margaret Powers is again quite characteristic. On hearing the unexpectedly compelling "girl's voice" the two men turn and see her: "She was dark. Had Gilligan and Lowe ever seen an Aubrey Beardsley, they would have known that Beardsley would have sickened for her: he had drawn her so often dressed in peacock hues, white and slim and depraved among meretricious trees and impossible marble fountains. Gilligan rose." (*SP*, 31). This evocation of the Beardslean imagery providing an obvious link to Faulkner's early poetry and painting is not just a formal indication of artistic continuity. Faulkner's poeticality is much more "substantive." What it comes to represent in this context is the characteristic inner gesture of Faulkner's male protagonist, who tries to use "words" to shield himself from reality, to "domesticate" the striking new phenomenon, to reduce it to something known, manageable (the two framing short sentences giving away his authentic reaction). Well, he fails. Faulkner's woman would not be reduced to a stereotype, however flattering. Ironically, "meretricious trees and impossible marble fountains," signifying the imposition of an artificial, egocentric pattern on reality, are rather the domain of his male heroes—the rector, seeking escape from life in his rose garden; Januarius Jones, trying to make life "conform" to a classical "text"; Cadet Lowe, seeking in vain to impose on the world his inflated and hopelessly inadequate ego. Such a psychological disposition naturally translates itself into the perception of a woman as "the Passive and Anonymous whom God had created to be not alone the recipient and receptacle of the seed of *his* body but of *his* spirit too, which is truth or as near truth as he dare approach" (*LA*, 350, italics mine).

I am alluding to these words for the second time now but from a different perspective. How really "passive and anonymous" and consequently "impervious to the mire" of "reality" is Faulkner's woman? Not nearly so much as Hightower (who is eventually taught by his wife to know better), or Horace Benbow (thus trying to pacify his bad conscience) would have it, or the Compson brothers, who each in his own way is trying to control Caddy, to "isolate [her] out of the loud world" (*SF*, 220).[21] In order to fulfill her mission in the novel Faulkner's woman has to overcome such ostensibly idealizing yet repressive impulses. She definitely wouldn't conform to Gordon's "feminine ideal"— "'a virgin with no legs to leave me, no arms to hold me, no head to talk to me'" (M, 26). She would, on the contrary, indulge in running, or rather, "going between"—a paradoxical yet seminal manifestation of her independence and versatility.

Understandably Cecily Saunders's scurrying between the houses of her parents and of the rector, the town drugstore and George Farr's car occasions an "arresting" close-up on her "long legs, not for locomotion but for studied completion of a rhythm carried to its *nth:* a compulsion of progress, movement" (*M*, 186). Yet she will continue "tapping her delicate way" on the souls of her male victims and on different venues of the novel, thus fulfiling her basic "integrating" function.

In a similar fashion Caddy Compson would run errands for her frivolous uncle, which causes Benjy's bewilderment. She would then try to bridge the unbridgeable worlds of "the flower tree" and of the "hitting" strangers, the "blackguards," to the mixed feelings of admiration, anger, and grief of her brothers.

In Temple Drake, Cecily's and Caddy's running is brought to an abrupt stop by a perverse "humanoid" of a gangster who yet partakes of that inextricable monastic quality of Faulkner's men—trying to seclude himself in an artificial world of his own, guarding the real one with whatever means are at hand. The underlying paradox, however, is that despite all dramatically accentuated distinctions, which would seem to set Faulkner's men and women apart as representatives of different species, the existential gap between them is far from being insuperable. What I mean is certainly not just Temple Drake's "teaming up" with Popeye. Neither Cecily's nor Caddy's running takes them very far from their male counterparts. Cecily's flights end in inevitable returns. Caddy's threat "to run away and never come back" is just as proud as it is untenable and in no way different from her brothers' abortive attempts to flee their doom. Neither she nor Faulkner's other women are "impervious to the mire" of reality, as the famous metaphor of Caddy's "muddy drawers" overhead in the tall tree[22] so graphically indicates. Caddy's ambivalence, her being "of two worlds," relates not only to her enigmatic charm but also to her inner conflict and eventually to her personal disaster. Margaret Powers, Emmy, even Cecily Saunders—they all have a "story" to tell that would render the myth of their "imperviousness" to human delusions, hope, and grief superficial fiction. The same is true of such later characters as Addie Bundren or Mrs. Gail Hightower or Joanna Burden or Charlotte Rittenmeyer—this list could be amplified to include female characters from Rosa Coldfield through Nancy Mannigoe to Eula Varner and Linda Snopes.

Even Lena Grove who seems to be tailored to the "Passive and Anonymous" definition[23] is hardly "impervious" to anything. If she seems imperturbed by that bizarre world charged with "impossible" masculine passions, she is still part of this world for the obvious reason that she carries it in herself.[24] So men would virtually run from her all-knowing stare (as Lucas Burch does), or say, as Byron Bunch does, "with a kind of musing astonishment: 'I never even had any need to keep it from her, to lie it smooth. It was like she knew beforehand what I would say, that I was going to lie to her. . . . But that part of her that knew the truth, that I could not have fooled anyway'" (LA, 226–27). What Byron Burch is "fumbling" and "groping" for could be Harry Wilbourne's realization that the woman was "a better man" than he was or, to translate it from "the male," that she was just as human.

What it all adds up to is that from his outset as a novelist Faulkner's inner tendency in the depiction of women has been from stereotype to individuality, from superficial mythologizing to the realistic comprehension of their full-fledged humanity. Also, this could clinch a much debated problem of Faulkner's recurrent allusions to the concepts of the "epicene" or the "androgynous." The reasons the "epicene girl," to quote Cleanth Brooks again, so "powerfully engaged" Faulkner's imagination are certainly manifold. If I were to name the chief one, I would say that she helped him to pinpoint and dramatize what was to become the main ethical premise in his artistic "dealings" with women. Transgressing, as it were, the codified gender boundaries and thus puzzling her male counterpart, the "epicene girl" enables the author to put across this basic idea: that woman is substantively human and adjectively female. Eventually this metaphoric idea dissociates itself from its original "carrier"—the particular kind of woman—and acquires a wide range of specific and general artistic-philosophical applications.

On the one hand, it retains its original function, symbolizing those qualities that in psychological terms keep Faulkner's women apart from men—their "self-sufficiency" and versatility, their being of the present and of eternity, of nature and of society. Yet even in this specific sense, it expands to include women in general, not just the "marginal" type. What Byron Bunch is actually trying to tell Hightower is that Lena is "androgynous": that there are male and female "parts" in her, and "one of them knows that he is a scoundrel. But the other part believes that when a man and a woman are going to have a child, that the Lord will see that they are all together when the right time comes" (*LA*, 227). This paradoxical realization virtually becomes a clue to the *feminine enigma*—a recurrent motif throughout Faulkner's work—bringing together even diametrically opposed characters. Thus, Byron's experience with Lena is foreshadowed by Christmas's encounter with Joanna Burden: "My God. How little I know about women, when I thought I knew so much. . . . It was like I was the woman and she was the man" (*LA*, 177).

On a still higher level of abstraction, which actually the latter quotation pertains to, the initial metaphor becomes a symbol of man and of the human condition. Part of its general meaning is summarized by Thomas McHaney: "This repeated ambiguous sex differentiation functions in a number of ways. In the strongest sense, it is part of the paradox inherent in nature, which is emphasized by other means as well, a denotation of the one-ness of life beneath the apparent diversity of individuality. Male and female, like birth and death, are merely aspects of a continuing and integral thing-in-itself, the will to live."[25] What McHaney says is certainly true, yet, to my mind, not enough. The will to live is a human property, yet not specifically human. At the same time striving as they do to achieve harmony with nature, Faulkner's men and women would not forfeit their human, social identity. Like Joe Gilligan and Margaret Powers, they will be trying hard to "help nature make a good job out of a poor one" (*SP*, 303). Harry Wilbourne's choice of "life" has very little or nothing to do with the "will to live" and, in fact, is similar in motivation to, for instance, Socrates' choice of *death*[26]; they both merely adhere to their human principle. The sphere of the metaphor under discussion embraces both natural and social worlds, the latter dominating. Just as the depiction of the tragically "divided" human nature in Faulkner bears the memory and dream of a whole person and "homogeneous" society, the gender incarnations of human beings are imbued with the memory of their mythical "androgynous" progenitors.

In his perceptive and erudite discussion of *The Wild Palms* in general and of this specific problem in particular, McHaney, among other things, adduces Schopenhauer's *World as Will and Idea* as a source of possible influence or compatible configurations of thought. At the same time he seems to be quite aware of its limited applicability to the novel.[27] I would rather suggest the "gloss" I have already hinted at.

It is difficult to say how extensive was Faulkner's knowledge of Plato, though as we know from Joseph Blotner, some of the great philosopher's works featured on that truck-load of books which Phil Stone used to turn over to the future great writer.[28] But even if he hadn't read "Symposium" he would have undoubtedly listened to what Aristophanes had to say there—with no less interest than Plato himself:

> "And so, gentlemen, we are like pieces of the coins that children break in half for keep sakes—making two out of one, like the flatfish—and each of us forever seeking the half that will tally with himself. . . .
>
> And so all this to do is a relic of that original state of ours, when we were whole, and now, when we are longing for and follow after that primeval wholeness, we say we are in love. For there was a time, I repeat, when we were one, but now, for our sins, God has scattered us abroad, as the Spartans scattered the Arcadians."[29]

A lot of Faulkner's artistic "theory" of love and of man's general condition seems to be condensed here. To appreciate this fact, it would suffice to recall the conclusion of *Soldiers' Pay* in which all the "impossible heart's desires" of the characters are "absorbed" into the words of the black prayer and those of the author: "Feed Thy Sheep, O Jesus. All the longing of mankind for a Oneness with Something, somewhere. Feed Thy Sheep, O Jesus" (*SP*, 319); or to remember Byron Bunch speaking of Lena and her fugitive lover as of "two parts" ("and if Lord don't see fit to let them two parts meet and kind of compare" [*LA*, 227]), which almost verbatim reproduces Plato's image.

Whatever the source, we can say that the metaphor of androgyny became for Faulkner a somatic symbol of woman's humanity. This spawned a series of full-blooded and highly original women characters, making Faulkner's achievement singular in twentieth-century American literature. Working through diversified plastic realizations, the metaphor also became a vehicle for the basic idea of human sameness—in the inner if not in the outer forms of being, in spirit if not in flesh. Hence the characteristic *spiritual* quality of Faulkner's work which, incidentally, enables us to see him as at least a double heir: to the stock American—white and black—puritan moral and artistic tradition as well as to the tradition of Russian classical literature of the nineteenth century.[30] This "oneness" in spirit is paradoxically implied in the ambiguous "sex differentiation" and finds its ultimate artistic expression in the *reversal* of the traditionally male and female "parts" in the novel. The latter is quite disorienting and annoying to the male characters, which may result in "aggressively" sexual discourse (as in *Sanctuary* and *The Wild Palms*). Yet, it is of cardinal importance to the author and, I would suggest, to the critic as well.

Thus, the appreciation of the intentionally reversable or "transitive" nature of male-female artistic functions in Faulkner might throw some additional light on the original structure and meaning of *Sanctuary*. This effect is suggested in Michael Millgate's perceptive critique, specifically when he states that "Faulkner perhaps had in mind a crude juxtaposition of Horace's superficially humdrum but obsessively internalised emotional life with the much more violent experiences undergone by Temple Drake."[31] Yet, Millgate doesn't grant sufficient artistic justification to this pairing, and in fact holds it responsible for "the principal weakness of the original version," which is "one of balance and structure."[32] "Crude" as this opposition might be, it could contain some original meaning (which so often has turned out to be the case with Faulkner's other "brilliant failures"). So it is only natural for another outstanding Faulkner scholar, Noel Polk, rating the original *Sanctuary* as "a highly serious work, with an integrity all its own, by America's greatest novelist,"[33] to pursue the case further. The questions he puts are most pertinent: "Why does Temple's tale affect [Horace] so personally, so physically?" Why does he identify with her in the climactic scene of the novel so completely as to become "at one and the same time male, female, androgynous?"[34] Consistent with his general view of the novel as "essentially . . . a heavily Freudian study of Horace's sexual and emotional problems,"[35] Polk concludes that Horace is thus fulfiling "his own rape fantasy," originating in his childhood traumatic experience of the "primal scene."[36]

I find Polk's hypothesis difficult to accept as an answer precisely because I wholly agree with him that "the early text is far more than the 'Freudian mishmash' Linton Massey called it" and is "a significant addition to the Faulkner canon."[37] Elaborating on these important remarks, I would like to suggest that it is not just the male protagonist, Horace Benbow, who forms a clear-cut continuity with his predecessors, "Prufrockian idealists" Quentin Compson and Darl Bundren, thus undermining the notion of the novel as an offspring of a "cheap idea." Of no less importance is Temple Drake.

Obviously enough, she is essentially the "epicene" girl of the Cecily Saunders-Caddy Compson type. Just like them, she is constantly "on the move," "her long legs blonde with running, in speeding silhouette against the lighted windows" (S, 80). Her empty eyes, "like the holes in one of these masks" (S, 111–12) would not contradict the "shallow fool" definition accorded to Cecily. At the same time, as between Caddy and Benjy there is an immediate rapport established between Temple and the "feeb" Tommy, who look "at one another soberly, like two children or two dogs" (S, 91). Tommy's devotion costs him his life, while Benjy's leads to castration and imprisonment in an asylum. And, of course, Temple's disposition as a concubine of a gangster in Reba's whorehouse is not dissimilar to Caddy's connection with a Nazi general in occupied Paris.

However, there is more to the hero and the heroine than just those continuity "credentials." The original *Sanctuary* is not only like Faulkner's earlier novels; it is also different—and thus makes a really "significant addition" to Faulkner's artistic-philosophical canon.

However closely the relationship between Horace and Narcissa parallels that of Quentin and Caddy in *The Sound and the Fury*, it is important to stress the *reversal* or sharing of symbolic roles. It is now the sister and not the brother who stands guard to the family pride, being unwilling or unable to understand the other's moral predicament. Just like Quentin or, for that matter, Jason of *The Sound and the Fury*, Narcissa cannot conceive of a relationship between man and woman in terms other than a vulgarly sexual or commercial one. In any event she wouldn't have her "brother mixed up with a woman people are talking about" (*S*, 197).

Narcissa's social rigor as well as her basic unscrupulousness recalls Temple Drake (with her repeated incantations of "my father is a judge"). She in turn carries on "Quentin's" theme through her "narcissism," her obsessive preoccupation with codes of behavior and "mechanic" time. The following passage could be transplanted—style, imagery, and all—from the story of Temple Drake to the Quentin section of *The Sound and the Fury*:

> There was still a little light in the room. She found that she was hearing her watch; had been hearing it for some time. She discovered that the house was full of noises, seeping into the room muffled and indistinguishable, as though from a distance. A bell rang faintly and shrilly somewhere; someone mounted the stairs in a swishing garment. The feet went on past the door and mounted another stair and ceased. She listened to the watch. A car started beneath the window with a grind of gears; again the faint bell rang, shrill and prolonged. She found that the faint light yet in the room was from a street lamp. Then she realised that it was night and that the darkness beyond was full of the sound of the city. (*S*, 177–78)

All these attendant factors suggest that the culminating identification of male and female protagonists in the original *Sanctuary* can be seen as realization of their substantive functional similarity rather than of a psychic disorder of one of them. This view is corroborated by the fact that in the course of narration the author quite consciously works towards eventual identification from "both ends": beginning with the clear-cut parallelism in the characters' plot-lines (from their "cultural shock" experiences at the moonshiners' hideout to Horace's imaginary and Temple's actual flight to Europe); through "accidental" details, like Clarence Snopes's calling Horace "Judge," the unavoidable picture of Little Belle calling Temple to Horace's mind, or the "lighted clock face" that looms in his face after he visits Temple at Reba's; to the "reciprocal" male reincarnations of the female protagonist, who first imagines herself to be a "boy" and then "an old man with a long beard" (S, 214, 217). All this artistically necessitates their eventual merging into one, making it highly meaningful in terms of socioethical and not just psychoanalytical symbolism.

This identification of male and female characters brings to the fore the somewhat obscured generic nature of the book, which essentially is an *initiation* novel, pitting the aggregate, "androgynous" human being against social reality. To quote Millgate, the action of the novel affords the protagonist an "occasion to measure the gulf that divides his palely chivalric idealism from the unpalatable realities of a society which he discovers to be corrupt at every level . . . intricately criss-crossed by soiled bonds tying the brothel to the State capital, the jail to the courthouse."[38] It should be pointed out that intricate and, to be sure, no less "soiled" links bond social reaction and the "traditional" attitude to women, forming for Horace Benbow the "logical pattern to evil" (S, 218).

This is still more vividly and painfully realized by the hero of a later novel, Harry Wilbourne, who opines that "if Venus returned she would be a soiled man in a subway lavatory with a palm full of French post cards" (WP, 106–7). Strikingly revealing is not just *what* he says here but also the way he puts it. The identification of masculine and feminine characters or the reversal of their "traditional" functions (which is at the core of this paradox) forms a graphically defined pattern in the novel as a whole. It is Charlotte, of course, who seduces Harry, yet is reluctant to marry him; it is she who is the breadwinner and has "strong hands," and who dies a violent and unnecessary (one might say) death. And it is Harry who virtually becomes prisoner of love, who not only writes pulp stories from the woman's point of view but seems to have learned from them how to "cope with death . . . envelope it in one soft and instantaneous confederation of unresistance."[39]

Such "crossgender" transitions bring into focus some of the essential ambiguities inherent in Faulkner's attitude to women. One the one hand, he seems to have most vehemently disapproved not just of the times that tend to turn Venus into a "soiled man," but also of women who, however malicious the times might be, fail to hold their own, to stay true to their "nature." It is not by chance, I would suggest, that Joanna Burden and Charlotte Rittenmeyer are chosen to die. On the other hand, it is the "traditional" attitude toward women that he haltingly yet all the more furiously sought to exorcise in his fiction (the ultimate, however unexpected, example of this is Linda Snopes who nearly converts Jefferson to "communism").

As far as Charlotte and Harry are concerned, despite all their "sexual ambiguity," they are a perfectly plausible pair, and their love story is one of the most poignant and bitter in modern literature. Equally "strange" yet compelling, however different, is the "abortive" love affair of Gavin Stevens and Linda Snopes in *The Mansion*. What these two couples have in common is that the "oceans" of their love are troubled *not* by "hemingwaves," entailing the radical redefinition of traditional "male" and "female" roles. Both Harry and the tall convict remain men despite the fact that apparently they refuse to "fight back and have their brains trampled out" (*R*, 47). Both Charlotte and Linda remain women despite their sometimes affected "manliness." The reason is that they are made not "out of their own clay," but are measured against "something somewhere that . . .

made them all"[40]—against one, human dignity, endurance, and courage.

Speaking about Linda Snopes, Faulkner called her "one of the most interesting people I've ever written about."[41] "People," Faulkner said, not "women." What stands behind this phrase as well as behind all of Faulkner's artistic strategy is the recognition of woman's humanity: not just her equality to man, but her original, lost oneness with him.

NOTES

1. René Wellek and Austin Warren, *Theory of Literature* (New York: A Harvest Book, 1956), 25.

2. A. S. Pushkin, *Sobranie sochinenij*, 10 vols (Leningrad, 1979), 10: 96.

3. William Faulkner, "Address upon Receiving the Nobel Prize for Literature," in *William Faulkner: Essays, Speeches, and Public Letters*, ed. James B. Meriwether (New York: Random House, 1965), 119.

4. *Lion in the Garden: Interviews with William Faulkner, 1926–1962*, ed. James B. Meriwether and Michael Millgate (New York: Randon House, 1968), 255.

5. *The Faulkner-Cowley File: Letters and Memories, 1944–1962* (London: Penguin Books, 1978), 14.

6. *Faulkner in the University*, ed. Frederick L. Gwynn and Joseph L. Blotner (Charlottesville: University of Virginia Press, 1959), 145.

7. Ibid., 3.

8. *The Faulkner-Cowley File*, 14.

9. *Light in August* (London: Penguin Books, 1970), 350. Hereafter cited in the text as *LA*.

10. *The Wild Palms* (New York: The New American Library, 1968), 79. Hereafter cited in the text as *WP*.

11. *Sanctuary: The Original Text*, ed. Noel Polk (New York: Random House, 1981), 274. Hereafter cited in the text as *S*.

12. Cleanth Brooks, *William Faulkner: Toward Yoknapatawpha and Beyond* (New Haven: Yale University Pres, 1979), 124.

13. Ibid., 127.

14. Evans Harrington, "Faulkner and Mississippi," a paper presented at the Soviet-American symposium "William Faulkner and the Literary Traditions of the American South" (Moscow, 1984).

15. *Soldiers' Pay* (New York: Liveright, 1954), 7. Hereafter cited in the text as *SP*.

16. Basil Cottle lists Power[s] as "an occupational name common in Ireland, meaning 'herald' OF (One em*power*ed to do something)" in *The Penquin Dictionary of Surnames* (London: Penguin Books, 1967), 224.

17. See my essay "Word and Idea in *The Sound and the Fury*," in *New Directions in Faulkner Studies*, ed. Doreen Fowler and Ann J. Abadie (Jackson: University Press of Mississippi, 1984), 296.

18. *Mosquitoes* (New York: Liveright, 1955), 339. Hereafter cited in the text as *M*.

19. For this observation I am indebted to N. I. Balashov's important article "On Structural-Relational Differentiation between a Linguistic and a Poetic Sign" ("Strukturno-relyatsionnaya differentsiatsiya znaka yazykovogo i znaka poeticheskogo") in

Izvestiya Akademii Nauk SSSR. Seriya Literatury i yazyka, 60, 2, (1982), 128. Following the line of derivation from "Versus" through "Vertex, icis" to "verticalis," he specifically suggests that "the poetic sign is fully realized as a sign not in linearity, but in the sphere of conception, possessing vertical dimensions as well." This, I believe, has immediate bearing on Faulkner, who is all too often being read in a linear, that is, strictly "prosaic," fashion.

20. *The Sound and the Fury* (New York: Vintage Books, 1956), 143. Hereafter cited in the text as *SF*.

21. What is a latent psychological tendency in Benjy's and Quentin's sections (they both *don't want* to tell the story of Caddy) becomes an obvious factor in the plot of Jason's section as he tries to "contain" her, or at least to keep her out of town. For elaboration, see my essay in *New Directions in Faulkner Studies*.

22. *Faulkner in the University*, 1.

23. Ilse Lind has pointed out to me that even the name of the heroine could be not quite "personal," for there was a small village of that name in northeast Mississippi that Faulkner might have known.

24. It is certainly not by chance that the "roads" of the two runaway orphans Lena Grove and Joe Christmas finally merge and that the child she gives birth to is thought to be Christmas himself, at least by his grandmother.

25. Thomas L. McHaney, *William Faulkner's "The Wild Palms": A Study* (Jackson: University Press of Mississippi, 1975), 147.

26. I rely on Plato's account in "Phedo."

27. McHaney, 147, 191. He notes that *The Wild Palms* is not the first place to look in Faulkner's fiction for a conception of existence that is compatible with Bergson or Freud or Schopenhauer or Nietzsche.

28. Joseph Blotner, *Faulkner: A Biography*, 1-vol. ed. (New York: Random House, 1984), 45.

29. Plato, "Symposium," in *The Collected Dialogues of Plato*, ed. E. Hamilton and H. Cairns (Princeton: Princeton University Press, 1978), 544–45.

30. Much has been written on Faulkner and Dostoevsky. Less prominence, however, have been given to his ties with Tolstoy. I briefly mention here that the epical tendency in Faulkner, his preoccupation with the moral-ethical dimension, and his profound interest in the "plain folk" are certainly compatible with those elements in Tolstoy. Both *Soldiers' Pay* and *A Fable* bear comparison to "Sevastopol Stories" and *War and Peace; Light in August* and *The Wild Palms* are just as "Tolstoyan" as they are "Dostevskyan" in their reproduction of the folk mentality, most noticeably in Lena Grove and the tall convict and, of course, in the story of Charlotte Rittenmeyer being a twentieth-century version of the Anna Karenina story. The problem of "Tolstoy and Faulkner" is tackled in greater detail in the article of the same name by my colleague at the Gorky Institute, Tatyana Morozova, in *Tolstoy i Nashe Vremya* (Moscow, 1978), 223–44.

31. Michael Millgate, *The Achievement of William Faulkner* (Lincoln: University of Nebraska Press, 1978), 117.

32. Ibid.

33. Noel Polk, "Afterword," in *Sanctuary: The Original Text*, 295.

34. Noel Polk, "'The Dungeon Was Mother Herself': William Faulkner: 1927–1931," in *New Directions in Faulkner Studies*, 68.

35. Polk, "Afterword," 304.

36. Polk, "'The Dungeon Was Mother Herself,'" 72.

37. Polk, "Afterword," 305–6.

38. Millgate, 119.

39. *The Reivers* (New York: Random House, 1962), 47. Hereafter cited in the text as *R*.

40. *Essays, Speeches, and Public Letters*, 193.

41. *Faulkner in the University*, 195.

Meditations on the Other: Faulkner's Rendering of Women

Philip M. Weinstein

"Sir," asked the undergraduate (gender unknown) at the University of Virginia, "do you find it easier to create a female character in literature or a male character?" "It's much more fun to try to write about women," Faulkner replied, "because I think women are marvelous, they're wonderful, and I know very little about them."[1] In the energetic debate about Faulkner's portrayal of women, this remark has been often cited (by Cleanth Brooks among others),[2] as evidence, amply supported by the books themselves, that Faulkner's fictional women are as richly portrayed as his men. As I reflected upon Faulkner's statement, however, I realized that its terms are unthinkable if applied to men: what male author would speak of men as "marvelous . . . wonderful": "I know very little about them"? Taking Faulkner at his word (though his tongue may have been somewhere near his cheek), I have sought in this paper to identify what is "marvelous" or "wonderful" in Faulkner's women, not in the moral sense of how they are evaluated, but in the narrative sense of *how they are deployed* in the fiction. Marvels and wonders are to be marveled and wondered at; they exist in a significantly different relation to the narrative voice than do more understandable phenomena. More precisely, they exist as *the other:* noteworthy, indeed remarkable, but continuously isolated within their own domain.[3]

I shall take my examples from four major Yoknapatawpha novels—*The Sound and the Fury, Light in August, Absalom,*

Absalom!, and *Go Down, Moses*.[4] Attention to these four novels, written over a thirteen-year period, allows me to generalize Faulkner's narrative habits as no single novel would permit. At the same time, by allowing a certain amount of sustained commentary on selected novels, it should keep me from irresponsible impressionism.

* * *

In Quentin's section of *The Sound and the Fury* there are two significant encounters with unknown characters, one with a group of boys interested in fishing, the other with a little girl whom he calls "sister." The vignettes are of roughly equal length, but Quentin experiences them in quite different ways:

> The trout hung, delicate and motionless among the wavering shadows. Three boys with fishing poles came onto the bridge and we leaned on the rail and looked down at the trout. They knew the fish. He was a neighborhood character.
> "They've been trying to catch that trout for twenty-five years. There's a store in Boston offers a twenty-five dollar fishing rod to anybody that can catch him."
> "Why dont you all catch him, then? Wouldnt you like to have a twenty-five dollar fishing rod?"
> "Yes," they said. They leaned on the rail, looking down at the trout. "I sure would," one said.
> "I wouldnt take the rod," the second said. "I'd take the money instead."
> "Maybe they wouldnt do that," the first said. "I bet he'd make you take the rod."
> "Then I'd sell it."
> "You couldn't get twenty-five dollars for it."
> "I'd take what I could get, then. I can catch just as many fish with this pole as I could with a twenty-five dollar one." Then they talked about what they would do with twenty-five dollars. They all talked at once, their voices insistent and contradictory and impatient, making of unreality a possibility, then a probability, then an incontrovertible fact, as people will when their desires become words. (145)

This scene is clearly located in space and time and understanding: by a bridge, with three boys and a trout, full of localizing details—the Boston store, the bet, the fishing rods. The boys chatter at length (they share a conviction, however fantastic), and Quentin enters into what they are saying, into both their motives and their delusion. He is at home in this scene; he understands its discursive rules. Some fifteen pages later he wanders into a bakery and encounters "sister." He buys her some bread and they walk outside together:

> "You'd better take your bread on home, hadn't you?"
> She looked at me. She chewed quietly and steadily; at regular intervals a small distension passed smoothly down her throat. I opened my package and gave her one of the buns. "Goodbye," I said.
> I went on. Then I looked back. She was behind me. "Do you live down this way?" She said nothing. She walked beside me, under my elbow sort of, eating. We went on. . . . She swallowed the last of the cake, then she began on the bun, watching me across it. "Goodbye," I said. I turned into the street and went on, but I went to the next corner before I stopped.
> "Which way do you live?" I said. "This way?" I pointed down the street. She just looked at me. "Do you live over that way? I bet you live close to the station, where the trains are. Dont you?" She just looked at me, serene and secret and chewing. (160)

This scene is as eery as the one with the boys is reassuring. The setting seems both to shift and to remain the same—to move away from this girl and yet, as in a dream, continuously to include her. Quentin cannot establish a relation to her, cannot discover who she is, who her family is, or even what tongue she speaks. Indeed, her tongue is doing something more eloquent than speaking: it is participating in the methodical pulverization of the food—cake, bun, bread, ice cream—that she never ceases to put into her mouth. She is *other* throughout this scene, a silent body all of whose engulfing motions are intently observed, as though they had an unspeakable connection with Quentin's own fantasy life. As indeed they do. She is as conventionally unplaced in a foregrounded social setting as she is scandalously implicated in Quentin's incestuous memories and desires. As such, as a solitary female "marvelously" attached to the psychic stresses of her observer yet deprived of the component parts of her own subjective setting, "sister" serves, I would propose, as a model for the three Compson brothers' rendering of their sister Caddy, as well as an indication of Faulkner's broader narrative stance toward his "wonderful" women.

Within the context of "sister" we can make more sense of Faulkner's often cited reason for not making Caddy a narrator: "because Caddy was still to me too beautiful and too moving to reduce her to telling what was going on, that it would be more passionate to see her through somebody else's eyes, I thought."[5] Like "sister," a Caddy wholly presented through male optics is a Caddy wholly answerable to male emphases. She is "more passionate" because more focused: there is no leakage here, nothing expressed that is not relevant to the sibling crises through which she is perceived. Had Faulkner entered her mind and allowed *that* movement of thought and feeling to pace his own narrative, Caddy would have become inevitably more diffused, more tangentially implicated—through the promiscuous impetus of stream of consciousness itself—in the lives of other figures. And in becoming a character whose narrative reality was not entirely a function of the love and hatred of her three brothers, she would have become less "beautiful," less "wonderful," and more free.[6]

The contrast between "sister" and the three boys fishing reveals another narrative principle apparently commanded by gender. The female is essentially alone, whereas the male is granted the privilege of same-sex company. Caddy, her daughter Quentin, and "sister" are of course surrounded by males—they move through a male world as through a gauntlet—but this is a context that stifles (rather than enables) the female at the center. Deprived of female "correspondents," these figures are defined by, and at the mercy of, the brothers, fathers, uncles, and lovers who surround them. By contrast, the three boys going fishing and swimming speak a common language, engage in common activities. The narrative's mode of encountering them does not automatically put their gender identity under pressure or at stake. In like manner, Quentin and his father are free to *talk* to each other throughout *The Sound and the Fury*. (That they disagree is immaterial: they share a common language; they ratify each other's identity through argument.) Mrs. Compson is not similarly empowered; the words that pour forth unceasingly from her may meet resistance or acquiescence, but they rarely issue into dialogue. Who would she talk to (rather than at)? Like the other "wonderful" women in *The Sound and the Fury*, she is essentially on display, dramatized not through any bond with others but through her impact on them.

The exception is of course Dilsey. The narrative somehow manages to render her as other and interrelated at the same time. It can do so, I believe, because blackness is not only not problematic in *The Sound and the Fury*, it permits narrative escape from white problems of sexuality and gender both. (If this is so, it would help to explain Faulkner's extraordinary access to Dilsey's social behavior—her words and gestures within the Compson precincts.) The aristocratic retainer model looms large in this arrangement: an undisturbed black family devotes their daily energies to taking care of an unsalvageable white one, and nothing appears amiss to anyone involved. Since the two bloods are innocently imagined as *separate*, the two families may be innocently imagined as together. Dilsey (as well as Roskus, Frony, Versh, T. P., Luster) is fully contained within her role as black servant/helper/advisor/mother to the Compsons. Those three white brothers and their white author see in her only a loving (and immovable) domesticity. Free of Nancy's aggressive sexuality, untainted as well by the scandalous possession of Clytie's Sutpen blood or the menacing possibility of Molly's liaison with Zack Edmonds, Dilsey is (so to speak) a portrait conceived in innocence. She fulfills a white fantasy of a black women essentially at ease and functioning within a patriarchal world. Hers is a voice whose range and effectiveness (with white and black, male and female) are purchased by both an exclusion of private desire and a willingness to leave Southern race relations unprobed. (On matters of desire and race she can tell them—and us—nothing.) Given the price paid, it is all the more remarkable—it is indeed mysterious—that her voice be among the most compelling in all of Faulkner's fiction.

*   *   *

"Joe Christmas is the most solitary character in American fiction, the most extreme phase conceivable of American loneliness."[7] For over twenty-five years these words of Alfred Kazin have seemed persuasive, but scrutiny of *Light in August, from a narrative perspective,* would as easily show that the most solitary figure is Lena Grove. Not that she is "lonely"; one of the reasons we have persistently gone to the Faulkner males as figures of isolation—Bayard, Benjy, Quentin, Darl, Joe Christmas, Sutpen, Ike—is that in them loneliness and isolation are thematically conjoined and proclaimed. The narrative itself is designed to emphasize their predicament. But this move on the part of the narrative, which socializes their isolation by inviting the reader imaginatively to share it, is denied to the women. Conceived as (comparatively) gregarious beings, the women are not often portrayed as lonely. Yet they are solitary inasmuch as the narrative itself neither enters their lives on their own terms nor dramatizes them enacting their lives in each other's company.

Consider the opening of *Light in August.* The first six pages are a *tour de force* that establishes, for the duration of the novel, Lena's "marvelous" quality. Her refrain of "a fur piece," her summarized past in which childhood, adolescence, pregnancy, and departure are all related without either demur or a word of dialogue with others, her lyrical meditation that "if he is going all the way to Jefferson, I will be riding within the hearing of Lucas Burch before his seeing. He will hear the wagon but he wont know. So there will be one within his hearing before his seeing" (6)—all these Lena-notations are interwoven into poetic third-personal descriptions of the "evocation of *far,*" of "something moving forever and without progress across an urn" (5). The result is a lyrical celebration of Lena Grove as a "wonderful" creature who communes with herself, who imperturbably sustains the vicissitudes of her life, and who moves with more than human grace and tranquility across a heightened landscape. These six pages eloquently tell us that she inhabits her own space, that there is no one like her.

There is no one like her, but Armstid and Winterbottom (whom she meets up with on page 6) appear as almost exactly like each other. Their setting is matter-of-fact rather than poetic, their activity is the quotidian one of arranging (in a studiedly offhand way) the sale of a cultivator, and their medium is talk. They understand each other perfectly. The transaction they are embarked upon is part of the immemorial business of country life, and the unhurried, articulate rhythm of such communal activities carries (more than anything else) this novel's powerful sense of traditional values.

In the next sixteen pages Armstid takes Lena home and we witness a dialogue that follows quite different premises from the one between him and Winterbottom. Mrs. Armstid and Lena engage in a comic ballet of cross-statements, the two of them speaking out of opposed and inarticulable centers:

> Mrs Armstid watches the lowered face. Her hands are on her hips and she watches the younger woman with an expression of cold and impersonal contempt. "And you believe that he will be there when you get there. Granted that he ever was there at all. That he will hear you are in the same town with him, and still be there when the sun sets."
>
> Lena's lowered face is grave, quiet. Her hand has ceased now. It lies quite still on her lap, as if it had died there. Her voice is quiet, tranquil, stubborn. "I reckon a family ought to all be together when a chap comes. Specially the first one. I reckon the Lord will see to that." (18)

Passages such as this suggest not only that Lena protects what she is carrying in her womb, but that she herself is *in* a womb. An invisible shield seems to intervene between her and her interlocutors, permitting her to draw upon hidden resources and effortlessly to ward off the attempts of others to penetrate her space. The comic effect of these interchanges, based upon incompatible perspectives, is exactly the reverse of the comic effect of the following:

> The others had not stopped work, yet there was not a man in the shed who was not again watching the stranger in his soiled city clothes. . . . The foreman looked at him, briefly, his gaze as cold as the other's. "Is he going to do it in them clothes?"
>
> "That's his business," the superintendent said. "I'm not hiring his clothes."
>
> "Well, whatever he wears suits me if it suits you and him," the foreman said. "All right, mister," he said. "Go down yonder and get a scoop and help them fellows move that sawdust."
>
> The newcomer turned without a word. The others watched him go down to the sawdust pile and vanish and reappear with a shovel and go to work. The foreman and the superintendent were talking at the door. They parted and the foreman returned. "His name is Christmas," he said.
>
> "His name is what?" one said.
>
> "Christmas."
>
> "Is he a foreigner?"
>
> "Did you ever hear of a white man named Christmas?" the foreman said.
>
> "I never heard of nobody a-tall named it," the other said. (28–29)

As in the earlier dialogue between Armstid and Winterbottom, this comic interchange is premised upon a common understanding. The shared dislike of and acquiescence in work, the common awareness of what clothes one wears for this job, the general conviction that "Christmas" is not a name befitting a white man—these settled matters constitute a minimal social space within which jokes may be both uttered and understood. Joe Christmas may be lonely, but he is, by way of contrast, nicely placed in a scene like this one. Because the novel proliferates its male scenes of camaraderie, showing us in relaxed detail how the menfolk of Jefferson talk to each other, Joe's social ostracism is precisely identified. We know what he is not like. Further, the novel tirelessly tells us, through symbolic parallels, what he *is* like: he is like McEachern and Hines in their unbending misogyny, like Grimm in his impatience with natural processes, like Burch in his being on the run, like Hightower in his latent homosexuality. The point is that Faulkner knows so richly what is normal, abnormal, and in between in male behavior that his novel teems with analogues and foils to Christmas's descent into murder and self-immolation. His loneliness is illuminated at every stage.

Lena, by contrast, is like no one else. Comparisons with the Virgin or with the Magdalene only emphasize the point: her arena is not social but "marvelous." Here is the scene of crisis with Lucas Burch:

> She did not speak at all. She just lay there, propped on the pillows, watching him with her sober eyes in which there was nothing at all— joy, surprise, reproach, love—while over his face passed shock, astonishment, outrage, and then downright terror. . . . She watched him, holding his eyes up to hers like two beasts about to break, as if he knew that when they broke this time he would never catch them, turn them again, and that he himself would be lost. She could almost watch his mind casting this way and that, ceaseless, harried, ter-rified, seeking words which his voice, his tongue, could speak. "If it aint Lena. Yes, sir. So you got my message. Soon as I got here. . . ." His voice died somewhere behind his desperate eyes. Yet still she could watch his mind darting and darting as without pity, without anything at all, she watched him with her grave, unwinking, unbear-able gaze, watched him fumble and flee and tack. . . . (406)

Burch is as clearly understood—his expressions, his gestures, his language, his motives—as Lena is mysterious. Her "unbeara-ble" gaze suggests an absolute register beyond the bounds of social life, and we do not meet that word again until Joe Christ-mas also transcends the communal boundaries, lying castrated and bullet-ridden upon Hightower's kitchen floor: "For a long moment he looked up at them with peaceful and unfathomable and unbearable eyes" (439). Lena is beyond relationship, a "won-derful" figure whose psyche is never reduced to articulation. Her all-portending blankness reminds us of Judith in *Absalom, Absalom!* and of Lion in "The Bear": likewise figures of inex-pressible significance, representations of the other. It is no more surprising that Burch runs from her than that Bunch, when last seen, is still trying, hopefully but without much confidence, to discover access to her.

Another way of indicating *Light in August*'s narrative comfort with its males is to point out how often it pairs them. Males are connected throughout the novel, linked either legitimately or scandalously. The females seem to hover on the edge of these male pairings. For example, there are Hightower and Byron, Hightower and his grandfather, Hightower and the black male servant whom the townspeople beat, Hightower and Christmas whom they kill. What chance does Mrs. Hightower have in this structure? Likewise, there is Mrs. Hines kept from her husband by his passionate preference for his grandson, Mrs. McEachern kept from her husband by *his* passionate preference for his adopted son, Joanna Burden kept from her own family history by its relentless four-generational focus on males (Nathaniel and Calvin, Nathaniel and Calvin: Joanna's mother is not even named). And finally there is the suggestive homosexual pairing of Christmas and Burch, sleeping in the same cabin, a couple whose violence is peaceful compared to the heterosexual violence in the big house. In these instances the novel finds its way into the one male by silhouetting him against the other male, hearing them talk to each other, establishing their narrative history and domesticating them both through these comparisons.[8]

Women in *Light in August* are granted no such satisfying narrative space. Either they are given a top-heavy masculine history, like Joanna; or they are given a casually summarized history, like Lena; or they are cursed with their husband's history, like Mrs. Hines and Mrs. McEachern; or they have no history, like Bobbie the prostitute or that poor little girl Alice who vanished from the orphanage in the middle of the night: "Vanished, no trace of her left, not even a garment, the very bed in which she had slept already occupied by a new boy. He never did know where she went to" (127–28).

*   *   *

That was why it did not matter to either of them which one did the talking, since it was not the talking alone which did it, performed and accomplished the overpassing, but some happy marriage of

speaking and hearing wherein each before the demand, the require-
ment, forgave condoned and forgot the faulting of the other. (316)

This passage has been justly celebrated as intimating *Absalom, Absalom!*'s response to the irreversible doom embodied
in Sutpen's design. That response is *narrative:* the Sutpen saga
may be made bearable only by being interrogated, probed, and
pondered. Sutpen himself is narratively impotent: even when he
rehearses his earlier history with Grandfather Compson, "he was
not talking about himself. He was telling a story" (247). Incapable of probing himself or discovering his repressed motives
through dialogue with another, Sutpen must be reclaimed
through the imaginative narration of others. What is usually not
observed, however, is that such narration, in order to "overpass
to love," must be *shared,* and that only males are allowed to
share it.

Mr. Compson talks *to* Quentin, whereas Rosa talks *at* him
(perhaps a better phrasing would be *"through* him"). Chapter 5,
the most lyrical in the novel and the one that establishes Rosa
unforgettably, is told in uninterruptible Rosa-ese. Thirty-eight
pages of italicized intensity pass through Quentin, pass through
the reader. It is neither processed through intermittent response
nor punctuated by interrogation. The first chapter as well gives
us an inexplicably urgent Rosa, a woman whom Quentin can
only assent to ("'Yessum,' Quentin said. *Only she dont mean
that,* he thought. *It's because she wants it told"* [10]). The demur
must be silent. Rosa cannot be questioned, nor does she herself
raise questions. But this condemns her to being rendered
throughout *Absalom, Absalom! as an essentially questionable
figure,* a case history, an unconsciously eloquent witness, often
most eloquent because unconscious. Since she only talks
through others, it is hard to avoid reading *through* her. There is
no likelihood that Quentin or Shreve will mistake each other's
voice for hers, as they do for Mr. Compson's ("'Don't say it's just
me that sounds like your old man'" . . . "'*Maybe we are both
Father'"* [261]). They neither say nor think this about Rosa's voice
because, in its shrill and "marvelous" uninterruptibility, that

voice verges on a state of feeling all too easily associated with the female: hysteria.

Her utterance courts hysteria because it is so inattentive to its audience as a *participant*, so unaware of its status as a *narrative*. Rosa never solicits a response from Quentin, never says "maybe," never punctuates her discourse (as Mr. Compson does his) with phrases such as "I can imagine them as they rode" (107). She does not ponder. Being aware of oneself as a teller and interacting verbally with another person, however, are the hallmarks of the present narrative moment in *Absalom, Absalom!* Thus Rosa's discourse is curiously poised between the telling and the told, the still-emerging present and the already-completed past. We read it as both subjective and objective; it carries her spontaneous feeling yet remains impenetrable. Her narrative can receive the living speculations of others only as an object receives them, unresponsively, rather than as a subject does, dialectically altering in relation to what she hears.

Rosa is not the only woman caught between the extremes of vatic speech and silence. Judith Sutpen is given almost no voice in this novel, but when she does speak (as in passing on Bon's letter to Grandmother Compson), her words are gnomic in their intensity and resonance.[9] In related fashion, Eulalia Bon hardly opens her mouth in *Absalom, Absalom!*, yet others imagine her as (all during Charles Bon's childhood) "a kind of busted water pipe of incomprehensible fury and fierce yearning and vindictiveness and jealous rage" (298). If Eulalia's state is akin to hysteria, Rosa's aunt is nearer to it yet, a "grim virago fury of female affront" (54) who descends upon Jefferson society with her incoherent invitations to Sutpen's wedding. And there are women more vocally eccentric than these: the octaroon who weeps rather than speaks, Wash Jones's granddaughter who is given a total of one and a half broken lines to say (just before she is decapitated), and Sutpen's daughter Clytie whose role in the novel is as significant as her voice is irrelevant. Indeed, these are all major figures—even Milly Jones plays her part in Sutpen's downfall—but their importance is symbolic and objective: symbolic insofar as they are counters in a male design, objective insofar as they approached from without, as objects. Few characters speak *to* these women; none speaks *with* them. Deprived of a wider subjective frame within which they might think their spontaneous thoughts and speak their unpredictable words, they are all representations of the other, beyond relationship.

By contrast, how easily the men can be imagined talking to each other. Sutpen may be Faulkner's isolated demigod, but he nevertheless accommodates fairly easily to a number of narrative situations: in a hammock talking with Wash Jones, by a campfire with Grandfather Compson, later in a law office with Grandfather Compson. Henry and Bon are tirelessly envisaged together, and the novel may be said to reach its crescendo of inventiveness as it seeks to imagine Bon and Sutpen together (that, rather than Bon and Judith, becomes the privileged scenario, the relationship most worth exploring). Quentin and his father achieve a satisfying narrational relationship; Quentin and Shreve achieve a sublime one. It is sublime because each accepts the other as a subject, not an object, and between subjects capable of forgiving, condoning, and forgetting the faultings of each other—capable therefore of responding creatively to each other's differences—there arises the possibility of a "marriage of speaking and hearing." In *Absalom, Absalom!* this marriage seems limited to males.

*   *   *

There is no Caddy nor Lena nor Rosa in *Go Down, Moses,* and what women there are—with the minor exception of Miss Worsham in the final chapter—have little to say.[10] Most of them suffer the fate of the distaff side: their history of breeding is beside the genealogical point. The pathos of this novel, of course, lies in Faulkner's passionate rehearsal of that distaff history, especially in its scandalous moments. But the obvious corollary to such an approach is that the women come into focus mainly *as* potential or successful breeders.

Sometimes, however, they do not attain even this much narrative importance. Consider the first appearance of Sophonsiba Beauchamp:

> But at last a hand began waving a handkerchief or something white through the broken place in an upstairs shutter. . . . Then they stood in the hall, until presently there was a jangling and swishing noise and they began to smell the perfume, and Miss Sophonsiba came down the stairs. Her hair was roached under a lace cap; she had on her Sunday dress and beads and a red ribbon around her throat and a little nigger girl carrying her fan and he stood quietly a little behind Uncle Buck, watching her lips until they opened and he could see the roan tooth and he remembered how one time his grandmother and his father were talking about Uncle Buddy and Uncle Buck and his grandmother said that Miss Sophonsiba had matured into a fine-looking woman once. Maybe she had. He didn't know. He wasn't but nine. (10)

Handkerchief, perfume, cap, ribbon, fan, roan tooth: these component things establish Sophonsiba as a composite thing, a creature of surfaces and effects. Granted that the narrator is only a nine-year-old boy and that nothing in this first chapter is openly treated in a problematic fashion, Sophonsiba is nevertheless singled out for uniquely distortive narrative rendering. Her pattern of speech summarized on the next page, with its bumblebees and flowers and desert air and honey and queen bee, is "marvelous" as no other speech is in "Was." (Hubert and Buck and Buddy are permitted to speak an unremarkable English; they immediately understand each other.) Sophonsiba here emerges as a grotesque, and the question may arise: how can this woman be Ike McCaslin's mother? I think that to ask the question is to see that Faulkner's text bypasses rather than answers it. Sophonsiba has no narrative reality whatsoever as Ike's mother; this dimension of her being is wholly omitted. Although he is amply supplied with four fathers who all enjoy a substantial narrative history—Buck, Buddy, Cass, Sam Fathers (and we could add Boon and Hubert to this list)—Ike has no mother. The interesting thing is that he doesn't miss one.

Less bizarre than Sophonsiba, but equally represented in the narrative as irreconcilably *other,* is Ike's unnamed wife. This woman appears as though out of nowhere: he is married to her within four lines of our first hearing of her (311), and in bed with her a page later. The narrative interest in her is as intense as it is limited. It focuses entirely on her archetypal sexual identity and her localized sexual gestures and utterance. "Lock the door. . . . Take off your clothes. . . . Promise": these terse phrases punctuate Ike's furious cerebration. She is rendered as the unthinking desire of the body, he as the tempted but scandalized witness to the spirit. They are worlds apart. At the end of their intercourse (and of the five pages of *Go Down, Moses* that attend to her), we read:

> . . . he thought she was crying now at first, into the tossed and wadded pillow, the voice coming from somewhere between the pillow and the cachinnation: "And that's all. That's all from me. If this don't get you that son you talk about, it won't be mine": lying on her side, her back to the empty rented room, laughing and laughing[.] (315)

"Cachinnation" suggests so much: a woman who laughs violently (it could be mistaken for crying), a word one needs the dictionary for, a scene riddled with nonrecognition. Ike neither gets his son nor keeps his wife; neither event later receives emphasis. Like Lorraine in *The Sound and the Fury*, like Bobbie or Mrs. Hightower in *Light in August*, this woman can enter the narrative only as a nonrelational and disruptive fragment of the male protagonist's continuing history. All bodily desire and cunning, archetypally complete in herself, she has no story of her own.

The women that *do* matter in *Go Down, Moses* are black. Cleansed of sexual threat by the role of the victim that they are forced to play, these women—Eunice, Tomasina, Fonsiba, and especially Molly—are portrayed with dignity and pathos. But insofar as the victimizer is white, male, and McCaslin, the narrative significance of their stories is wrested away from them. Despite the teeming black population of this novel, the women are rarely seen in relation to each other. Carothers McCaslin intervenes between mother and daughter, causing the former's suicide; his great-grandson Zack intervenes between husband and wife, almost wrecking their marriage. The narrative logic of *Go Down, Moses* simply does not permit Eunice and her daughter to make common cause (if only in the form of commiseration) against this intruder, nor can it attend to Molly's dilemma as anything other than the tripartite male struggle (narrated at great length) between Lucas on the one hand, Zack on the other, and old Carothers somewhere in the middle. Molly herself appears as virtually a foil, a figure reduced to the single quality of breeder, an indiscriminate breast for children black and white. She is denied the complications of either desire or outrage. (These responses are left to the males.) Not, of course, that she necessarily *is* innocent of desire, outrage, or any other motive of her own. Rather, like Lucas (through whom we read her), we cannot know:

> She went on, neither answering nor looking back, impervious, tranquil, somehow serene. . . . He breathed slow and quiet. *Women,* he thought. *Women. I wont never know. I dont want to. I ruther never to know than to find out later I have been fooled.* (59)

And so even Molly—insistently described throughout this novel as small and weightless, preternaturally aged, wizened, and resignedly maternal—even Molly turns out, through the narrative deployment of her sexual difference, to be inscrutably other: a sister of "sister." Like the other women examined in this essay, she too appears as "wonderful" and "marvelous," with the attendant narrative posture, the combination of isolation and display, that these adjectives imply.

*　　*　　*

I should like to conclude speculatively. The patterns I have traced do not detract from Faulkner's greatness; indeed, they make it more interesting. His women *are* marvelous. But they are marvelous in the service of a narrative urge, present throughout his career, to probe the deepest recesses of his men. His ways of doing the one involved ways of doing the other. For his men to become themselves, his women had to take the shape they have. And in this creative move he shares in a larger Western project, eloquently summarized by Simone de Beauvoir: "what he [man] really asks of her is to be, outside of him, all that which he cannot grasp inside himself . . . because he must project himself into an object in order to reach himself. Woman is the supreme recompense for him since, under a shape foreign to him which he can possess in her flesh, she is his own apotheosis. Treasure, prey, sport and danger, nurse, guide, judge, mediatrix, mirror, woman is the Other in whom the subject transcends himself without being limited, who opposes him without denying him; she is the Other who lets herself be taken without ceasing to be the Other, and therein she is so necessary to man's happiness and to his triumph that it can be said that if she did not exist, men would have invented her."[11]

De Beauvoir goes on to say that men *did* invent her, and that many of her subsequent troubles come from this imposed and unwanted form. But this last is a story more properly our own than Faulkner's—that is, he can be seen to reveal it whereas we are eager to tell it—and I want to close these remarks by suggesting in what ways the biases I have been tracing do and do not matter. They *do* matter because Faulkner approaches his women differently from his men: only a New Critical insistence on universality, on the work of art as heroically complete in itself, could have blinded us to the differences made by gender.[12] Seen for the most part from outside, deprived both vertically in time and horizontally in space of their own subjective history, Faulkner's women move through their world as "wonderful" creatures, but considerably handicapped, from a narrative perspective, when compared with his men. Next to Tolstoy, though, these differences ascribable to gender will seem mild, and are we willing to give up Tolstoy because of *his* biases?

I come now to the sense in which his biases do not matter. They do not make him a lesser writer. No writer, no text, can be free of biases, complete, for completeness is a notion incompatible with the lineaments of achievement itself. It is we, not

Faulkner, who have wanted him complete, wanted him not only to say it all but to say it all right. What he wanted—and what he achieved—was not completeness but delivery, the delivery of his "impossible heart's desire." Faulkner became Faulkner by making his mark upon the stone, by having the courage not to be all the things that make up not-Faulkner. His every literary move, both voluntary and involuntary, is enabled by other moves not made. This ratio looks different now from the way it looked twenty-five years ago; in twenty-five years it will look different again. The array of useful critical commentaries and perspectives upon his work is therefore inexhaustible, and each of these (whatever its intention) constitutes a testimonial to his impact upon us.

NOTES

1. *Faulkner in the University*, ed. Frederick L. Gwynn and Joseph L. Blotner (New York: Vintage, 1965), 45.

2. Cleanth Brooks, "Introduction" to Sally R. Page, *Faulkner's Women: Characterization and Meaning* (DeLand, Fla.: Everett/Edwards, 1972), xi–xii.

3. The concept of "the other" is an important counterterm in most philosophic discussions of the self or the subject, and this has been especially true in the line of European philosophy that moves from Hegel's master-slave dialectic through twentieth-century existentialism and phenomenology. The major texts on this topic are Hegel's *Phenomenology of Spirit*, Heidegger's *Being and Time*, and Sartre's *Being and Nothingness*. Contemporary psychoanalytic theory, influenced by Lacan, likewise approaches the subject by way of a massive concern with "the other." For my purposes, the clearest formulation of "woman as the other" is Simone de Beauvoir's:

> Now, what peculiarly signalizes the situation of woman is that she—a free and autonomous being like all human creatures—nevertheless finds herself living in a world where men compel her to assume the status of the Other. They propose to stabilize her as object and to doom her to immanence since her transcendence is to be overshadowed and forever transcended by another ego [the man's] . . . which is essential and sovereign" (*The Second Sex*, trans. H. M. Parshley [New York: Knopf, 1968], xxix).

The crucial terms here are immanence and transcendence: woman, by being defined extrinsically, by being known only as the object of the male gaze, loses the intrinsic, moment-by-moment freedom of own subjective self-awareness. In place of this unpredictable transcendence, she assumes her identity from without—as a foreclosed immanence, a completed symbolic text whose terms are imposed by the male.

4. I cite from the Vintage editions of *The Sound and the Fury* and *Light in August*, and from the Modern Library editions of *Absalom, Absalom!* and *Go Down, Moses*.

5. *Faulkner in the University*, 1.

6. Sartre explains succinctly this movement of (male) subjective consciousness through which the freedom of the other is foreclosed: "Thus at one and the same time I have regained my being-for-itself through my consciousness (of) myself as a perpetual center of infinite possibilities, and I have transformed the Other's possibilities into dead-

possibilities by affecting them all with the character of '*not-lived-by-me*'—that is as *simply given*" ("The Encounter with the Other," in *The Philosophy of Jean-Paul Sartre*, ed. Robert D. Cumming [New York: Vintage, 1965], 205).

7. Alfred Kazin, "The Stillness of *Light in August*," in Frederick J. Hoffman and Olga W. Vickery, eds., *William Faulkner: Three Decades of Criticism* (New York: Harcourt, 1963), 253.

8. In a passage relevant to Faulkner's narrative practice, de Beauvoir posits that the incapacity to render woman as a subject is intimately allied to the incapacity to render women as a group: "For the male it is always another male who is the fellow being, the other who is also the same, with whom reciprocal relations are established. The duality that appears within societies under one form or another opposes a group of men to a group of men; women constitute a part of the property which each of these groups possesses and which is a medium of exchange between them. . . . To the precise degree in which woman is regarded as the absolute Other—that is to say, whatever her powers, as the inessential—it is to that degree impossible to consider her as another subject" (*The Second Sex*, 71). Something like this irremediable marginality explains the isolation of the women in *Light in August*, especially those like Mrs. Armstid, Mrs. McEachern, and Mrs. Hines, whose every thought, feeling, and gesture are constrained by a male code of expectations and requirements.

9. The closest Judith comes to being spoken to is Bon's letter to her: an occasion when she is both solicited and absent. The eventless period between Bon's murder and Sutpen's return is shared by Rosa, Judith, and Clytie; but there is neither purpose nor discourse among them: "We were three strangers" (157).

10. Miss Worsham strkes me as the egregious false (because sentimental) note of "Go Down, Moses." "It's our grief" (381), she tells Gavin Stevens, but that haunting black chorus of woe has no white voice in it.

11. *The Second Sex*, 186.

12. Jane Gallop suggests the way in which, behind the common discursive model for discussing "subjects" as universal and sexually neutral—a model that dominated New Criticism—there lurks a far from universal male paradigm: "The neutral 'subject' is actually a desexualized, sublimated guise for the masculine sexed being. Woman can be subject by fitting male standards which are not appropriate to, cannot measure any specificity of femininity, any difference. Sexual indifference is not lack of sexuality, but lack of any different sexuality, the old dream of symmetry, the other, woman, circumscribed into woman as man's complementary other, his appropriate opposite sex" (*The Daughter's Seduction: Feminism and Psychoanalysis* [Ithaca: Cornell University Press, 1982], 58).

Mothers and Daughters in Endless Procession: Faulkner's Use of the Demeter/Persephone Myth

Mimi R. Gladstein

Our literature, both ancient and contemporary, is replete with plots that concern the relationships of fathers and sons, fathers and daughters, and mothers and sons. *Oedipus Rex, Hamlet, King Lear, Sons and Lovers,* and *Portnoy's Complaint* come immediately to mind. We all could list dozens of others, great works and lesser works, which focus on these three sets of the parent/child relationship. The masculine element is always present. The solely female set, the mother/daughter relationship, however, has received little development in Western literature. This fact has not escaped the attention of feminist scholars, who reecho Simone de Beauvoir's complaint that since even our mythology is male-devised and male-oriented, woman is always Other and only perceived in relationship to some man.

One classical myth that does present mother and daughter in primary roles is the Demeter and Persephone story. Both Susan Gubar and Phyllis Chesler have written about the ramifications of this myth for the female psyche.[1] Women writers as diverse as Doris Lessing, Margaret Atwood, and Virginia Woolfe have seen the rich possibilities in the story of grieving mother and ravished daughter and recreated their own versions of the paradigm.[2] Male writers who have been inspired to stamp their signatures upon the Demeter/Persephone archetype are few and far between.[3]

William Faulkner is one, however, who used the myth a number of times. For him the mother/daughter relationship was endlessly provocative, fecund for interpretations. While ultimately it embodies an optimistic message because of its implications of continuity and immortality, still, the ravishment and only partial restoration of the daughter also suggest a dark side of the paradigm.

In his use of the myth, Faulkner develops both the bright and the dark aspects of its message. His emphasis, however, is on the positive; he uses the paradigm to suggest the endless renewal of the Eternal Feminine. It is one of a variety of techniques he employed to communicate his sense of female strength. Often in his characterization of women Faulkner emphasized their great endurance. His "unvanquished" elderly aunts and grandmothers are clearly representative of female indomitability. So are the many "earth mother" characters in his works. However, it is in his manipulation of the Demeter/Persephone myth that some of his strongest affirmative messages are transmitted, an affirmation inherent in the continuity embodied by the mother/daughter relationship. Caddy Compson and her daughter Quentin of *The Sound and The Fury*, Addie and Dewey Dell Bundren of *As I Lay Dying*, and Eula and Linda Snopes of *The Hamlet*, *The Town*, and *The Mansion* are three examples of Faulkner's Demeter/Persephone-like mother/daughter combinations.

Carvel Collins, Richard P. Adams, and Walter Brylowski are three critics who have noticed Faulkner's use of this myth. Collins concludes that whereas Joyce and Freud were strong influences in the writing of *The Sound and the Fury*, James Frazer's *The Golden Bough* is a primary source for *As I Lay Dying*. (I will argue in this paper that Frazer is also an important influence in *The Sound and the Fury*.) Collins claims that Faulkner presents "Addie, Dewey Dell, and Cora in a detailed and significant parallel with the Greeks' three-in-one goddess Demeter-Persephone-Kore."[4] Collins makes many ingenious comparisons between characters and events in the myth and in the novel, concluding that Addie is an inverted Demeter in that rather than being, among other things, buxom and all-loving as Demeter is, she is thin and rejects some of her children.

Whereas in the myth Persephone is carried away by Hades, in Faulkner's inversion Dewey Dell's trip to the woods with Lafe can hardly be called rape. Collins never does explain how Cora fits into the pattern. The only connections I can assume are linguistic ones; Cora sounds like Kore. However, in Greek, Kore means Maiden and the term is used to refer to Persephone. Cora can hardly be seen as Maiden in *As I Lay Dying*. She is more like a witness, such as Hecate was, but a witness who misinterprets the meaning of everything, a nice comic, ironic inversion consistent with the way Faulkner played with mythic patterns.

According to Richard P. Adams, Faulkner used the Persephone paradigm in a number of novels, with *Sanctuary* as the strongest example of its use.[5] Adams's witty explication of Faulkner's appropriation of the myth focuses on how Faulkner used the myth as organizing structure or form. Adams points out that the Persephone myth is but one of many myths at work in Faulknerian characterizations, symbolism, and plot patterns.

Brylowski, distinguishing among the various levels of myth apparent in Faulkner's works, calls the comparison of Caddy Compson and Eula Varner to Persephone the "simple" level of myth, that level which is allusion and analogy.[6] He sees the rape of Temple Drake as analogous to the rape of Persephone. In Brylowski's interpretation of *Sanctuary*, Horace Benbow becomes Demeter, the grieving mother, searching for her daughter, a curious interpretation even at a "simple" level.

Brylowski, Adams, and Collins are instructive. By exploring some of the ways Faulkner used the Demeter/Persephone myth they lay the groundwork for further development of the subject. For, in addition to using the myth's basic plot patterns and characters, Faulkner also uses the Demeter/Persephone relationship as a paradigm for what he saw as an essential truth of existence, the significance of female endurance and continuity. In the stories of Caddy Compson and her daughter Quentin, Addie and Dewey Dell Bundren, and Eula Varner Snopes and Linda Snopes, Faulkner presents varying rhapsodies on the theme from the Eleusinian mysteries, all of which sing of the perpetuation of life through the reunion of mother and daughter.

Frazer, whom Faulkner most certainly read, saw Demeter and Persephone as personifications of corn, who in the course of religious evolution also became symbols for rebirth: "Above all, the thought of the seed buried in the earth in order to spring up to new and higher life readily suggested a comparison with human destiny, and strengthened the hope that for man too the grave may be the beginning of a better and happier existence in some brighter world unknown."[7] More recent scholars have interpreted the myth in similar ways. Kerenyi, embellishing on the "bud-like" qualities of the mythical truths that were the undergirding of the worship of Kore, insists on the oneness of the two women. Though they are mother and daughter, their unity is a central fact of the mystery. They must be reunited for there to be life. They are pictorially represented as a double figure, sometimes indistinguishable from each other. "Persephone is, above all, her mother's Kore; without her, Demeter would not be *Meter*,"[8] Kerenyi observes. Demeter and Kore, mother and daughter, are symbolic extensions of the feminine consciousness, extending it both backwards and forwards in time. As they merge into one, the myth suggests "that every mother contains her daughter in herself and every daughter her mother, and that every woman extends backwards into her mother and forwards into her daughter."[9] Thus the myth has implications of continuity and immortality. Erich Neumann sees it as the mystery of the endless renewal of the Eternal Woman, for as Kore is restored to Demeter, she becomes identical with her, and so as each daughter ceased to be Maiden, she then becomes Mother.[10]

Faulkner's works demonstrate his sensitivity to the "bud-like" qualities of myth, that borderline balance of extremities at the heart of the paradox of the mythological idea. He repeatedly plays on these paradoxes, developing ambiguities, inverting patterns to demonstrate the oneness of opposites. Such is his use of the Demeter/Persephone myth. In one of his inversions, when both the mother and daughter are present in the story, it is the mother not the daughter who must undergo the trip to the underworld or "death" to insure the endurance of the daughter. Faulkner acknowledged this kind of literary tampering openly: "the writer, as I say, never forgets that [what he has read], he stores it away—he has no morals—and when he needs it, he reaches around and drags it out, and if it doesn't quite fit what he wants to say he'll probably change it just a little."[11] And change it Faulkner does. But his changes do not violate the integrity of the myth.

Caddy must exile herself to insure Quentin's future. In effect she, like Persephone, becomes the bride of the Lord of the Underworld, a Nazi officer's mistress. The oneness of Caddy and Quentin is underscored in many ways. Jason calls them both "bitches." Other canine imagery is used in their descriptions. Quentin's eyes are described as hard as a fice dog's. When Caddy is frustrated and angry, her upper lip jerks higher and higher on her teeth like a snarling cur. Jason states emphatically that Quentin is "just like her mother" (267).

Quentin identifies herself with her mother and against Jason. Rather than wear a dress bought with Jason's money she is ready to tear it off. This is not a pose, though Jason thinks it might be initially. For he soon realizes, "Then I saw that she really was trying to tear it, to tear it right off her" (233).

Both women are treated similarly by Jason; he controls them through blackmail. They both escape the Compson domain of sickness and sterility in similar ways, by climbing out of the window. The merger of the two women is also accomplished in the mind of their creator. A 1956 interview with Jean Stein dealt with Faulkner's assessment of *The Sound and the Fury*. For him it was the story of two lost women. Explaining the meaning of the muddy drawers, he said, "And then I realized the symbolism of the soiled pants, and that image was replaced by one of a fatherless and motherless girl climbing down the rainpipe to escape the only home she had, where she had never been offered love or affection or understanding." Quentin's image replaces or is superimposed on Caddy's in Faulkner's mind, and the "soiled" pants are replaced by the soiled girl.

Though Quentin repeats the tragic circumstances of her mother's life, as in the myth spring and summer give way to fall and winter, the implication is also that though she runs away, she is not defeated or destroyed. Unlike her mother who must leave her behind, a hostage in Jason's care, Quentin makes a complete escape. Not only that, but she defeats Jason by taking the only thing that is meaningful to him, "his" money. By taking the money, which was sent for her care by Caddy, Quentin symbolically and literally comes into her birthright. Her vehicle for escape is also significant; she climbs down on a blossoming pear tree, an obvious symbol of life and fruition which combines flower and fruit, mother and daughter, as the myth does.[12] After a period in the underworld each year, Persephone is returned. In one interview, Faulkner suggested the possible rejuvenation of Quentin in a future book. Neither death nor damnation is permanent for Faulkner's characters. Temple Drake is one of his Persephones who undergoes a time in the underworld only to be resurrected to motherhood and redemption. When needed, Caddy's brother Quentin was plucked from his watery grave to narrate *Absalom, Absalom!*

The perpetuation of female generations in *The Sound and the Fury* is not limited to Caddy and Quentin. It can also be read into another mother/daughter pair in that novel. The pattern of caring and sacrifice and endurance is readily seen in the relationship between Dilsey and her daughter Frony. Frony seems destined to continue in her mother's caretaking role. The men in the Gibson family may be troublesome, but not Frony. She cares about her mother, hoping that the Easter sermon will "give her the comfort en de unburdenin" (364). Dilsey is Demeter-like in her ability to love all living creatures, for Demeter is an all-loving mother, making no distinctions among her children. Dilsey is, in deed if not in fact, more of a mother to the Compson family than is Caroline Compson. Another way of reading the novel posits Dilsey in the Demeter role with Caddy as her Persephone. If she is read as mother and Caddy as daughter, the Demeter/Persephone analogy still works. A characterization of Dilsey as the Earth Mother is appropriate. She provides food for both the Compson and the Gibson families. At one juncture in the story, she is described as standing like a cow in the rain. The connections of women to both water and milk-producing animals is suggestive of their nourishing capabilities. Like Demeter, Dilsey grieves for her "lost" daughter. Symbolically, that daughter is returned to her in the person of Caddy's daughter Quentin. She has her for a season, and then loses her again, just as in the myth Persephone must return to the underworld after a period with her mother.

Addie and Dewey Dell Bundren also fit into the Demeter/Persephone archetype. Numerous critics have explored the Earth Mother images that are used to characterize both of these women.[13] As in the case of Caddy and Quentin, there is a fusion of mother and daughter. Both engender illicit children in the woods; both are nurturers, serving their family of men. In Dewey Dell's perception, Addie must die, in this case be literally consigned to the underworld, so that Dewey Dell can accomplish her purpose. Ironically, Dewey Dell wants not to sustain life, but to abort it. In keeping with the macabre sense of humor that is the dominant tone of As I Lay Dying, Dewey Dell's trip through hell will sustain life. In the myth, Persephone is raped by Hades, Lord of the Underworld. In As I Lay Dying Dewey Dell is taken advantage of by both her father, Anse, who takes her money, and by the druggist, who uses her sexually. Dewey Dell describes herself with a simile that suggests Persephone's role as the incarnation of the acorn: "I feel like a wet seed wild in the hot blind earth" (61).

Throughout the nightmarish occurrences of Dewey Dell's trip through and to hell, Dewey Dell acts in many nurturing and life-sustaining ways. She is first seen fanning Addie on her deathbed. She is next seen preparing food for the family. She cares for Cash when he is hurt. She takes over the care of Vardaman, who even accompanies her to her rendezvous with the druggist's assistant, which takes place appropriately in the underworld, a cellar.

Just as the Persephone of the myth is not as active a character as her mother, Demeter, so none of Faulkner's Persephones quite measure up to their mothers. Linda Snopes may be the exception, but then there is no other woman in all of Faulkner who measures up to Linda Snopes. Like the Persephone of the myth, Dewey Dell is mostly passive. Demeter searches all over heaven and earth for her daughter; her grief lays waste the land; she effects the rites and ceremonies to commemorate the re-union. Persephone is merely victim, the acted upon. Yet, it is she who is the embodiment of spring, she who is the renewal; it is her return which is celebrated. Thus Addie, in the active role, "takes" Anse, sets up elaborate codes of word and deed, aloneness and unaloneness, sets into motion the revenge of the journey to Jefferson. But it is through Dewey Dell that the "duty to the alive," the preservation of the species, is effected.

Howe dismisses Dewey Dell as "vegetable," "concerned only with her ease," a depiction which is hardly borne out by her actions.[14] Perhaps "vegetative" would be a better description since it would convey a sense of her fertility. Fiedler sees her as malevolently destructive: "Faulkner's dewiest dells turn out to be destroyers rather than redeemers, quicksands disguised as sacred groves."[15] One critic despises her for her inertness, one for her aggression. Stonesifer has come to her defense by interpreting her as the guardian of her mother's decree.[16] What none of these critics have noted is that, at the end of the book, Dewey Dell is the only Bundren who represents possibilities for the renewal of life. Cash is crippled, and if he hasn't shown much interest in women prior to the funeral trip, he is not likely to begin at this point. Jewel's sexual interest has been his horse, which he has now lost. Darl is in an insane asylum, hardly a fruitful possibility. Vardaman is still a child. One of the final images in the novel is of Dewey Dell, still pregnant, munching on a banana, an image rich with implications of continuity and renewal.

Faulkner's use of the Demeter/Persephone pattern in the Snopes trilogy clearly explores the moral dimensions of the myth. The forces of evil, death, impotence, and destruction are personified in Snopesism against which Gavin Stevens, V. K. Ratliff, and Charles Mallison have joined forces. Like Popeye, Faulkner's earlier incarnation of Pluto/Hades, Flem Snopes is an impotent bridegroom from the underworld. Popeye's Persephone, Temple Drake, is not fertile while in his care. Her fecundity is not realized until *Requiem for a Nun*. In *The Hamlet* Eula Varner is already pregnant when Flem Snopes marries her. Because of Flem's impotence and the lovelessness of their relationship, their marriage is sterile, a symbolic Land of the Dead.

In Eula, Demeter and Persephone are one. She is Persephone who is carried away by the Lord of the Underworld, but she is also the Great Earth Goddess who is worshipped wherever she is known. Labove, one of the first worshippers at her shrine, compares her "to the very goddesses in his Homer and Thucydides: of being at once corrupt and immaculate, at once virgins and the mothers of warriors and of grown men" (*H*, 128). In *The Town* she is likened to Lilith; in *The Mansion* she is described as Venus (*M*, 211). Ratliff calls his room the Eula Varner room, but Charles Mallison says it is more like a shrine (*M*, 232).

As the pattern of Persephone's removal from her mother is repeated every year, and Demeter, after the blossoming of spring and summer, sorrows through the coldness of winter, so Eula becomes the sorrowing goddess because of the loss of her daughter. Just as Persephone is ransomed by Pluto because of the pomegranate seed she ate while in the underworld, so Linda is ransomed to Flem because of the lie of her parentage. In order for Linda to have her chance for happiness, to escape Flem, Eula thinks she must die. In terms of the mythic pattern, the earth (in this case the Earth Mother) must die so that spring can return. This and other death/rebirth imagery abound in the Snopes trilogy.

The oneness of the mother and daughter is underscored in

various manners. Linda is continuously seen as Eula reborn. The three point-of-view characters, through whose perception the story is told, V. K. Ratliff, Gavin Stevens, and Charles Mallison, all switch their adoration from mother to daughter. At the end of the final book, when Linda leaves Jefferson, the theme of continuity is articulated by Ratliff. He says: "I don't know if she's already got a daughter stashed out somewhere, or if she jest aint got around to one yet. But when she does I jest hope for Old Lang Zyne's sake she dont never bring it back to Jefferson. You done already been through two Eula Varners and I dont think you can stand another one" (*M*, 434). The implications of this statement are in keeping with the message of the myth. The image is one of a continuously renewable line of mothers and daughters: Demeter and Persephone reunited anew for each year and each generation. Ratliff does not suggest a male child, and in terms of both Faulkner's use of the myth and his other symbolism in the trilogy, this is significant. Sally Page's study of Faulkner's women argues for a pattern of life-nourishing representatives of the female principle, particularly in the maternal role in opposition to life-destroying representatives of the male principle. The Snopes domain—the land of death and destruction, the land of the Lord of the Underworld—is male; the earth—the land of fecundity and motion—is female, and it is the return of the daughter which renews it. As Gavin Stevens explains: "So that was not the first time I ever thought how apparently all Snopeses are male, as if the mere and simple incident of woman's divinity precluded Snopesishness and made it paradox" (*T*, 136). David Williams, though his reading of the significance of Linda's character is less positive, agrees that "Linda suggests the archetypal feminine's potential for re-emergence."[17]

Prior to his Nobel Prize Acceptance Speech, most criticism of Faulkner's work emphasizes its negative aspects, its pessimistic world view, its presentation of "defeat and the consequences of defeat."[18] Much of the post-prize criticism, almost as if in response to the speech, has attempted to find evidence in the works for the optimistic message of the Nobel laureate: "I believe that man will not merely endure: he will prevail. He is immortal, not because he alone among creatures has an inexhaustible voice, but because he has a soul, a spirit capable of compassion and sacrifice and endurance." When I first read those words I was puzzled. Who was Faulkner describing? Jason Compson? Darl Bundren? Flem Snopes? And then I realized that part of the problem was that, like Addie, I had been tricked by words—"words that don't ever fit even what they are trying to say at" (163). Maybe if Faulkner had said, "I believe that woman will not merely endure, she will prevail," the proper image would have been created in my mind. For in Faulkner's greatest works, it is more often than not the women who show spirits capable of compassion; it is the mothers and the sisters and the aunts who sacrifice or are sacrificed for the needs of others. Faulkner's characterization of women is one of the areas in which the search for optimistic messages bears fruit, for his women are often personifications of the human will to endure. His "unvanquished" older maiden ladies and grandmothers are clearly characters whose spirits prevail. His many Earth Mothers, like the matter they symbolize, seem nigh indestructible. However, it is in his manipulation of the Demeter/Persephone myth that some of his strongest optimistic messages are transmitted, an optimism inherent in the continuity embodied in the mother/daughter relationship.

NOTES

1. Susan Gubar, "Mother, Maiden and the Marriage of Death: Women Writers and an Ancient Myth," *Women's Studies*, 6 (1979), 301–15; Phyllis Chelser, "Demeter Revisited—An Introduction," *Women & Madness* (New York: Avon Books, 1972), xiv–xxiii.

2. Gubar also analyzes how Mary Shelley, Elizabeth Barrett Browning, H.D., Virginia Woolf, and Toni Morrison have utilized the Demeter/Persephone myth.

3. I am utilizing the Leslie Fiedler's definition: literature comes into being when signature is stamped on archetype.

4. Carvel Collins, "The Pairing of *The Sound and the Fury* and *As I Lay Dying*," *Princeton University Library Chronicle* 18 (Spring 1957) 119–20.

5. Richard P. Adams, *Faulkner: Myth and Motion* (Princeton: Princeton University Press, 1968), 59.

6. Walter Brylowski, *Faulkner's Olympian Laugh* (Detroit: Wayne State University Press, 1968), 12.

7. Sir James Frazer, *The Golden Bough*, 1 vol., abr. (1922; reprint ed., New York: Macmillan, 1951) 460–62.

8. C. G. Jung and C. Kerenyi, *Essays on a Science of Mythology*, trans. R. F. C. Hull (Princeton: Princeton University Press, 1959), 109.

9. Ibid., 162.

10. Erich Neumann, *The Great Mother*, trans. Ralph Manheim (Princeton: Princeton University Press, 1972), 309.

11. Frederick L. Gwynn and Joseph L. Blotner, eds., *Faulkner in the University* (Charlottesville: University of Virginia Press, 1959), 251.

12. In Faulkner's appendix to a later edition of *The Sound and the Fury*, he seems to have forgotten his own scene. He states that Quentin climbed down a drainpipe. In the novel, however, the scene reads, "The window was open. A pear tree grew there, close against the house. It was in bloom." Luster later explains, "Me and Benjy seed her clamb out de window . . . clamb right down dat pear tree."

13. Karl Zink, Sally Page, David Williams, and Robert Kindrick are names that come immediately to mind. The list of critics who have noted Faulkner's Earth Mother imagery would fill this page.

14. Irving Howe, *William Faulkner: A Critical Study* (New York: Random House, 1952), 131.

15. Leslie Fiedler, *Love and Death in the American Novel*, rev. ed. (New York: Criterion, 1966), 320.

16. Richard Stonesifer, "In Defense of Dewey Dell," *Educational Leader*, 22 (July 1958), 27.

17. David Williams, *Faulkner's Women: The Myth and the Muse* (Montreal: McGill-Queens University Press, 1977), 225.

18. Gustaf Hellstrom, "Presentation Address," *Nobel Prize Library* (New York: Alexis Gregory, 1971), 4.

Desire and Despair:
Temple Drake's Self-Victimization

ROBERT R. MOORE

Temple Drake's story has shocked, titillated, and provoked the indignation of *Sanctuary*'s readers since its 1931 publication. From the opening scenes of her girlish coquetry, through her night of terror at the Old Frenchman place, her rape, and her apparently willing (even enthusiastic) collusion with evil at Miss Reba's and in the Goodwin trial perjury, readers respond to Temple with a complex mixture of arousal, sympathy, horror, and finally, disgust. By the end of the novel she appears no longer victim but rather, in words of one critic, a "representative of a spiritually impotent society."[1] As she sits amid the silken decadence of Miss Reba's Memphis whorehouse retelling to Horace Benbow the story of her night at the Old Frenchman place, "in one of those bright, chatty monologues which women can carry on when they realise that they have the center of the stage,"[2] Temple seems almost to relish the texture of the experience and the effect of the telling on her audience. Her attitude is unexpected, inappropriate for a young girl so brutalized. George Toles, explaining Horace's response to Temple's manner, speaks for many readers as well: "What Temple communicates to Horace is something he would prefer not to comprehend: how she has managed to avoid being victimized in any way which would permit feelings of outrage, or even honest sympathy, to emerge. Horace is defrauded of the emotional response which he felt was necessary to draw the perpetrated evil back somehow into an intelligible sphere of humanity."[3] "Defrauded" of his

ability to feel sympathy for Temple, Horace concludes that she—
all of them—would be better off dead: "Better for her if she were
dead tonight, Horace thought, walking on. For me, too. . . . all
put into a single chamber, bare, lethal, immediate and profound" (213-14). To Horace, Temple's response exemplifies the
pervasiveness of evil as he has come to understand it. To many
readers, Temple has revealed what they always suspected to be
her true nature. She, more than Popeye, becomes Faulkner's
intended representative of evil, one critic goes so far as to
argue.[4]

But Faulkner is less interested in *Sanctuary*, I would suggest,
with evil as a static reality than he is in how evil comes about. By
the end of the novel, Temple Drake *is* part of the evil from which
there is no sanctuary. Certainly, the girl who gives testimony at
Goodwin's trial and who gazes vainly into her compact mirror in
the Luxembourg Gardens was potentially present in the young
flirt who taunted the watching town boys at the college dance.
She is, nonetheless, a victim of evil as well. The process by
which victim becomes victimizer is the story Faulkner tells in
Sanctuary. Temple's unexpected, inappropriate behavior is not
the enigma it has too often been made out to be. It is, instead, a
key to understanding Faulkner's vision of evil.

Faulkner creates his most discomfiting effects using the symbolic imagery of defilement. Temple is touched, tainted,
stained, violated by an evil which is positive, external, and
infecting in the most literal sense. Paul Riceour, in *The Symbolism of Evil*, observes that the symbolism of defilement retains
its strongest impact today in its association with illict sexuality;[5]
and, certainly, Faulkner uses Temple's rape to evoke in his
readers powerful emotional responses. The sudden awareness
that comes with Eustace Graham's presentation of the bloodstained corncob at Goodwin's trial elicits our revulsion. We feel
in some way soiled ourselves; and it is, perhaps, this ability of
the book to affect us on a subrational level that explains the moral
indignation with which *Sanctuary* has been greeted.

Dominated by images of impurity—stain, disease, contamination, dirtiness—the expression of defilement identifies evil as external. One is made impure when touched by evil; consequently, evil is initially separate from self. Images of defilement are accompanied by multiple interdictions, "thou shalt nots," conceived to restrict the possibilities of potentially corrupting experiences. There attends, then, some sense that if one is tainted by contact with evil, it is because one has violated the interdictions.[6] More than a simple contagion in its implication of moral corruption, defilement possesses something of the power of literal disease to create fear and horror.[7] Evil is tied to active sexuality which, in turn, is associated with outward stain (prostitutes, for example, have been called "painted women" as if they bear the outward sign of their defilement in the make-up they wear) and inward, consuming disease.

In Temple Drake, Faulkner has created the archetypal ingenue, exuding a dewy innocence, magically attractive to men, yet possessing that instinctually manipulative quality Faulkner finds characteristic of women. To her father and brothers, she is the "temple" her name implies, an object of worship, a fleshless principle to be protected. Any association, however, of this Temple with a life removed from the temptations of the flesh does not take into account the girl we first meet at the college dance. She is not the ideal Southern lady,[8] no vestal virgin in unsullied white. She will not allow herself to be frozen on anyone's pedestal, escaping at every opportunity to play with boys who would be men, becoming the saucy flirt with "bold painted mouth" and eyes "cool, predatory and discreet" (29). She violates the community's "thou shalt nots," sneaking out at night to ride in the town boys' cars or on the weekends to dance and party with Gowan Stevens.[9] She enjoys the game—for to Temple, before her experience at the Old Frenchman place, such flirting is only a game with its own rules and without heavy moral implications.

We find ourselves on a roller coaster ride of ambivalence as we respond to Temple. If she demands our sympathy and protective impulses, she is also fair game for our sexual fantasies. Faulkner captures this paradox in the casual conversation of the drummers after Goodwin's trial has ended:

> "They're going to let him get away with it, are they?" a drummer said. "With that corn-cob? What kind of folks have you got here? What does it take to make you folks mad?"
>
> "He wouldn't a never a got a trial, in my town," a second said.
>
> "To jail, even," a third said. "Who was she?"
>
> "College girl. Good looker. Didn't you see her?"
>
> "I saw her. She was some baby. Jeez. I wouldn't have used no cob." (286–87)

Like the town, we respond to Temple both as virgin and whore; our horror at what befalls her mingles with an undefinable, leering attraction. We are disgusted and fascinated as we watch the process of Temple's degradation, seeing her as an ambiguous participant in her own debasement. We want to turn away from what we see and we want to see more.

Until the violent act of the rape, in fact, our watching her becomes a metaphor for Temple's defilement. Faulkner builds his atmosphere of terror not with physical acts so much as with a cloying voyeurism. He introduces Temple, even before the Old Frenchman place episode, as an object watched and admired. Her car passes; boys watch. She meets Gowan Stevens at the train station; "overalled men chewing slowly" watch (36). She is desired, and possessing that flattering knowledge, she controls the men around her. But at the Old Frenchman place, the watching changes from flattering to sinister. Voyeuristic scenes accumulate. Tommy sneaks a glimpse of her thigh as she struggles with her high-heeled shoe and later that evening, as she undresses, he crouches outside her bedroom window. The next morning an unidentified figure lurks in the bushes as she seeks privacy in the absence of a bathroom. As she huddles beneath the makeshift covers of the bed provided her, Faulkner offers us a scene of layered voyeurism, repeating it three times from different points of view as if to emphasize the significance. Popeye gropes at Temple beneath her nightgown as Tommy squats within the darkened room, watching. Ruby stands just

inside the door, overseeing the entire scene; and soon we become aware that Faulkner has made us, as audience, the final
circle of voyeurs for this sordid tableau.

This watching creates an atmosphere of terror, both for the
characters and for the reader. Voyeurism becomes more than an
annoying invasion of one's privacy; it becomes the psychological
equivalent of the act of rape.[10] The self is penetrated by an
undefined other, by a foreign quality which insinuates itself into
the sanctity of one's being. And, like the rape itself, this voyeurism conveys a sense of defilement. To the extent that
Faulkner has exposed us to ourselves as a final circle of voyeurs,
he causes us to see that we participate in the defilement, that we
in some sense are morally culpable here.

Significantly, watching in this world replaces talking; words, in
the sense of meaningful communication, are abandoned.
Faulkner presents these scenes at the Old Frenchman place
increasingly as tableaus that we *must* watch from without. He
transforms the voyeurism into a palpable evil first symbolically
when Temple returns to the crib:

> Her hand moved in the substance in which she lay, then she
> remembered the rat a second time. Her whole body surged in an
> involuted spurning movement that brought her to her feet in the
> loose hulls, so that she flung her hands out and caught herself
> upright, a hand on either side of the corner, her face not twelve
> inches from the crossbeam on whcih the rat crouched. For an instant
> they stared eye to eye, then its eyes glowed suddenly like two tiny
> electric bulbs and it leaped at her head just as she sprung backward,
> treading again on something that rolled under her foot. (90)

The eyes confront her on her own level, blazing unnaturally as if
they were lit by the fires of hell, the culmination of all those eyes
that have followed her movements since she left the dance. But
Faulkner now presents an aggressive rather than a passive voyeurism. When the rat leaps, the nightmare potential of evil
springs into reality. What has been until this point a vague
though strongly felt atmosphere of terror is given form. Temple is
literally cornered. That rat serves well as a symbolic agent of

defilement, triggering associations with disease and filth. We experience Temple's violation here *before* the rape. Faulkner milks the scene for its melodramatic potential even to the gratuitous gesture of introducing the cob as an extraneous yet faintly menacing prop in the last line. The actual corncob rape by Popeye follows immediately; but because Faulkner chooses a radically subjective presentation which obscures the details, we do not feel the emotional terror of evil there as powerfully as we do here in the penetrating stare of the rat.

The physical acts of Tommy's murder and Temple's rape finally give evil form in the figure of Popeye, a man alienated from everything natural in the world. But the evil Faulkner presents cannot, of course, be reduced to a single character. In *Sanctuary*'s world evil is not simply present—it is pervasive. It is not simply powerful—it is omnipotent. What then is the nature of man's existence within such a world? Faulkner creates an apt metaphor for that condition as Temple sees it in the situation of the two dogs, Miss Reba and Mr. Binford, which cower beneath her bed at the Memphis whorehouse: "She thought of them, woolly, shapeless; savage, petulant, spoiled, the flatulent monotony of their sheltered lives snatched up without warning by an incomprehensible moment of terror and fear of bodily annihilation at the very hands which symbolized by ordinary the licensed tranquillity of their lives" (151). The insidious quality of evil's threat lives not only in its physical action but also in the "terror and fear" generated by the uncertainty of the "without warning" and the arbitrariness of "the very hands." Temple interprets the dog's condition as emblematic of her own. She sees men, who under normal circumstances have represented and secured the "licensed tranquillity" of her life, as responsible for her present state, which is, in a very real sense, "incomprehensible" to her. In learning she cannot control men as she has been accustomed to doing, she feels she has also lost control over her own life. The analogy extends even further than Temple is willing to consider. This pervasive, omnipotent, arbitrary threat reduces the two dogs to snarling, snapping, thoroughly repulsive animals that command not our pity but our disgust. So, too, Faulkner seems to imply, man is diminished by his fear as much as by his actual contact with evil. The menace that stalks Temple at the Old Frenchman place, like the threat to the dogs, is real; but its power to reduce Temple derives as much from its uncertainty and its potential as from its actuality.

So, just as the two dogs cringe in the shadows under Temple's bed in an attempt to escape their fate, Faulkner depicts his characters scrambling for refuge—sanctuary—from the crushing presence of evil. Once they become aware that evil is a real and active possibility in their world, they react immediately by trying to erect walls in the hope that they might keep this force from visiting them personally. Frantically and futilely they search for asylums, physical, social, institutional, and moral. Inevitably they fail.

Faulkner allows us some distance from Temple as she scurries around by making her vision of evil that of a child, bound up with fears of the dark and of bogeymen. The shuffling appearance of Blind Pap triggers much of Temple's flight; he seems to become the object upon which she heaps all the fears she has not otherwise been able to place. Even at the moment of the rape, she visualizes not Popeye with the corncob but "the old man with the yellow clots for eyes" (99). Popeye, Van, Lee, and Tommy, for all their rough and crude sexual overtones, finally are only men to Temple, men whom she assumes can be manipulated with girlish pleas and coquettish smiles. Still, like a child, she reserves her greatest fears for the unknown—for the impenetrable mysteries of darkness and the freak.

But Temple's search for protection is more than a physical one. She arrives at the Old Frenchman place secure that she carries the protective mantle of social position. For all her flirting and running around after hours with town boys, she has always been Judge Drake's daughter; and when it serves her purpose, she invokes his title as another means of attempting to control others. She implies first to Popeye and then to Lee and Ruby that certain rewards or punishments will be forthcoming from her father depending upon how she is treated. However, in *Sanctuary's* world, proper society labels Goodwin, Ruby, and Popeye, bootlegger, prostitute, and thug, and dismisses them accordingly. If they accept this system, they accept with it their low status. So these outcasts who inhabit the Old Frenchman place have long since chosen not to be bound within the structure of this society. Alienated as they are, the rewards or punishments of the community carry little weight with them. To the extent that Popeye is the most alienated, he is also the least threatened by its power. Faulkner exposes social position with its supposed status and protection as a convenient fiction, gaining a tenuous reality only insofar as its illusion is shared. When Temple's fears begin to overwhelm her and she prays, not with the usual invocation to God the Father, but with an incantation to her father the judge,[11] we have already understood that social position is no more adequate as a sanctuary from evil than all those corners and cribs she searches out.

Ironically, then, Temple is more trapped within her so-called asylums than she is protected by them. She expects evil to operate by a certain logic and erects her defenses according to those expectations, but inevitably her attention is directed the wrong way at the moment evil strikes. Faulkner confounds his readers' assumptions as well in portraying an evil which refuses to play by the rules. When Temple survives the terror of that first night at the Old Frenchman place and awakens to a sunlit spring Sunday, we feel with her a conscious relief. Raised in the tradition of Gothic horror tales, we share her belief in evil as something that goes bump in the night. With her we relax our guard momentarily against their natural backdrop of a spring morning. The scene with the rat followed by Tommy's murder jars us into recognizing evil does not comply with our expectations.

Temple's ill-fated search for sanctuaries recalls something of the language Ricoeur associated with a second symbolic pattern, the evil of sin. Sin is pride, arrogance, or belief in self-sufficiency tied to the choice of false gods, Ricoeur explains.[12] To sin is to violate the preeminence of God in favor of the self. Temple's inability to pray points to her ruptured relationship with God; she has made of social position a false god which confers no protection. She may see herself as one of the "elect," but her election is only within a secular world. She understands her need to be "saved," but again it is only in the physical sense. Until the moment she is raped, she retains belief in her own self-sufficiency to escape the corrupting touch of evil. Her sin is a pride which entraps her. Thus, believing she is fleeing to a haven, she makes herself captive within the crib where evil discovers her.

The climactic moment of Temple's rape is a tableau. Faulkner uses it as the central metaphor for his understanding of man's ineffectuality in protecting himself from the encroaching reality of evil. He sets the scene carefully; at Temple's request Tommy crouches just inside the bolted door of the barn watching Lee Goodwin; Lee stands in the orchard watching the barn entrance; Popeye, meanwhile, circles the barn, watching them both, climbs into the loft, and lowers himself into the crib where Temple has withdrawn for safety. Temple erects her defenses against an evil external, casting about her concentric circles of watching. But evil—Popeye—awaits at the core of her sanctuary, immune to her efforts. In this scene Faulkner captures symbolically the essence of an evil which emanates from within as well as penetrates from without. It cannot be escaped because it lurks at the heart of any sanctuary man might devise. Temple, through her experiences at the Old Frenchman place, has awakened to the menace of an evil around her, but she has not yet understood that this evil is in some part within her as well. Nor, yet, have we as readers. It is the narrative following the scenes at the Old Frenchman place which reveals their metaphorical significance.

With the scene of Temple's rape, Faulkner has established the physical existence of evil as external and infecting in the most primitive sense of the imagery of defilement; but he has not finished with Temple. We are to understand her as more than just the object upon which evil is visited; her behavior in the latter half of the novel helps to define evil in a more complete sense. At the same time, as we come to understand these wider dimensions of evil through the actions and words of other characters, we begin to comprehend the motivations behind the perjured testimony Temple gives at Goodwin's trial.

Once Temple leaves the Old Frenchman place, her behavior perplexes many readers. Why does she shun the opportunities to escape Popeye for the protection of the community she so yearned for during her frantic scramblings before the rape? Why does she adapt so readily to the corrupt ease of Miss Reba's whorehouse? How can we explain the way she has accommodated herself to whatever happened back at Goodwin's? Why does she seem to take such relish in recounting to Horace Benbow the story of her night of terror? Finally, why does she condemn Lee Goodwin by her perjured testimony with so little apparent remorse? If we are to answer these questions, Faulkner demands that we become something more than voyeurs. Facts, Faulkner once wrote Malcolm Cowley, are to be regarded skeptically: "I don't care much for facts, am not much interested in them, you can't stand a fact up, you've got to prop it up, and when you move to one side a little and look at it from that angle, it's not thick enough to cast a shadow in that direction."[13] Truth, he believed, is the product of successive speculations about facts rather than something to be discovered in the facts themselves.

We are seldom privy to Temple's consciousness, yet we have clues to her motivations. The most obvious explanation is that she is controlled by Popeye. In other words, with the violation of the rape, she loses her autonomy as a human being, becoming an extension of his will. The fear he engenders in her saps her spirit and reduces her to cowering impotence. Her speculations on the fearful insecurity of Miss Reba's dogs suggest this would be how she sees herself. But in limiting our explanation to Temple's fear of Popeye, we restrict ourselves to a vision of evil as only external, a defilement so powerful and pervasive it corrupts everything it touches.

But the representation of sin differs from that of defilement in that it is expressed as an absence rather than a presence. To have sinned is to be nothing; the sinner is said to be alienated from God and from himself. "Sin makes [you] incomprehensible to [yourself]," Ricoeur explains.[14] Mankind is said to be lost in sin. Signified most powerfully by the slavery of the Hebrews in Egypt, the cosmic idea of sin is brought into historical context to depict the human condition under the influence of evil. The symbolic pattern is that of captivity:

> The sinner is "in" sin as the Hebrew was "in" bondage, and sin is thus an evil "in which" man is caught . . . it is a power which binds man, hardens him, and holds him captive; and it is this experience of the impotence of captivity that makes possible a taking over of the theme of defilement. However "internal" to the heart the principle of this bondage may be, the bondage in fact constitutes an enveloping situation . . . and so something of unclean contact is retained in this idea of the "captivity" of sin.[15]

If man is passive and impotent within this representation of evil as a captive condition, it is because he recognizes that he is in some sense possessed by an inclination toward evil. God seems to have consigned man to evil by creating him with an unmanageable will. One's desires become almost an instinct for evil action.[16] Man is at once caught in sin and the initiator of sin through his uncontrollable will. Evil is once more a palpable, external reality, but now there is a suggestion of man's responsibility for its existence.

When Temple leaves the Old Frenchman place, the character of her search for sanctuary changes. She is no longer fleeing a threat from without. Now she is passive, withdrawing from the so-called good people, seeking refuge from the prying eyes of the community she has left behind. When Popeye stops for food on the way to Memphis, Temple bolts from the car, not to escape from Popeye, but because she fears she might be seen by a boy she has known at school. She makes no attempt to reach her father or brothers though she can get to a telephone to call Red when she needs to. The boy from school, the doctor at Miss Reba's, her father and brothers all represent to Temple the world from which she came, a world in which "sin" was an abstraction the Baptist ladies concerned themselves with. She cannot escape the awareness of what has happened to her. She perceives what has happened as a stain immediately evident to anyone from that innocent world. The rape has made her "incomprehensible" to the self she has assumed herself to be; she now sees herself as caught within a state of sin, alienated from the community. This state becomes in time her new self-definition. Faulkner, in other words, initiates the process by which Temple internalizes the evil visited upon her.

Faulkner's characterization of Temple in Memphis is straight out of a grade B movie. She becomes a cheap twenties flapper, swilling gin, chain smoking, drinking and dancing at a local speakeasy until she works herself into a frenzy of sexual desire with Red. Our first impulse may be to criticize Faulkner for giving us the stereotyped "fallen woman" as the result of the interlude with Popeye on the floor of the crib. His imagination would seem to have faltered, yielding no more than this stock figure of moral melodrama if we conclude his purpose has been to show an evil so powerful and pervasive that it corrupts, absolutely, everything it touches. If, however, we see Temple's actions as reflecting feelings of guilt, Faulkner's portrayal becomes much more complex and interesting. "Man is guilty," explains Ricoeur, "as he feels himself guilty."[17] Guilt arises from the individual's willing assumption of responsibility for acts he has come to perceive as evil. Temple seems to accept that the experience has transformed her into a whore, unfit for the company of the so-called good people of Jefferson. "That which is primary is no longer the reality of defilement," Ricoeur says in outlining the birth of the guilty conscience, "but the evil use of liberty, felt as an internal diminution of the value of the self."[18] Faulkner has characterized her from the start as a passionate, headstrong girl, but one protected, or at least checked by the limits of the role the community has defined for one of her status. Her unruly will has carried her beyond the bounds of that community, however; and her almost instinctual flirtatiousness, reflecting desires that are part of her nature, has involved her in the violation of one of her community's most sacred interdictions. Now she feels cut off from any return to that community and partially responsible for her own isolation. She feels sinful so she abandons herself to acting as she naively supposes a "sinful woman" would act: gin-swilling, chain-smoking promiscuity. Her behavior is a sort of role-playing, a casting about for a new self-definition. This posturing also explains in part her "bright, chatty monologue" as she recounts to Horace the story of her experiences at the Old Frenchman place. She has given herself to this new identity. There is self-contempt in what she does, for it reflects that she has submitted to an identity which treats only a part of her nature—physical desire—as if it were the whole. Seeing herself as alienated from that community she has known before, Temple adapts to Miss Reba's world, which offers a license to the exercise of desire; but, in doing so, she fans the self-consuming flames of her guilt.

Miss Reba recognizes that Temple is engaging in a kind of self-destruction: "'I wish you'd get her down there and not let her come back. I'd find her folks myself, if I knowed how to go about it. . . . She'll be dead, or in the asylum in a year, way him and her go on up there in that room. . . . She wasn't born for this kind of life'" (213).

At the center of Ricoeur's circle lies despair, the consequence of which is the generation of evil. Temple murders Lee Goodwin with her false testimony as surely as if she were to shoot him with Popeye's gun. Why? Again, the most frequent explanation is that she acts from fear. Throughout her time on the stand, her eyes fix on the rear of the courtroom, and she cringes as she is led from the room by her family. Like Goodwin huddled in his cell before the trial expecting a bullet from Popeye's revolver to find its way through the barred windows, Temple, it is reasoned, seems to believe that Popeye awaits her just beyond the door. Like the two dogs at Miss Reba's, snarling and snapping in anticipation of some undeserved fate, she is reduced by the uncertainty of Popeye's avenging evil. The enormity of what she does—not simply absolving the guilty party but actually condemning a man she knows to be innocent—and the detachment with which she does it cannot be fully accounted for by this explanation, however. In the language with which he describes her actions and appearance in court, Faulkner suggests her experiences have reduced Temple to a shell: "Her face was quite pale, the two spots of rouge like paper discs pasted on her cheekbones, her mouth painted into a savage and perfect bow, also like something both symbolical and cryptic cut carefully from purple paper and pasted there" (277). Temple appears in public for the first time since the rape, not as the innocent ingenue who left a few weeks before, but in her assumed role of "fallen woman," wearing the paint emblematic of her defilement. Faulkner describes her in abstract impressionistic terms of shapes and colors which deny her an element of humanity: "she gazed at the District Attorney, her face quite rigid, empty. From a short distance her eyes, the two spots of rouge and her mouth, were like meaningless objects in a small heart-shaped dish" (279). She stares vacantly as if drugged, her eyes blank and lifeless. The woman Faulkner gives us in this scene is not really there; she is without substance, sleepwalking through a role she thinks expected of her. The earlier Temple is lost. She has made of herself a prisoner within her own consciousness, dead to an outside world. As her father leads her from the courtroom, she moves "in that shrinking and rapt abasement" (282). Neither her testimony nor Lee Goodwin has any reality for her. Abject as she is, retaining no sense of self-worth, nothing she does or says can, in her eyes, matter. She has been caught within the web of despair. Her single, meaningful reality is a sense of isolation from the world she once knew—the world of her father, the judge, of her four brothers, and of the townspeople who fill the courtroom.

Temple and her father sit in the Luxembourg Gardens at the novel's end apparently oblivious to the world around them, bored with life. After the intensity of the trial and lynching scenes, Faulkner mutes the tone here. The electric tension which has permeated the atmosphere of *Sanctuary* is replaced by "a gray day, a gray summer, a gray year" (308). No one watches Temple now; instead, she watches herself, gazing vainly into her compact mirror, a Narcissus wrapped up in her own image. As we find her here, Temple does seem finally lost, a victim of her own self-involvement. Through her story Faulkner has suggested the process by which evil begets evil. Temple has been changed by her contact with the evil that Popeye represents but also by her reaction to that contact, by her passivity, her surrendering of self to guilt and, finally, to despair. Confronted with the violence and sordidness of evil, she gives herself up to the pride that characterizes her worst nature. She isolates herself within a circle of her desires and guilt—the sanctuary of her impenetrable consciousness a prison that cuts her off from humanity.

NOTES

1. William R. Brown, "Faulkner's Paradox in Pathology and Salvation: *Sanctuary, Light in August, Requiem for a Nun*," *Texas Studies in Literature and Language*, 9 (August 1967), 433.

2. William Faulkner, *Sanctuary* (New York: Random House, 1958), 208–9; hereafter cited parenthetically within the text.

3. George Toles, "The Space Between: A Study of Faulkner's *Sanctuary*," *Texas Studies in Literature and Language*, 22 (Spring 1980), 41.

4. Brown, 433.

5. Paul Ricoeur, *The Symbolism of Evil*, trans. Emerson Buchanan (New York: Beacon Press, 1969), 8.

6. Ibid., 27.

7. Ibid., 35.

8. Anne Firor Scott, "Women, Religion, and Social Change in the South, 1830–1930," in *Religion and the Solid South*, ed. Samuel S. Hill, Jr. (Nashville: Abingdon Press, 1972), 92. Scott explains that the definition of the ideal Southern woman closely paralleled that of the ideal Christian woman. Thus when the Southern woman perceived herself as falling short of what we might call the social expectations of her culture, she was quite likely to see herself as sinning. "The biblical verse most frequently quoted in southern women's diaries," Scott writes, "was from Jeremiah: 'The heart is deceitful above all things and desperately wicked: who can know it?'" (96).

9. Kenneth K. Bailey notes certain of the "thou shalt nots" typical of the Southern Protestant church in the 1920s: "A Southern Presbyterian committee deplored 'unchaperoned automobile riding at night,'" and the Southern Baptist Social Service Commission warned: "'Accompanied, as it is, by immodest dress, by close physical contact of the sexes, and by its lack of restraint . . . [dancing] is undoubtedly doing much to undermine the morals of our young people'" (*Southern White Protestantism in the Twentieth Century* [New York: Harper and Row, 1964], 46). Temple, as we first see her, is

clearly flouting the standards of conventional behavior young girls of the day were expected to adhere to.

10. Toles, 31. Referring to Karl Abraham's essay on voyeurism in his excellent discussion of how Faulkner uses these scenes of voyeurism and the language of sexual violence to create an atmosphere of alienation, Toles concludes: "the voyeur [is] locked to [his] object by a power of alienation that has all but destroyed the power of identification."

11. Samuel S. Hill, Jr., points out that Southern Protestants typically characterize God as the Holy Judge or the Righteous Judge (*Southern Churches in Crisis* [New York: Holt, Rinehart & Winston, 1966], 77). Thus, Temple's association of her father, the judge, with God the Father shows that in some almost instinctual way she perceives with the eye of the Southern Protestant.

12. Ricoeur, 57, 75–76.

13. Malcolm Cowley, *The Faulkner-Cowley File: Letters and Memories, 1944–1962* (New York: The Viking Press, 1966), 89.

14. Ricoeur, 70–71. Looking again at the scene in which Temple is raped, we see that her repeated words "something is happening to me" (99) show a split of consciousness from the body which is being defiled. Faulkner, in turning to this radically subjective point of view, lays groundwork for a shift in focus from the objective event of the rape to the subjective response of Temple, from defilement to a sense of having sinned.

15. Ricoeur, 93.

16. Ibid., 88.

17. Ibid., 104.

18. Ibid., 106.

In Praise of Helen

ANDRÉ BLEIKASTEN

One can say that beauty is present wherever light and matter, the ideal and the actual are in touch.
                                                    —F. W. G. SCHELLING

[*Light in August*] began with Lena Grove, the idea of a young girl with nothing, determined to find her sweetheart. It was . . . out of my admiration for women, for the courage and endurance of women. As I told that story I had to get more and more into it, but that was mainly the story of Lena Grove.[1]

Whether *Light in August* is "mainly the story of Lena Grove" is highly debatable, and there is good reason to question the accuracy of Faulkner's account of its genesis.[2] If not literally true, however, the statement has its own truth, the truth of its maker, the poet's truth, and it is indeed in Lena, a young pregnant woman on a dusty summer road, that the novel has its beginning and its ending. More than that: Lena holds the novel together, enfolds it in her monumental serenity, makes it what it is: a story full of sound and fury set against a background of pastoral stillness, a tale of darkness fringed with light.

And in a tenderly humorous way *Light in August* is indeed a homage (from the French *homme,* man, male) to Woman, an invocation to Venus Genitrix in the tradition of Homer and Lucretius,[3] a graceful tribute to feminine fertility, feminine endurance, and feminine triumph. Lena is the radiant figure at the novel's gates, and from one to another her trajectory draws a straight line, as economical as light itself—a straight line which would be at the same time the most accomplished circle.

Lena comes to us, comes back to us from the plumbless depths of a time before time, prior to the nightmares of history, a time slow and simple, ruled by the regular rhythm of mere alternation: "backrolling now behind her a long monotonous succession of peaceful and undeviating changes from day to dark to day again, through which she advanced in identical and anonymous and deliberate wagons as though through a succession of creakwheeled and limpeared avatars, like something moving forever and without progress across an urn."[4] Lena moves in the timeless time of eternal recurrence, along a soft curve retracing and rejoining itself in a circle ever rebegun. As to her own time (if we can credit her with a time of her own), it is like a smaller circle within the large one, closed in upon itself, throbbing with the pulse of living matter, and so quite naturally attuned to the unchanging cycle of days, months, and years. For Lena and in Lena life flows smoothly and slowly, following its predetermined course, "with the untroubled unhaste of a change of season" (47). In sharp contrast to Dewey Dell, her rebellious and tormented sister in As I Lay Dying, she "is waging a mild battle with the providential caution of the old earth of and with and by which she lives" (23, italics added). Of and with and by: Lena is but another name for natura naturans.

Her swollen body shows nature at work in the fecund field of female flesh, and Lena hears and feels "the implacable and immemorial earth, but without fear or alarm" (26). Nothing can hurt her. No need even for her to fight to achieve her ends. Her ends are in her beginnings, the harvest is in the seed, it is all a matter of growing and ripening. Lena has just to wait, and her patience is inexhaustible. Contrary to Joe Christmas's journey, her own is not a restless, aimless wandering, nor is it a true quest. Her destiny bears her along, and she bears it within herself, like the child soon to be born.

Everything for her comes at its appointed hour, in the appointed place. Lena has no permanent dwelling, but why should she care? She is at home wherever she goes. Her puzzled pleasure in measuring the distance she has already traveled—

"My, my. A body does get around" (26)[5]—clearly indicates that to her space is not at all the ever-receding, inaccessible horizon which it will be to Christmas. Hers is the realm of *immanence:* she is as safely inside space as she is inside time, cradled in its folds like the foetus in her womb. Conversely, space appears to be the cosmic double of her own body: both welcoming, hospitable, and closed, concentric—space as it was described by Plato in the *Timaeus,* that is, a receptacle, a vessel, a matrix, as though it were the mother or nurse of all becoming. Significantly, all its predicates—luminosity, stillness, warmth, and a unique combination of torpor and alertness—also apply to Lena herself. Woman's body and the world's body call for each other and respond to each other in preestablished concord, joined by a happy complicity which nothing, apparently, will ever be able to break. *Mundus muliebris.*

Lena therefore never stands out *against* the landscape. The natural world at peace with itself (in other words the pastoral world) is her true milieu, gathering around her as if to shelter her in its seamless and boundless mantle. And if her habitat seems to be a solid earth, it is infused by light, a light which lightens matter, slows down motion, and in which time itself almost comes to a standstill: "The wagon moves slowly, steadily, as if here within the sunny loneliness of the enormous land it were outside of, beyond all time and all haste" (24).

* * *

The first chapter of *Light in August* celebrates the victory of light and space over the darkness of time, and this victory might be called as well the triumph of the mythic over the actual. "Mythological Antiquity," writes Catherine Clément, "is precisely that: *the privilege of space over time.* . . . Mythology cancels time, and opening up space, renders human achievements indefinite. Immortality finds there its foundation." And she adds that with the advent of Christianity space lost this privilege and ceased to be a locus of life: "Time and its tragic consequences—sin, guilt—then became the straight gate to immortality."[6]

Lena belongs to this pure mythic space prior to the fall into time, and as has often been pointed out, she turns out to be herself a mythic figure, a new avatar, in Faulkner's fiction, of the primal mother or earth goddess. Admittedly, she is a very earthy earth goddess, a deity mildly astonished at finding herself in the young body of a very ordinary mortal woman, yet in her absolute serenity she is assuredly Olympian.

Faulkner called her after Helen, the Spartan princess who caused the Trojan war, the daughter of Zeus whose bewitching beauty equalled that of the fairest goddesses. He thereby associated Lena even more closely with the symbolism of the novel's title, since etymology links "Helen" to Greek words denoting the brightness of light.[7] As to *Grove*, her patronym, it is likewise loaded with mythic connotations, bringing to mind the Ephesian Diana (or Diana Aricina), the Roman goddess described by Frazer in the first pages of *The Golden Bough*, whose cult used to be celebrated in a sacred grove of the Alban hills. Yet Lena not only evokes pagan goddesses. The "faded blue" of her sunbonnet and her dress, and her "palm leaf fan" (7) may remind one as well of the Virgin Mary, as she might have been portrayed by Bellini, and once Lena has found her meek Joseph in Byron Bunch, there will be another Holy Family on the road.

Helen and Diana were originally goddesses of vegetation and fecundity, and if the Virgin Mary has not been divinized, she came to hold in the Christian West the place which the Great Mothers of earlier cultures had left vacant. The mythological configuration in which Lena is embedded is then clearly that of the archaic *Magna Mater.* It will not do, however, to catalogue her as another earth mother and let it go at that. As a character in a novel, Lena is both more and less than a replica of her mythic models. Myth and fiction belong to different cultural registers, and whenever a novelist uses mythic figures and mythic patterns, it is to pervert and subvert them for his own private

purposes. It is therefore important to see how myth is deflected
and transformed in the writing process, and to begin with, one
should perhaps take a closer look at the mythic material itself.

In their search for large and simple truths, Jungian critics
would have us believe that all mythic figures can ultimately be
reduced to stable, monolithic archetypes.[8] In·fact, nearly all
gods and goddesses, especially when they involve themselves in
human affairs, turn out to be ambiguous and contradictory figures. This duality holds true for Helen and Diana as well as for
the Virgin Mary. Helen was believed to be a daughter of Zeus,
but there was no consensus as to the identity of her human
mother, who may be have been Leda, a daughter of Oceanus, or
Nemesis, the goddess of retribution, who was herself the daughter of Nyx (Night). Helen, in her unsurpassed beauty, is the
"bright," the "shining" one, and yet her half-divine, half-human
origins are wrapped in mystery and darkness, even as there is
darkness in her fate and in the fatality she became to thousands
of Greeks and Trojans in provoking, albeit involuntarily, a murderous war, and lastly, as Aeschylus suggests in *Agamemnon*,
there is also darkness in "that name for the bride of spears and
blood, Helen, which is death . . . death of ships *(helenas)*, death
of men *(helandros)* and cities *(heleptolis)*."[9] Diana is no doubt a
different figure, but she too has a double face: at one and the
same time a woman and a robust huntress, a fierce virgin,
inviolate and inviolable, and the patron goddess of brides, wives,
mothers, and children. As to the Virgin Mary, she stands for a
similar duality in the Western Christian tradition: a woman born
of woman, and yet conceived out of sin, a second Eve exempted
from the first Eve's evil inheritance, the mother of Jesus, and yet
an immaculate virgin.

After this short detour through mythology, let us come back to
Lena. There is darkness, too, in her name, at least in her last
name, through its association with the groves referred to in the
novel, all of which are somehow related to sex and/or death, and
it is certainly not fortuitous that it is in the vicinity of the oak
grove surrounding Joanna Burden's house that Joanna is slain and

Lena gives birth to her child. Furthermore, Lena obviously also partakes of the paradoxical myth of the virgin mother, in which the role of sexuality and the male's procreative function are blandly ignored. Of course, the reader soon learns that the girl is pregnant, and he is even told under what circumstances she was seduced, yet everything seems to suggest that the identity of the father does not really matter and that there is no need to find him promptly. If it is not Burch, it will be Bunch. In the novel's comic epilogue, the family triad is at last completed, order is restored, but even then Byron Bunch, the future husband and father, is still like an intruder, an alien to the primordial and autarchic couple formed by mother and child.

*   *   *

Lena is unique because she is one, and she is one because she is two, one in two, two in one—thanks to the child-supplement or, as Freudians would put it, to the child-phallus which makes her whole. She is the one who lacks nothing. Fulfilled and intact: mother *and* virgin.

Her exceptional status is confirmed by her privileged relationship to *light*, the importance of which in the novel, especially in connection with Lena, Faulkner himself pointed to in one of his interviews:

> . . . in August in Mississippi there's a few days somewhere about the middle of the month when suddenly there's a foretaste of fall, it's cool, there's a lambence, a luminous quality to the light, as though it came not from just today but from back in the old classic times. It might have fauns and satyrs and the gods and—from Greece, from Olympus in it somewhere. It lasts just for a day or two, then it's gone, but every year in August that occurs in my country, and that's all that title meant, it was just to me a pleasant evocative title because it reminded me of that time, of a luminosity older than our Christian civilization. Maybe the connection was with Lena Grove, who had something of that pagan quality of being able to assume everything, that's—the desire for that child, she was never ashamed of that child, whether it had any father or not, she was simply going to follow the conventional laws of the time in which she was and find its father. But as far as she was concerned, she didn't especially need

any father for it, any more than the women that—on whom Jupiter begot children were anxious for a home and a father. It was enough to have had the child. And that was all that meant, just that luminous lambent quality of an older light than ours.[10]

Here we are back at the place and time of beginnings: in Greece, under its sky and sun, in its light. Faulkner's Greece is not quite his own invention; he inherited it from a dream which has been with us for centuries. From the Renaissance through Romanticism to the Symbolists Greece kept haunting the Western imagination like the nostalgic memory of a lost world of innocence and wholeness, and it is indeed as a lost "home" that young Faulkner, the enthusiastic reader of Keats, Swinburne, and Mallarmé, redreams it in his early poems. The first chapter of *Light in August* thus echoes the texts of Faulkner's literary apprenticeship, but it is also easy to see how much he has moved away from them. The Greece of his poems was a highly formalized and rather conventional Greece. In the novel, Arcadia has become a part of Yoknapatawpha County. The light of August in Mississippi, as Faulkner himself notes, *"might have fauns and satyrs and the gods"* of Greece in it, but the landscape and the figures in the landscape are now recognizably Southern. The imaginary, this time, resurges from within the densely textured reality of Faulkner's fiction.

What it refers back to is a golden age, the time "of a luminosity older than our Christian civilization," and, we might add, poles apart from Christianity and its somber world of sin and retribution. Lena-Helen partakes of that "luminosity" and has "something of that pagan quality of being able to assume everything," which sets her apart from all the other characters in the novel, especially from her negative double, Joanna, sadly weighed down by her "burden" of inherited guilt. Lena draws all her strength from her spontaneous and total acquiescence to the cosmic order. Hers is not an abject submission, like that demanded by the harsh Puritanical God of Jefferson, but a serene and joyful acceptance of her destiny as a woman and a mother: *amor fati.*[11] Since her innermost will coincides with the world's will, how could she ever enter into conflict with the law? Lena is Helen, Hellenic, and Greek is her world, a world where the gods are still close, a true cosmos where the severance of the human and the divine has not yet been consummated.[12] So she can paradoxically be a docile handmaiden of the species as well as a living example of *autarkeia*, the virtue of self-sufficiency which Greek wisdom valued over all others. Lena travels by herself, but hers is "the sunny loneliness of the enormous land," under the benevolent gaze of the gods of the Olympus, and not at all the barren solitude in which Christmas, Joanna, and Hightower live out their desperate lives.

*   *   *

The first chapter of *Light in August* offers us another version of Faulkner's pastoral. The model is still Greek. However, if the tamely erotic texts of Faulkner's youth were full of lusting fauns and tantalizing nymphs, Lena is anything but a maenad. The Greece she comes from is certainly not that of the drunken cohorts of the goat-god, the nocturnal and riotous Greece of the bacchanalia. Serene and simple Lena walks in the light of day, the "lambent" light of a late summer day, clear, soft, and warm. There is not the faintest touch of the Dionysian in the evocation of her world. This Arcadia is utterly chaste, and if a tutelary god were needed, it could only be Apollo, the "bright one," the god of measure and wisdom, and master, according to Nietzsche, of "the beauteous appearance of the dream-worlds."[13]

Space around Lena is indeed in a state of dreamlike suspension: "Fields and woods seem to hang in some inescapable middle distance, at once static and fluid, quick, like mirages" (24–25). And amidst this dreamscape in broad daylight Lena herself appears as a mirage, a "fair appearance," a dream woman, too fair to be true.

Lena was no doubt meant to represent Nature in its generous fertility, yet, as in all pastorals, the "good" nature which she is assumed to embody is no longer there, has in point of fact never been there except as a gratifying illusion conjured up by the wistful staging of a myth. Besides, when the procession of identical wagons in which Lena is traveling is likened to "something moving forever and without progress across an urn" (5), Faulkner's pastoral calls attention to itself as a *work of art*. And revealingly, the reference here is to the *plastic* arts, the arts of space, whose privileges Faulkner must have sometimes envied, and with which he seems to have competed more vigorously in *Light in August* than in any of his other novels. We know, however, that the image of the *urn*, used by Faulkner in other texts and other contexts, is also a *literary* allusion or, if you prefer, an intertextual effect, the first emergence in *Light in August*, that is, of Keats's "Ode on a Grecian Urn," a poem in many ways reread and rewritten in and by the novel.

At this point it may be worth recalling that the Keatsian ode is already a work of art on a work of art, a word-shaper's tribute to a sculptor of marble or, to put it more pedantically, a reflexive and interrogative text in the *ut pictura poesis* tradition, in which the function of art and its relations to life and truth are already crucial issues. The answer is given laconically at the close of Keats's poem: "Beauty is truth, truth is beauty." This aphoristic statement has given rise to much speculation, but in essence it is an idealistic equation in the Platonic spirit of Greek philosophy and in the Apollonian spirit of Greek art. Keats seems to endorse it, and yet Dionysus is not missing from his ode:

> What men or gods are these? What maidens loth?
> What mad pursuit? What struggle to escape?
> What pipes and timbrels? What wild ecstasy?

These eager questions, the first prompted by the contemplation of the urn (the poem will leave them unanswered), all evoke the dark god of music, dance, and madness, and it is quite remarkable too that most of the semantic oppositions patterning the ode could be subsumed under the antithesis Dionysus/Apollo: the disorder of the "mad pursuit" is contrasted with the fixed order of the represented scene, the turbulence of unleashed passions with the "silent form" of the Attic vase, the transient ardor of life

with the permanence of the "Cold Pastoral." Apollo cannot do
without Dionysus, for from the Dionysian depths comes the
dark, as yet unshaped and uncontrolled *matter* from which all
Apollonian works of art, be they urns, odes, or novels, ultimately
proceed. A reversal takes place, however: the "wild ecstasy"
gives way to aesthetic stasis, its savagery caught in the eternity of
the fair *form*. The first tableau engraved on the urn is clear
evidence of this reversal and offers an eloquent example of the
Apollonian representation of the Dionysian: an amorous pursuit,
yet petrified; the arrested motions and suspended gestures of a
human passion forever unfulfilled; a stilled scene set against the
green foliage of perennial spring. Immune to the ravages of time
and change, sheltered from aging and death, but also barred
from all earthly bliss, the lovers on the urn are the mute,
transfixed impersonators of desire or rather of the *idea* of desire,
a pure idea dwelling in marble, the truth of which is made
visible through the beauty of a semblance. "Beauty is truth,
truth beauty," but for the equation to become effective the
mediacy of the ideal is indispensable. Reality must be cleansed
and refined into the incorruptible ideality of art. Whence these
silent forms, these "unheard" melodies, not meant for the "sensual ear," but for the eye or the soul. Keats's urn exemplifies the
victory of the sculptor-god over the god who dances. Or, again,
the triumph of light over darkness.

*   *   *

If we now turn back to the first chapter of *Light in August* and
reread it through the "Ode on a Grecian Urn," it will appear that
both are steeped in the same light, and that in both the light
source is the sun of a twice mythic Greece. True, the opening
scene in the novel is to some extent an obverse reflection of the
poem's scene of desire: the partners have exchanged roles, from
pursued the maiden has become pursuer, and for the time being
there is no "bold lover" in sight. Yet again day prevails over
night. What night? The primal night associated by all my-

thologies with the uncanny and terrifying "realm of Mothers," the dark chaos from which all life springs and to which all life returns. As a pregnant woman, Lena might be expected to have her share in the darkness. Faulkner's *mise en scène*, however, is handled in such a way that darkness almost never reaches her, and that she nearly always *appears* to be flooded with light, from both without and within.[14]

Lena is light, as "Helen was light,"[15] and she is also, according to one of the oldest metaphors of womanhood, an urn, a body-vessel destined to receive man's seed. It is interesting to note that it is precisely in such terms that Hightower, in chapter 20, evokes, "*The* woman. Woman . . . : the Passive and Anonymous whom God had created to be not only the recipient and recepta-cle of the seed of his body but of his spirit too, which is truth or as near truth as he dare approach" (441–42). Again Keats's ode is close to the textual surface, with its beautiful truth and its truthful beauty. Lena is the emblem of their union. It is impor-tant to note, though, that for Hightower—and perhaps for Faulkner too—truth comes *to* woman but does not come *from* her: she may represent it to man; she is neither its seeker nor its finder. Only man, as Hightower suggests, carries the *spiritual* seed capable of transmuting matter and of generating the sub-lime clarity of beauty and truth.

To the binary oppositions we have detected so far (darkness/light, matter/form, nature/art), we must therefore add that of feminine and masculine, which is probably the most decisive of all insofar as it points to the deeper meaning of the others, and subsumes them in the process of idealization, the wily trick of white magic through which both pastoral landscape and the figure of Lena are produced in the text.

Lena is the woman who casts no shadow, the woman subjected to light, to its measure and order—the Apollinian order of visible forms. Being a maternal figure, she is of necessity related to the earth, yet what determines her significance more than anything else is her relationship to light. Lena is the Mother wed to the Sun, and this mythic wedding is not without ideological

implications: what it actually amounts to is a roundabout reassertion of the phallocentric principle of feminine dependence and
subordination, a surreptitious way of putting woman back into
her place, under the absolute sovereignty of the sun-father.

The mother supplies matter; the father inseminates and informs it, gives it a shape and a name, promotes it to a higher
order. The idea or, rather, the fantasy is by no means new, and
can be found in philosophers like Plato and Aristotle as well as
with the Aranda tribe or the Trobriand Islanders studied by
Malinowski.[16] It probably also permeates most male fictions
about women, and *Light in August* is no exception: female
characters have to be imaginatively reappropriated and reshaped
according to the demands of male desire. A woman cannot be
apprehended in her unique, irreducible individuality; she must
be made to stand for something else, something larger, so as to
be more effectively diminished. Lena is both a real woman (or, to
be more specific, a woman rendered according to the realistic
code) and a metaphorical woman, an unmarried pregnant girl
and "the still unravish'd bride of quietness," even as the urn is at
once an image of natural fertility, a symbol of the work of life,
and, through Keats's intercession, a paradigm of the work of art.
Denied as desiring body and dissociated from the "act of
darkness," which would jeopardize her mythic purity, she is, at
least in the first pages, a mother *not yet* a mother, still at one
with her child: the ideal mother, the mother ideal, suspended
out of time, prior to birth and death, a pure mirage of "inwardlighted" stillness and togetherness.

Moments of euphoria are rare in Faulkner, but the opening
scene of *Light in August* is one of them. From the outset it holds
us spellbound as few openings in Faulkner's novels do, and its
spell is the exact reverse of what we experience in reading the
first pages of *Sanctuary*: not a dark spell, not the eerie power of
an evil eye, but a slow vertigo, a happy languor, in which
perhaps something repeats itself of the little child's fascination
with its mother, and something, too, of the later fascination of
adults with childhood. As Maurice Blanchot argues:

If our childhood fascinates us, it is because childhood is the age of enchantment—an enchanted age—and this golden age seems to be suffused in a wonderful, invisible light. But in fact this light is foreign to visibility, has nothing to make it visible, is no more than a reflection. Doubtless the mother-figure's importance derives from this enchantment. It could even be said that if this figure is so fascinating it is because it first appears while the child still inhabits the reflected light of enchantment and the mother is the essence of such enchantment.[17]

Interestingly, Blanchot's evocation of the enchanting mother of childhood calls in turn for the light metaphor, and it is noteworthy too that the quoted passage is part of an essay on the specific spell of writing. Could it be that the enchantments of literature all originate in the clear or dark enchantments of childhood, and that writing is always an attempt to retrieve the plenitude of the origins by re-membering the resplendent body of the lost, forgotten and unforgettable mother? "To write," Blanchot contends, "is to accept that solitude where fascination lurks."[18] This is indeed what writing was for Faulkner at his most daring: a solitary venture into the twilight territories of the unknown, a single-handed confrontation with the alluring and fearful powers arising out of an ever present and ever pressing past—a fascination both surrendered to and heroically resisted. For us, his readers, however, there can only be the radiance of words, the spell of a text, the incantations of a book called *Light in August*.

Perhaps one should also note that in the novel itself the enchantment of luminous motherhood is short-lived, that it is only one moment in its unfolding, and that even in the first chapter, it works only intermittently. The pastoral note is not sustained; as early as the second page the description of an abandoned sawmill compromises the image of the peaceful, well-tended garden. Moreover, at the close of the first chapter, when Lena's wagon crests the last hill before Jefferson, she sees two tall yellow columns of smoke. A house is burning. Light has already turned into devouring fire.

Soon there will be other women, women of another otherness, dark women in dark houses in dark groves, and other urns, cracked and foul. Even Lena will be deprived of her magic aura, briefly but significantly, when she is about to give birth to her child. As Byron Bunch runs to the cabin where Lena lies in labor, he still believes that he will be "met by her at the door, placid, unchanged, timeless" (377). But

> then he passed Mrs. Hines in the door and he saw her lying on the cot. He had never seen her in bed before and he believed that when or if he ever did, she would be tense, alert, maybe smiling a little, and completely aware of him. But when he entered she did not even look at him. She did not even seem to be aware that the door had opened, that there was anyone or anything in the room save herself and whatever it was that she had spoken to with that wailing cry in a tongue unknown to man. She was covered to the chin, yet her upper body was raised upon her arms and her head was bent. Her hair was loose and her eyes looked like two holes and her mouth was as bloodless now as the pillow behind her.

The bright screen image has momentarily dissolved. Paradoxically, at the moment when Lena is about to give life, life has deserted her, and it looks as if she had withdrawn into another alien and barely human world, speaking now in "a tongue unknown to man" not unlike that of "the bodiless fecundmellow voices of negro women" (107) in Freedman Town, from which Joe Christmas had fled in revulsion and terror. Indeed, with her loose hair, her empty eyes, and her bloodless mouth, Lena has become in turn a figure of disquieting strangeness.[19] One might argue, of course, that she only appears as such to Byron Bunch, and that for him this is a decisively sobering moment, compelling him at last to acknowledge the harsh laws of reality. Whether it leads him to recognize Lena as a woman with a mind, a body, and a life of her own, and whether Byron will ever conquer the blindness of his romantic love, remains however extremely doubtful. The point is that Lena—like nearly all of Faulkner's women—is held throughout in a male's gaze, and that insofar as this gaze fails the test of reciprocity, it precludes the possibility of true insight. Woman's otherness, in Faulkner's fiction, is seldom the otherness of another's self; more often than not woman turns out to be merely a male self's other, the fantasmal projection of its secret desires and fears. Whether praised or disparaged, idolized or demonized, she never comes into her own, and Faulkner's consoling, motherly Eve figures are just as equivocal as his lurid Lilith figures, for they ultimately belong to the same private fantasmagoria. The celebration of Lena in the role of earth goddess is in the last resort little more than a precarious rite of exorcism, and the scene of her delivery gives it away. Take off the fair mask of light, and all that is left is the stark enigma of spawning flesh.

NOTES

1. *Faulkner in the University: Class Conferences at the University of Virginia, 1957–1958*, ed. Joseph Blotner and Frederick Gwynn (Charlottesville: University of Virginia Press, 1959), 74.

2. On this point, see Carl Ficken, "The Opening Scene of William Faulkner's *Light in August*," *Proof*, 2 (December 1972), 175–84; Regina K. Fadiman, *Faulkner's "Light in August": A Description and Interpretation of the Revisions* (Charlottesville: University Press of Virginia, 1975), 31–32.

3. See for instance the superb invocation to Venus in the opening lines of *De Rerum Natura:* "Aeneadum Genetrix, hominum divomque voluptas, / alma Venus, caeli subter labenta signa." Lucretius's lines are echoed by Spenser in the *Faerie Queene*, Book *IV*, Canto 10, Stanzas 44–46.

4. *Light in August* (New York: Harrison Smith and Robert Haas, 1932), 5. Subsequent page references appear parenthetically in the text.

5. Like the first chapter, the novel begins and ends with the expression of Lena's naive amazement. See *Light in August*, 1, 26, 94, 480.

6. *Miroirs du sujet* (Paris: 10/18, 1975), 174–75.

7. On the etymology of the name, see Ch. Daremberg and E. Salia, *Dictionnaire des Antiquités grecques et romaines, III*, 56. There are allusions to Helen in Faulkner's work from his early writings to *The Town* and *The Mansion*, and in one of their conversations in the latter novel, Ratliff and Stevens explicitly identify Helen with light. It is also worth recalling that among the women Faulkner loved there was Helen Baird.

8. For a Jungian reading of *Light in August*, see for example David Williams, *Women: The Myth and the Muse* (Montreal: McGill-Queen's University Press, 1977).

9. From Aeschylus to Ronsard, poets have derived "Helen" from "helein" (to take away, to steal, to ravish). The poets' etymology is not the philologists'.

10. *Faulkner in the University*, 199.

11. See Faulkner's comments in his interview with Jean Stein: "I would say that Lena Grove in *Light in August* coped pretty well with [her fate]. . . . She was the captain of her soul"; *Lion in the Garden: Interviews with William Faulkner, 1926–1962*, ed. James B. Meriwether and Michael Millgate (New York: Random House, 1968), 253.

12. See Faulkner's reflections after his visit to Greece, in *Faulkner in the University*, 129–30.

13. *The Birth of Tragedy*, trans. W. A. Haussmann (New York: The MacMillan Company, 1924), 23.

14. On page 15 Faulkner calls her "inwardlighted."

15. *The Mansion* (New York: Random House, 1959), 133.

16. On this point, see Jean-Joseph Goux, "Matière, différence des sexes," in *Matière et pulsions de mort* (Paris: 10/18, 1975), 123–67.

17. "The Essential Solitude," in *The Sirens' Song: Selected Essays by Maurice Blanchot*, ed. and intro. Gabriel Josipovici, trans. Sacha Rabinovitch (Brighton: The Harvester Press, 1982), 107–108.

18. Ibid., 108.

19. Her loose hair reminds one of the dishevelment of the Medusa-like Joanna. The comparison of her eyes to "two holes" is also used in *Sanctuary* to describe Temple Drake.

Joe Christmas and "Womanshenegro"

DOREEN FOWLER

From the very beginning of his career, Faulkner has been the target of censure for the allegedly antifeminine sentiments that pervade much of his fiction. In fact, some critics, including such well-known authorities as Leslie Fiedler, Irving Howe, and Albert Guerard, have even charged Faulkner with harboring a deep-seated and thinly veiled hatred of women. Fiedler, for example, calls Faulkner "a serious calumniator of the female," and Howe finds in Faulkner's texts "an inclination toward misogyny."[1] Such accusations should perhaps not be taken too seriously; as Judith Wittenberg observes in her study, "William Faulkner: A Feminist Consideration," critics who locate misogyny in Faulkner's texts may be projecting their own concealed aversion.[2] Nevertheless, these assertions of misogyny are not entirely groundless; a number of male characters in Faulkner's novels undeniably exhibit antifeminine sentiments ranging from mild condescension to overt repugnance. In *The Sound and the Fury* Jason Compson's feelings about women are summarized in the unforgettable phrase "Once a bitch always a bitch";[3] in this same novel Mr. Compson, from whom we might expect a somewhat more liberated attitude toward women, observes: "Women . . . have an affinity for evil for supplying whatever the evil lacks in itself for drawing it about them instinctively as you do bedclothing in slumber";[4] in *As I Lay Dying* Darl Bundren describes Dewey Dell's breasts as the "mammalian ludicrosities which are the horizons and valleys of the earth";[5] in *Light in August,* when Joe Christmas learns that women are "doomed to be at stated and inescapable intervals victims of periodical filth,"[6] he vomits

144

in disgust; in "Old Man" the tall convict couples the word "women" with an unprintable excremental epithet;[7] in *The Hamlet* Jack Houston finds the "waiting, tranquil"[8] Lucy Pate so terrifying that he flees her for twelve years before returning to marry her: and these are but a few examples; numerous other instances of a male aversion to the female could be cited.

Of course, the attitude of any particular fictional character is not necessarily the author's attitude and should not necessarily be attributed to the author; nevertheless, the obtrusive and pervasive woman-censuring attitude in Faulkner's fiction inescapably raises a troubling question—if Faulkner is not a woman-hater, why, then, do so many of his male characters hate women?

The simplest and most obvious answer is, of course, that Faulkner described the world he knew and that world was rife with contempt for women. The problem with this answer is immediately apparent if we compare Faulkner with his contemporaries. For example, was there so much more malice for women in Faulkner's environment than in Wolfe's, or in Steinbeck's, or in Dos Passos's? And, if not, why do we not find in the fiction of these authors, as we do in Faulkner's, numerous and striking examples of antiwomanism? Of course, one might counter that none of these authors experienced precisely the same set of environmental influences that Faulkner did, but this argument would seem to beg the question, because if we say that a particular and unduplicatable set of circumstances caused Faulkner to write about men who loathe women, what is to prevent us from acknowledging as true a corollary statement— that a particular set of circumstances caused Faulkner to be a misogynist? In other words, this argument merely attributes cause, shifts responsibility (blame, if you will) for whatever is in Faulkner's texts from Faulkner to his unique behavioral history and avoids addressing the crucial question—is there misogyny in Faulkner's fiction?

A better way perhaps to attempt to understand what appear to be antifeminine attitudes in Faulkner's texts is to examine in detail the particular instances of apparent misogyny in the context of the novels in which these statements are found. In fact, those who have charged Faulkner with antiwomanism typically have made their case with isolated quotations taken, out of context, from a number of Faulkner novels—a method which is more provocative than it is sound.[9] I propose, therefore, to assess Faulkner's text fairly, to consider one novel and one of Faulkner's alleged misogynists, and to attempt to answer the questions: What is the reason for this masculine aversion to the feminine? What is the context for it? What purpose does it serve in Faulkner's narrative? And, finally, does Faulkner's rendering of antiwomanism accept or critique this attitude?

Before addressing these questions, however, one caveat is in order. The issue of antiwomanism in Faulkner's fiction is far too large and too multifaceted to be dealt with in a comprehensive way in one study. All I can attempt to do here is to shed some light on the misogynistic attitude of one of Faulkner's characters, but what holds true for one particular character does not necessarily apply to another, not even if both characters utter similar antifeminine statements. Each of Faulkner's characters is a separate case and needs to be studied separately. For example, while Jason Compson, Mr. Compson, Joe Christmas, and the tall convict all make, at one time or another, woman-slighting remarks, clearly these are dissimilar characters, and the causes of their negative feelings toward women may be equally dissimilar.

Of all Faulkner's novels, none seems more disparaging of women than *Light in August,* and, of all Faulkner's characters, possibly none is more relentlessly contemptuous of women than Joe Christmas. Unlike some of Faulkner's male characters, Joe is not merely guilty of an occasional sexist slip of the tongue; to all appearances, he is the self-mandated enemy of the female sex. While still a youth, each week he takes from the wash his garments on which his foster-mother solicitously has replaced missing buttons and he cuts off the new buttons "with the cold and bloodless deliberation of a surgeon" (100). At the age of seven he dumps on the floor food which his foster-mother brings him; and many years later, at thirty-three, he repeats the same gesture of repudiation, hurling against a wall dishes of food prepared for him by Joanna Burden. At the age of fourteen he and some of his friends hire a black girl as a prostitute; when it is Joe's turn to copulate, he attacks the girl, kicking her violently and uncontrollably. On the night before his final deadly confrontation with Joanna, Joe's disgust for women drives him to sleep in a stable where the odor of "womanflesh" (353) will be masked by the smell of horses because, as he puts it, "even a mare horse is a kind of man" (101). And on that same night he exposes himself to a woman in a passing car in a show of male dominance and contempt. The question, then, is not—does Joe Christmas appear to hate women? The evidence indicating misogyny is overwhelming. The question is—why such an extreme and violent reaction, which seems so totally disproportionate to the creatures who provoke it?

Because, as Joanna Burden astutely observes, "a man [has] to act as the land where he was born . . . trained him to act" (241), before we can formulate an answer to this question we need to examine the society in which Joe lives, the status of women in that culture, and Joe's relationship to his environment. However, we can suggest here the general outlines of the argument which will be developed in this study. In his rejection of women, Joe, to a certain extent, represents his society and its attitude toward women; further, his feelings for women are related, in a complex way, to his attitude toward blacks; last and perhaps most important of all, Joe's apparent dread of women is rooted in confusion about his own sexual identity and in a terror of androgyny.

As André Bleikasten has argued convincingly in his essay "Fathers in Faulkner," the society of *Light in August* is the very distillation of the patriarchal.[10] What this means is that, in Jefferson, certain attributes, those which are usually labelled masculine, are admired and emulated, while another set of traits, commonly ascribed to women, have been almost totally extinguished. These ascendant male traits include willfulness, aggression, brutality, and imperviousness; while temporarily suspended female attributes are gentleness, tenderness, sensitivity, instinctiveness, a desire to nurture, and vulnerability. In this society dominated by male values, Lena Grove stands out conspicuously as a major exception to a masculine rule. As Bleikasten observes, Lena seems to "exist in a space of her own."[11] But apart from Lena, *Light in August* depicts a hard-nosed man's world where practically every human interaction is a power struggle in which one person dominates and another is victimized. In this world, Joe Brown jokes and chaffs with the very men who periodically rob him in Saturday night dice games; in this world, everything has a price tag, as the prostitute Bobbie discovers when she takes Christmas as her lover and finds herself the object of Max's derisive laughter for "giv[ing] it away" (181); and in this world, love, with the single and apparently unique exception of the love of Byron and Lena, seems to have practically no chance to survive. *Light in August* portrays a brutal and brutalizing social environment that gentle men try to avoid—so Hightower cloisters himself in his dark house and Byron Bunch works at the mill on Saturday afternoons trying to stay clear of folks' "meanness" (38). Above all, *Light in August* depicts a society in which a struggle for the whip hand is always in progress—between Joe and McEachern, between Joe and Joanna, between Joe and Percy Grimm; and the disputed issue—whether it be learning the Presbyterian catechism as McEachern commands, or kneeling in submission before an irate father-god as Joanna commands, or accepting societal retribution, as Percy Grimm commands—is not really important. What is important is who commands and who is forced to obey. The issue, however it is disguised, is always power.

In such an environment, human beings tend naturally to fall into one of two classes: the strong, who rule, and the weak, who obey. The members of each class are easily distinguished. The strong are male, adult, and white; the weak are women and children and blacks.

Faulkner neither dwells on this oppression nor offers any authorial comment; instead, he reports the facts and allows his readers to draw their own conclusions. For example, in the first chapter of the novel in a throwaway phrase, Lena Grove is described as "the youngest living child" (2) in her family. In other words, Lena had younger siblings, but they were unable to survive this harsh environment. And, of course, the novel closely traces the history of the lost, abandoned child, Joe Christmas, who always knew that the asking price for survival was all his endurance and will.[12]

Like children, women also belong to Jefferson's underclass, and, for the most part, their plight is similarly pitiable. Not surprisingly, the exaltation of masculine values in Jefferson appears to have a perverting effect on the sexual identities of women. In a society that reveres masculinity and scorns femininity, one option for a woman is to suppress and deny her own feminine nature and to adopt society's preferred masculine characteristics. One such defeminized woman is Mrs. Armstid, a "gray woman . . . manhard . . . in a serviceable gray garment worn savage and brusque" with a face like "those of generals who have been defeated in battle" (14); and another is Joanna Burden, who, prior to her affair with Joe which precipitates an explosion of long repressed sexuality, presents to the watching world the attitude of a "calm, coldfaced, almost manlike, almost middleaged woman who had lived for twenty years alone, without any feminine fears at all" (244). But male-emulating women like Joanna and Mrs. Armstid are few; most of the women in *Light in August* are victims, brutalized by a hard life and hard men until they seem to be almost neutered. The roster of women in this category reads like a list of battle casualties. Heading the list is Mrs. McEachern, "a patient, beaten creature without sex demarcation at all save the neat screw of graying hair and the skirt," a woman who "instead of having been subtly slain and corrupted by the ruthless and bigoted man into something beyond his intending and her knowing . . . had been hammered stubbornly thinner and thinner like some passive and dully malleable metal, into an attenuation of dumb hopes and frustrated desires now faint and pale as dead ashes" (155). Another sexually deformed creature is the "woodenfaced," "dead voice[d]" (351–52) Mrs.

Hines, who, after having suffered her domineering husband's brawling "two-fisted evangelism" (325) for forty years, now also presents to the eye no sign of her gender "save for the skirt which [she] wears" (340); yet another casualty of male power is Milly Hines, whose father, by ruling that no doctor will attend the delivery of her child, effectively consigns his own child to death; equally pathetic is Hightower's mother, whose frail flesh is forced to pay the price for her husband's stern, unyielding abolitionist principles, a price which he, in his robust strength, can survive but she cannot; still another female victim is Hightower's own "thin and gaunted" wife, whose "frozen look" (58) and pitiful affairs are unheard cries for tenderness or at least attention in a brutal male world; and, last of all, there is Lena Grove, woman-incarnate, who alone remains undefeated, but who nevertheless belongs to this sisterhood of victims having been shamed, betrayed, and abandoned by Lucas Burch.

A third group—blacks—also numbers along Jefferson's underclass. The abject status of the black inhabitants of Jefferson is self-evident to any reader of Faulkner's prose. For example, in the course of investigating the apparent murder of Joanna Burden, Sheriff Watt Kennedy wants to know who lived in the cabin behind the Burden place. To procure this information, a black man is picked at random ("Get me a nigger," [274] says the sheriff) and is beaten with a belt until he tells what he knows. As it happens, the black man knows almost nothing, but one of the presiding deputies observes that Christmas and Brown occupied the cabin, and remarks offhandedly that just about any drinking man in Jefferson could have told the sheriff as much. But Sheriff Kennedy never questioned his deputy or anyone else; his first impulse, it seems, was to beat the information out of a black man.

But the full extent to which a black person is considered inferior to a white is perhaps most strikingly apparent in the appalled reactions of Jefferson's citizens who had accepted Joe Christmas as a white man and then are told he is black. Watt Kennedy's reaction is typical. When told by Brown that Christmas is black, the sheriff replies, "You better be careful what you are saying, if it is a white man you are talking about. . . . I don't care if he is a murderer or not" (91). In other words, there is no greater slur than to call a man black. A murderer, if he is white, has some social stature in Jefferson; a black man, it seems, has none.

Two conclusions emerge from this brief survey of Jefferson's underclass. First, if, as often has been stated, all of Faulkner's characters are the "poor frail victims of being alive,"[13] in *Light in August*, at least, those who are frailer, women and children and blacks, are the victims not only of being alive, but also of those who are stronger than they. This victimization of the weak, of women and blacks especially, is directly relevant to Joe Christmas's misogyny, since some part of his hatred for women and blacks has to do with his dread of the subjugation which, to Joe, they seem almost to embody. A second conclusion to be drawn from this survey is that women and blacks in *Light in August* share a kinship: their common victimization. In a world ruled by white males, blacks and women are both oppressed and powerless. In addition, both women and blacks exhibit those attributes which are prohibited to white men: gentleness, sensitivity, instinctiveness, submissiveness, and vulnerability. This conjunction of females and blacks[14] is also relevant to a discussion of Joe's misogyny because his hatred of women is frequently paired with a hatred of blacks; in fact, Joe's most virulent hatred appears to be reserved for the black woman.

Before confronting directly the issue of Joe's misogyny, one last question needs to be answered—what is Joe's place in his social order? Given the divided nature of his society, this same question could be phrased another way: to which one of two groups does Joe belong—the ruling upperclass, composed of white males, or the subject underclass, composed of women and blacks? In answering this question, consider that Joe Christmas is, to all appearances, a white man, but he thinks/believes he is black so he might, with justification, cast his lot with either group—white or black, victimizer or victim.

Our first impulse might be to say that Joe doesn't know where he belongs in the social hierarchy. For example, on at least one occasion, he shuns white people and lives with blacks, living "as man and wife with a woman who resembles an ebony carving,"[15] but then even as he tries to "breathe into himself . . . the dark and inscrutable thinking and being of negroes . . . his whole being would writhe and strain with physical outrage and spiritual denial" (212). And at other times, Joe seems to long for membership in the white upperclass. For instance, on the same night that Joanna dies at his hand, he wanders the streets of Jefferson and passes through a white neighborhood; he sees white people sitting around a cardtable on a lighted veranda, and he thinks, "That's all I wanted. That dont seem like a whole lot to ask" (108). Given this contradictory behavior, it seems safe to conclude that Joe is confused about his social identity and that this confusion is to some extent justified since he, in fact, does not know if he is white or black.[16] However, amidst all this ambivalence about Joe's identity, one fact about his nature can be stated with certainty: while he may not know who he is, he is, nevertheless, committed to the assertion of self in defiance of all those who would control him. Thus, in a world composed of masters and victims, he categorically refuses to be a victim, and this repudiation ranks him, whether he will or not, with white males. From the day he refuses to learn the catechism his foster-father commands him to memorize, Joe refuses to be dominated. And, while he continually resists patriarchal authority, he opposes white males with entirely white male values: willfulness, ruthlessness, brutality, and imperviousness. For this reason, Joe resembles the white men whom he defies. For example, on that Sunday, burned into Joe's memory, when McEachern attempts to beat the seven-year-old child into submission, the two men, adult and child, seem to be doubles: "There was a kinship of stubbornness like a transmitted resemblance in their backs . . . the two backs in their rigid abnegation of all compromise more alike than actual blood could have made them" (139). However, Joe resembles not only McEachern but all of the countless other flesh-denying white males in the novel, whose exaltation of will and spirit over world and flesh is underscored by a trail of images of transcendence.[17] Thus, the little boy Joe Christmas, who stands unflinching as "wood or stone" (150) beneath McEachern's measured, mechanical blows, looking like a "monk" (140) or a "Catholic choir boy" (140), is a close relative to that other unearthly being, Percy Grimm,[18] who, years later, hunts down, shoots, and castrates Joe Christmas, all the while possessing "the luminousness of angels in church windows" (437).

Another series of signs suggesting that Joe has absorbed the values of a male-revering society is his association throughout *Light in August* with phallic symbols: he is like a "post" (150), a "tower" (150), a "telephone pole" (106), and the last monument to his unconquerable maleness is that "pillar of yellow smoke" (77) marking Joanna's tragic ending. Finally, his overt antipathy for women would also seem to ally him with those white male supremacists, Hines and McEachern, who, like Joe, see women as weak and foul vessels.

Having established the extent to which Joe, while confused about his own identity, nevertheless has assimilated the ruthless, retributive male code that prevails in Jefferson, we are ready to answer the question—why does Christmas hate women?

Joe Christmas hates women and blacks because he has internalized his society's values, and his is a society which idolizes strength and despises weakness.[19] Women and blacks are society's weak members and, therefore, deserve contempt. If this answer seems to be too simple, it is because, in Joe's case at least, there is a further complication. Joe Christmas is, to all appearances, a white man, who thinks he may have black blood, and who senses further that he harbors within him a potential for qualities that, in his culture, are associated only with women and blacks. Thus, Joe's vehement antipathy for women has deeply repressed psychic causes: when he lashes out at the women and blacks outside of him, he seems to be attempting to repudiate the womanliness and blackness within him.[20]

One of the earliest manifestations of Joe's hatred for "woman-flesh" occurs on that day when at seven years old he became a man by asserting his own will in defiance of McEachern's and, by extension, God's, and refused to memorize a passage from the Presbyterian catechism. After a day of fasting and stern punishment, Mrs. McEachern kindly brings Joe dishes of food which he dispassionately dumps on the floor. Why this show of contempt? Why does he hate worse the woman's "soft kindness" than he does "the hard and ruthless justice of men" (158)?—because womanliness threatens to crack his wall of resistance, to unman him, and to leave him defenseless. In order to oppose McEachern's indomitable male will, Joe Christmas must meet force with force, but Mrs. McEachern's soft kindness threatens to evoke answering tenderness in Joe's own nature. Once this affinity with the woman is exposed, Joe believes, McEachern would be able to crush him, as he has already crushed the woman. Seeing the fate of the weak in his world, Joe refuses to betray a sign of weakness. As he puts it, "She was trying to make me cry. Then she thinks that they would have had me" (158). All his life, Joe seems to be trying not to cry, not to show emotion, not to act like a woman, for to behave in these ways would be to let down his guard and give the pitiless man's world its opportunity to destroy him.

The circumstances surrounding each instance of Joe's overt misogyny suggest that his anger with women is largely directed at their state of subjugation and his own fear of implication in this state. For example, the most vicious and seemingly unforgivable manifestation of his misogyny occurs when he, a fourteen-year-old boy, without provocation, violently assaults a young black woman who lies awaiting his penetration. The language describing this episode stresses the girl's utter debasement and thus suggests that precisely those qualities which make the girl so pathetic elicit Joe's outrage. Blackskinned, young, a woman, and prostituted, she virtually embodies the helplessness which he repudiates. As the scene unfolds, Joe enters the duskfilled shed "smelling the woman, smelling the negro all at once." At first, he cannot see in the darkness and, helpless himself, must "wait until she spoke: a guiding sound that was no particular word and completely unaware." Then he sees "something prone, abject: her eyes perhaps. Leaning, he seemed to look down into a black well and at the bottom saw two glints like reflection of dead stars" (147). It is the sight of the girl's vacant eyes which, more than anything else, seems to evoke Joe's fury. Her eyes, which should be luminous with consciousness, are "dead stars," void, like her voice, of awareness. The extinction of consciousness here appears to be linked to the sexual act. The girl has just copulated with Joe's friends and is about to copulate with Joe. By her submission to sexual desire, then, she is reduced to nothing more than lifeless flesh, and, Joe believes, if he yields to his sexual desire he will be one with the black woman and similarly diminished.[21] The semen-laden black girl would seem to present Joe with a clear-cut choice between male will and female will-lessness. Not surprisingly, then, he opts for autonomy and lashes out at "womanshenegro" (147), at a condition of total degradation, as one might lash out at a reflection of one's own dreaded, prefigured fate.

On yet another occasion the text offers an insight into the repressed rationale for Joe's repudiation of the composite— "womanshenegro." Just before Joe goes to the Burden place for the last time, he wanders the streets of Jefferson until they slope down into a dell, Freedman Town, the black section of town. Here, he feels "surrounded by the summer smell and the summer voices of invisible negroes" (106). In this black community he has chanced into a world foreign to the white male principle with which he seeks to affiliate himself, and here the air is thick and rich, redolent of woman and blacks. As though he had been returned to the womb, Joe sees himself "as from the bottom of a thick black pit. . . . as though he and all other manshaped life about him had been returned to the lightless hot wet primogenitive Female" (107). Feeling his manhood overpowered, he resists, running in denial, "panting," "glaring," "his heart hammering," desperate for "the cold hard air of white people"

(107). Why does he run? What is so terrifying about the "lightless hot wet primogenitive Female" which he encounters in the black hollow? The text supplies a clue: Joe runs because "on all sides, *even within him,* the bodiless fecundmellow voices of negro women murmured" (107, my emphasis). Here the text seems explicitly to attribute cause. Joe flees in terror and furious repudiation because, against his will, the black women in the dell strike a responsive chord in him.

This reference to the "fecundmellow voices of negro women" within Joe is not, however, the only clue to the cause of Joe's misogyny that this passage yields. In addition, the apparent merger of two hatreds—a repudiation of women and blacks—also seems to identify the reason for Joe's antagonistic feelings toward women. As is demonstrated by this instance in the black community and also by the episode in the shed where the fourteen-year-old Joe assaults a black girl, his hatred for women often appears to be related to a hatred for blacks. Above all, Joe hates "womanshenegro," and, as if to underscore that fact, Faulkner coins this word apparently to suggest that some element common to both woman and Negro unleashes his fury.

Of course, the reason for Joe's racial hatred is not a mystery: he repudiates blacks, not only because he has internalized the values of a society that scorns blacks, but also because he suspects and fears he may be one of them; similarly, then, he may repudiate women, not only because he has assimilated the values of a society that disdains women, but also because he fears he may be, in some way, like them.

I propose, then, that Joe Christmas is committed to a pose of impenetrable maleness, a pose which necessarily entails a repudiation of women and blacks, a pose which, in the deepest recesses of his being, he suspects on two counts may be a sham. In light of this lifelong commitment to denial and suppression, Joe's complex feelings for women and blacks become understandable as do the events which constitute the final tragedy of his life—the death of Joanna Burden and Joe's castration and death. When Joe Christmas slits Joanna's throat, he performs

what he believes is an act of self-preservation. Joanna orders him
to acknowledge his kinship with a despised people, in Joe's own
words, to "tell niggers that I am a nigger too" (262). Further,
Joanna demands that he surrender his pose of defiance and kneel
in abject supplication before that ultimate Patriarch for whom all
the white men he has defied all his life have been mere surrogates. Joanna will be obeyed or she will die, and to do what
Joanna commands is tantamount, in Joe's eyes, to an act of self-
immolation. As Joe puts it, "If I give in now, I will deny all the
thirty years that I have lived to make me what I chose to be"
(250–51). For thirty years he has acted the male part, and now
Joanna demands that he surrender this pose which he equates
with his survival. Thus, it is not surprising that when he kills
Joanna he feels as though he has no choice, as though her death
had already been accomplished before he has performed the act.

Following Joanna's death, however, the immolation which Joe
has resisted all his life gradually overtakes him. And the sign of
this imminent immolation is a pair of Negro brogans. As he flees
after killing Joanna, in order to elude his pursuers he trades
shoes with a black woman who wears a man's brogans. To Joe, the
Negro brogans are emblematic of the very victimization which
pursues him. Thus, as he runs, he seems to carry with him that
same state of oppression and degradation from which he flees.
All his life he has fought for the preservation of his being, a
preservation which he associates with maleness; and he has
fought against obliteration of self, which he associates with
females and with blacks. Now, as Joe is hunted like an animal by
white men who demand his life, he is at the very brink of
extermination, and "the black shoes smelling of negro" on his
feet are a "gauge definite and ineradicable of the black tide
creeping up his legs, moving from his feet upward as death
moves" (321).

In the end, Joe appears to surrender and to accept as inevitable the immolation of self which he has resisted for longer than
knowing remembers, for as long as memory believes. For some
thirty years Joe has believed that if he ever gives up his male

pose of absolute imperviousness, he will be destroyed. The conclusion of his flight would seem to confirm his belief. The manhunt ends in Hightower's dark house where, for the first and last time in his life, Joe does not meet force with force. Instead he is passive, submissive, meek—behavior which his society expects only of women or blacks. With a loaded and unfired pistol in his hand, he lets Percy Grimm shoot him to death. And then, there is one more thing to be done. Joe has failed to act in accordance with the brutal male manifesto—"Do it to them before they do it to you"; the price exacted for this lapse is his masculinity. It is, after all, only what Joe had always expected.

All his life Joe Christmas has been running in terror from a "black pit" (107), a "black abyss" (313), a "black tide" (321). The pit from which he flees is a state of abject defilement which he associates with women, with blacks, and with weakness. All his life Joe Christmas had been running from himself, from those mild qualities in his own nature which ally him with women and blacks. Thus, he never could outrun the black tide because, as he always suspected, it ran in his veins, and, after thirty-three years of suppression and denial, as Joe dies, it finally "rush[es] out of his pale body" in a "black blast" of "pent black blood" expelled like a long "released breath" (440).

Having considered the deep-seated causes of Joe Christmas's misogyny, we can return to the charge of antiwomanism with which this study began. And, now, given the context of the world of *Light in August,* perhaps this charge does not seem surprising. *Light in August* is, after all, a feminist's nightmare. In this novel, Faulkner describes a society where a bloodless masculinity rules and where sexism and racism run so deep that they have become unchallenged ways of thinking. This society equates male will with god and spirit; and male will equates the world and the flesh with the devil, and equates women with the world and the flesh.

But, if we are to confront directly the issue of antiwomanism in *Light in August,* the crucial question to pose is this: how does Faulkner portray this social order? Does his portrayal defend, accept, or celebrate this patriarchal, authoritarian society? Has Faulkner, like Joe Christmas, succumbed to the white-male-supremacist values of his culture? The answer is no. *Light in August* is not a facile affirmation; *Light in August* is an indictment and a warning. In this novel, macho values are not blindly accepted; rather they are stripped of all bravado and show and exposed as hollow and death-dealing. At every turn in *Light in August* Faulkner reveals a society that prizes will above flesh and, thus, is willing to make any sacrifice of living flesh to appease an insatiable willfulness, a society that is steadily hacking away at its own roots, its own sources of new life, women and children, a society, then, that appears to be unswervingly committed to its own extermination.

In closing, one observation bears reiteration: while some of the characters in *Light in August* are sexist and racist, Faulkner's novel, I contend, is not. All of *Light in August* can be seen as a parable told to illuminate a truth which, most likely, would appall and outrage the bigoted, hidebound members of Jefferson's populace. This truth is embodied, I think, in Joe Christmas, the child and mirror-image of his civilization. Try as he will, Joe cannot extinguish in himself woman-like qualities; and, try as he will, he cannot deny a consanguinity with blacks. What, then, is the symbolic significance of this character who, in a sense, is both male and female, both white and black? With Joe Christmas, Faulkner implies that male/female, black/white distinctions are not irreconcilable opposites, but rather only the opposing ends of one continuum.

NOTES

1. Monte Cooper, Review of *The Marble Faun*, *Commercial Appeal* (5 April 1925), Section III, 10; Leslie Fielder, *Love and Death in the American Novel* (New York: Criterion, 1960), 333; Irving Howe, *William Faulkner: A Critical Study*, 2nd ed. (New York: Vintage, 1962), 143; Albert J. Guerard, "Forbidden Games (III): Faulkner's Misogyny," in *The Triumph of the Novel: Dickens, Dostoevsky, Faulkner* (New York: Oxford University Press, 1976), 109–35.

2. Judith Bryant Wittenberg, "William Faulkner: A Feminist Consideration," *American Novelists Revisited: Essays in Feminist Criticism*, ed. Fritz Fleischmann (Boston: G. K. Hall, 1982), 326.

3. William Faulkner, *The Sound and the Fury* (New York: Random House, 1929), 223.

4. Ibid, 119.

5. William Faulkner, *As I Lay Dying*, corrected and reset under the direction of James B. Meriwether (New York: Random House, 1964), 156.

6. William Faulkner, *Light in August* (New York: Harrison Smith and Robert Haas, 1932), 173. Subsequent page references to this edition will be shown in parentheses in the text.

7. William Faulkner, *The Wild Palms* (New York: Random House, 1939), 339.

8. William Faulkner, *The Hamlet*, corrected and reset edition (New York: Random House, 1964), 209.

9. See, for example, Ellen Douglas, "Faulkner's Women," in *"A Cosmos of My Own,"* ed. Doreen Fowler and Ann J. Abadie (Jackson: University Press of Mississippi, 1981), 149–67.

10. André Bleikasten, "Fathers in Faulkner," in *The Fictional Father: Lacanian Readings of the Text*, ed. Robert Con Davis (Amherst: University of Massachusetts Press, 1981), 133–35.

11. Ibid, 129.

12. Another child in *Light in August*, Lena's baby, seems to be emblematic of a whole society, and especially the young, who are parched for a mother's milk, for nurturing and nourishment. Lena says to Hightower of her baby (whom Mrs. Hines confuses with her grandchild, Joe Christmas), "It looks like he just cant get caught up. I think he is asleep again and I lay him down and then he hollers and I have to put him back again" (386).

13. Wittenberg, 336.

14. In *Writers in Crisis: The American Novel 1925–1940* (Boston: Houghton Mifflin, 1942), 169, Maxwell Geismar finds "a vicious conjunction in Faulkner's work of the Negro and the Female." For discussions of an underlying identification of blacks and women in *Light in August*, see Sally R. Page, *Faulkner's Women: Characterization and Meaning* (Deland, Fla.: Everett/Edwards, 1972), 146; Franklin G. Burroughs, Jr., "God the Father and Motherless Children: *Light in August*," *Twentieth Century Literature*, 19 (July 1973), 193; François Pitavy, *Faulkner's "Light in August"* (Bloomington: Indiana University Press, 1973), 98–104; and David Williams, *Faulkner's Women* (Montreal: McGill-Queen's University Press, 1977), 177.

15. Only after learning "that there were white women who would take a man with a black skin" (212) does Joe repudiate whites and turn to blacks. Thus, disgust for whites, specifically for white women who would sleep with black men, seems to drive Joe to cohabit with a black woman.

16. Bleikasten, 130. See also Eric Sundquist, *Faulkner: The House Divided* (Baltimore: Johns Hopkins University Press, 1983), 63–95.

17. Several critics have observed that in Faulkner's fiction women tend to be associated with fecundity and natural processes while men are associated with a quest for spiritual autonomy. See Karl E. Zink, "Faulkner's Garden: Women and the Immemorial Earth," *Modern Fiction Studies*, 2 (1956), 139–49; Page, 139–75; and Williams, 157–87.

18. Critics who have noted that Percy Grimm seems to be Joe Christmas's double include Cleanth Brooks, *William Faulkner: The Yoknapatawpha Country* (New Haven: Yale University Press, 1963), 62; Bleikasten, 132–33; and Burroughs, 198–99. Further evidence to suggest this doubling is Hightower's vision of a ring of faces in which Christmas's face blends and merges with Grimm's (465–66).

19. Bleikasten writes that all of the major characters in *Light in August*, with the possible exception of Lena Grove, "are at once aliens to their community" at the same time as they "have absorbed and internalized [their community's] values," 129.

20. Several critics have observed that Christmas's masculinity appears to be affronted and threatened by femininity: see Zink, 146; Page, 146–51; Pitavy, 96–108; and Williams, 164–76. However, none of these critics contend, as I do, that Joe's antipathy has its roots in recognition and in identification.

21. Burroughs points out that "Joe feels obliged to assert his blackness to every woman he encounters as though in tacit recognition of some mysterious alliance between it and femininity" (193). However, Joe asserts his black blood not to every woman he encounters, but to every woman he copulates with, suggesting, in Joe's mind, an association of sexuality, blackness, and femininity. See also Sundquist, 81. Similarly, Joanna seems to identify the unleashing of her own sexuality with black blood. Thus, in the throes of sexual surrender she calls Joe "Negro" (245).

Faulkner and Womankind—"No Bloody Moon"

WINIFRED L. FRAZER

When Faulkner published *The Unvanquished* (1938), it consisted of six previously published short stories and one new one at the end called "An Odor of Verbena," the last much less of a *Saturday-Evening-Post* type and much more filled with knotty Faulknerian questions than the first six.[1] In it, like Orestes and Hamlet, young Bayard Sartoris is called home to avenge the murder of his father. Unlike either of these, he decides that killing must cease and shows his courage, not by shooting the murderer but by facing him unarmed. The story also partakes of the legend of Phaedra, for Drusilla, Colonel John Sartoris's young widow and Bayard's stepmother, had previously insisted that he kiss her, and there are some intimations that Bayard is not as entirely repulsed as was Hippolytus. The legend of Eve in the garden is also intimated, as Drusilla in pulling his face close and yielding her lips had reminded Bayard of the "ancient and eternal Snake," who had tempted Adam and caused his fall. Of course the legend of Southern honor is central to the story, as Drusilla puts the Colonel's pistols in Bayard's hands and enjoins him to glory in revenge. Also the townsmen, his black servant Ringo, and Redmond, the murderer, all expect Bayard to revenge his father's death by killing the man who had killed Colonel Sartoris.

Unaccounted for by any of these legends is the attitude of Jenny Du Pre, the Colonel's young widowed sister, who urges Bayard to rebel against everyone's expectations and hide in the barn if necessary to reverse the chain of killings. At the climactic moment when Bayard is about to leave the house to confront

162

Redmond, Aunt Jenny briefly relates what appears to be a most
irrelevant story of an Englishman, a blockade-runner she knew
in Charleston, who was a David Crockett-like hero during the
Civil War, even though his interest was not in the cause of the
Confederacy but only in the profit made from contraband. This
unnamed individual "who must have been a gentleman once or
associated with gentlemen," according to Aunt Jenny "had a
vocabulary of seven words." "The first four were," she explains,
"'I'll have rum, thanks,' and then when he had the rum, he
would use the other three—across the champagne, to whatever
ruffled bosom or low gown: 'No bloody moon'" (281–82). Jenny
concludes by repeating, "No bloody moon, Bayard," and that is
the end of her story. With the repetition of this phrase Aunt
Jenny ends her story. With no comment on it, Bayard leaves the
house, rides to Jefferson with his childhood friend Ringo, meets
George Wyatt and the other waiting townsmen of his father's old
troop of soldiers, refuses their offer of help, and walks toward
Redmond's upstairs office. Then, as Bayard tells it, "I had started
on when suddenly I said it without having any warning that I was
going to: 'No bloody moon.'" George Wyatt's one-word question, "What?" expresses his bafflement (285). Bayard, however,
merely crosses the square, leaving the reader, as well, un-
enlightened and indeed uncertain as to whether Bayard himself
could explain the phrase. Then occurs what in a lesser story
might be called the happy ending: Redmond, not wanting to kill
an unarmed man, shoots two bullets over Bayard's head, puts on
his hat, walks down the stairs, and catches the train out of town,
never to be seen in Jefferson again. Bayard emerges a hero to his
father's old fighting companions for having the courage to face
Redmond unarmed, even though, as Wyatt says, "I wouldn't
have done it that way, myself" (289). Bayard returns home to find
Drusilla departed, after having laid a sprig of verbena on his
pillow, and Aunt Jenny with tears of relief streaming down her
face.

All this leaves unanswered many questions about the crucial,
thrice-used phrase, "No bloody moon." As a blockade-runner

(and since rum is one of his seven-word vocabulary, the mind tends to associate with him a rum-runner), this possible gentleman, who had changed his name for unknown reasons and who had enough manners to be accepted by the quality folks of Charleston, which the Du Pre family certainly was, either wanted a moon to see by during his undercover activities or more likely wanted a dark night, so he wouldn't be seen. If the first, he might be cursing the absence of a moon; but if the second, he should not be cursing but rejoicing that it was a good night to run whatever he was bringing through enemy lines— salt, weapons, rum, or the champagne which the ladies and gentlemen of Charleston were drinking. Furthermore, he never said the last three words until he had the rum in hand, and then he spoke, Aunt Jenny tells us, "across the champagne, to whatever ruffled bosom or low gown" was present, he uttered these words, which surprisingly seemed acceptable to the genteel company.

Somehow all seven words seem inappropriate for a gathering in the home of a respectable and wealthy Charleston family. Didn't the others drink champagne rather than rum? One could imagine the words spoken at a low-life bar with the barmaid or tavern owner, used to rough manners and hard drink, sliding a glass across the counter. "No bloody moon" would also make more sense in such a place, where David Crockett or frontiersman John Sevier, to whom Jenny also compares the blockade-runners, might have been found. If this character, his language, and the situation in Charleston society itself seem strange, how much more strange that Aunt Jenny should relate the story to her beloved nephew Bayard at the last moment she may ever see him alive.

If the young woman was allowed to sit in company with this blockade-runner and even in a romantic way admired his heroism, all the while knowing that his motives were not altruistic, but opportunistic, it would seem that as a widow of a Confederate soldier, living for six years with her much older brother in Mississippi, she would now take a more mature view of such a character. She can hardly be advising Bayard to be the kind of hero which she had once thought the blockade-runner to be. What possible relationship can there be between blockade-running and the tragic dilemma of Bayard, who must revenge his father's murder or live in shame? Since it is bright sunlight when he goes to confront Redmond, a moon, bloody or not, is hardly relevant, yet Bayard, unexpectedly even to himself, repeats the phrase just before he faces likely death.

Explications which politely skirt or metaphorically apply the meaning of the blockade-runner's phrase are those such as Hyatt Waggoner's: "With the help of Miss Jenny, Bayard has come to see that the courage so highly prized by the old code would not always stand up under close inspection. Like the daring of the blockade runners which Miss Jenny tells him about, it often depended on there being 'no bloody moon.' Bayard wants to exhibit a courage that can stand the light of greater awareness and broader and deeper sympathies."[2] Another critic, David Williams, describing Bayard's progress toward confrontation with his father's slayer, likewise skirts the question of the precise meaning of the phrase: "Later, on the way into Redmond's office, he recalls a fragment of something he has heard his Aunt Jenny say: 'No bloody moon.' There is, this once, no moon-driven destruction because Bayard believes, like his aunt, in a reasonable order."[3] Another critic, William E. Walker, assuming that the phrase has to do with blockade-running by boat, explains of Bayard: "He wanted 'no bloody moon' because he did not want the real nature of his mission to be discovered until he was safely inside the office, the harbor."[4]

As to the first critic, is the old code of the South equatable with blockade-running in requiring darkness, or is Faulkner implying that, although it may be out of the dark ages, the old code is all too much in the sunlight? About the second, one wonders if "moon-driven destruction" is what the blockade-runner fears as much as detection by enemy forces. As to the last critic, whereas there is a possible validity to equating Redmond's office with a harbor, it it hardly a "safe" harbor.

In examining Aunt Jenny's story, which she begins telling "quietly, pleasantly as if she were talking to a stranger, a guest," one should note that the blockade-runner never used the second three words until the request contained in the first four was satisfied. "When he had the rum," according to Jenny's account, "he would use the other three." If it were of a much later prohibition era, one might surmise that the blockade-runner distrusts illegal booze: "I'll have rum, please. No bloody moonshine." In any case, as Aunt Jenny tells it, the "moon," whatever it means, would seem to have more connection to the social drinking scene than to nefarious business ventures, to be contrasted, that is, to rum rather than to a good night or a bad night for blockade-running.

I suggest that "no bloody moon" really means "no bloody woman." Although Bayard had already made Drusilla understand instinctively that he would not use his father's pistols which she has held out to him, he reiterates half-consciously, as he goes to face Redmond, that "no bloody woman" will interfere in his method of demonstrating courage. No doubt the blockade-runner was a loner, who had found rum of much greater comfort than women. With drink in hand, he had the audacity to covertly denounce womankind in the grossest terms to the very faces of the ladies and gentlemen of Charleston. Sacrilegiously swearing by God's blood, at least according to folk etymology, and relating the monthly cycles of the moon to the female sex, the drinker could hardly vilify woman more thoroughly or show his disgust more intensely than by cursing her for the characteristic which makes her woman and fallen from Eden.[5] It would seem, especially in view of Bayard's later contrasting the aroma of cigar smoke to that of verbena, that the blockade-runner is thinking, "A woman is only a woman, but a good glass of rum is a drink." In writing of Faulkner as a modernist, Virginia Hlavsa points out how extensively Freudian slips of the tongue, jokes, dreams, and word play are part of the consciousness of the modernist. "The reason for these routine distortions," she writes, "is that they protect us from those thoughts that lie too deep for tears (or titterings). Given this, the artist's task is to pluck the words and set them vibrating in the mind to register a wider range of meaning."[6] The reader's task then is to experience this wider range.

In *The Sound and the Fury,* written almost a decade earlier, Mr. Compson had revealed to Quentin how mysterious is woman: "Delicate equilibrium of periodical filth between two moons balanced. Moons he said full and yellow as harvest moons her hips thighs. Outside outside of them always but. Yellow. Feet soles with walking like. Then know that some man that all those mysterious and imperious concealed. With all that inside of them shapes an outward suavity waiting for a touch to. Liquid putrefaction like drowned things floating like pale rubber flabbily filled getting the odour of honeysuckle all mixed up" (Vintage, 159). And Joe Christmas of *Light in August,* informed by an older adolescent of "the smooth and superior shape in which volition dwelled doomed to be at stated and inescapable intervals victims of periodical filth . . . to be discerned by the sense of smell and even of sight," is so distraught at this revelation as to kill a sheep and bathe his hands in the warm blood of the dying beast. Several years later, when his waitress friend informs him that she is "sick" that night, he runs off through the woods, seeing visions of "a diminishing row of suavely shaped urns in moonlight, blanched. . . . Each one was cracked and from each crack there issued something liquid, deathcolored, and foul." As he leaned against a tree, "seeing the ranked and moonlit urns," he vomited (Modern Library, 173, 177–78). King Lear's mad disgust with women is hardly more damning: "But to the girdle do the Gods inherit,/ Beneath is all the fiend's;/ There's hell, there's darkness, there is the sulphurous pit—/ Burning, scalding, stench, consumption" (IV, 6). Neither civet nor honeysuckle nor the blood of the lamb can sweeten Lear's or Quentin's or Joe's imagination. And the odor of verbena cannot conceal from Bayard the stench of putrefaction in the bloody, moon-regulated woman who has been his father's wife.

It was necessary for Aunt Jenny to use strong language to

combat Drusilla's equation of love with death in handing Bayard his father's pistols. "Do you feel them? the long true barrels true as justice, the triggers (you have fired them) quick as retribution, the two of them slender and invincible and fatal as the physical shape of love?" She is the Snake who will tempt a man to taste of the fruit of killing, for which once he gets a liking, his appetite never diminishes. "How beautiful," she exclaims, "young, to be permitted to kill, to be permitted vengeance, to take into your bare hands the fire of heaven that cast down Lucifer" (273–74). Unlike the men of his father's troop of soldiers, who expect Bayard to kill as the retributive act of a dutiful son, she is a bloody woman, carried away by the romance of love and death as a sexual experience for both the killer and the killed.

It took strong and telling words from Aunt Jenny to overcome the power of the amphora priestess Drusilla to work Bayard to her will. As the title indicates, it is an odor of verbena with which she magically surrounds Bayard and which in some twenty uses of the word he describes as almost making him immune to other influences or to his own best judgment. Drusilla has worn sprigs of verbena in her short, jagged hair above her ears since she rode into battle with Colonel Sartoris because only the scent of verbena can be stronger than "the smell of horses and courage" (253). When she had compelled young Bayard to kiss her, she had put the sprig from her hair into his lapel, and now four years later, she does the same after handing her stepson the Colonel's dueling pistols, as once more the scent seems to Bayard to have increased "a hundred times" (273). In this second instance the bloom from the other ear she crushes and drops, triumphantly abjuring verbena forever in the presence of Bayard, now in a position to be permitted to kill. Since he leaves the sprig in his lapel when he goes to town to face Redmond next morning, the odor is strong throughout his ordeal and even into the evening. In fact, moving across the town square, with eyes watching him from all directions, Bayard remembers, "I moved in a cloud of verbena" (283), and when he returns in the evening, he is aware of it in spite of the strong smell of the funeral bouquets. Finally after Drusilla's departure, he finds the sprig she has left on his pillow.

Throughout his ordeal Bayard has most of all sought the good opinion of his stepmother. Inquiring of Aunt Jenny in the morning about Drusilla, who having sensed Bayard's "cowardice" had madly fled from him the night before, he questions, "Maybe if she knew that I was going. Was going to town anyway." Reluctantly Jenny advises, "All right. She's awake." When Bayard mounts the stairs and finds his father's widow sitting by the window, she again laughs hysterically, shrieking, "I kissed his hand! I *kissed his hand!*" (280–81). When he returns from his trial in the evening, Drusilla is again the one he hopes to find. With prescient knowledge, Aunt Jenny answers his unspoken question: "She's gone. . . . She took the evening train" (292). Bayard starts to ask, "Then she didn't——" wondering whether Drusilla knew how he had faced Redmond, but knowing that even so she has gone from the house never to return. From her point of view, having failed to force Bayard to her will, she has left the Sartoris house defeated.

As Bayard looks at the sprig she has left on his pillow, which is "filling the room, the dusk, the evening with that odor which she said you could smell alone above the smell of horses," he omits the word "courage" (293). Her concept of courage represented in the verbena is not his, so that although he accepts the sprig, he does not accept the romance of killing, which to her it represents. Between the two women, one of whose presence is with Bayard throughout his ordeal because of the verbena which she has put in his lapel and because of her constant reminder of what it stands for, and one of whom is only with him through a brief phrase, the latter has won. Much as Bayard's thoughts are on Drusilla, whom he wants to "think well" of him, he is enabled to act with his kind of courage because Aunt Jenny reaches his subconscious with the warning that Drusilla, a moon-cycled, bloody priestess, is a symbol of destruction.

It might seem that Aunt Jenny's story, which she begins in a casual way but climaxes with language no genteel lady should use, is inappropriate for one of her sex and breeding. Bernard Shaw early in the twentieth century dramatized in *Pygmalion* the shock experienced by the aristocratic occupants of Mrs. Higgins's elegant drawing room (and by the British public) when flower girl Liza Doolittle forgets her careful training and exclaims, "Not bloody likely," to Freddie's polite question of whether she is walking across the park. American audiences, though not shocked by the word "bloody," were amused by Pickering's later suggestion that Higgins should try to eliminate the sanguinary element from Liza's conversation. It should be noted that the expletive "bleeding," an even more pertinent derivative, is used in the same sense and as frequently as "bloody" by Eugene O'Neill's cockney trader Smithers in the first scene of *The Emperor Jones*. In fact, in the same sentence, "The bloody ship is sinkin' an' the bleedin' rats 'as slung their 'ooks," he uses them both, as he does when he complains of Jones, "Ho—the bleedin' nigger—putting' on 'is bloody airs." The remarkable Aunt Jenny, however, not only recognized the several connotations of the words she used, but knew that nothing less shocking would overcome the Lilith, which was Drusilla.

In justifying the women of two extremes which he created, Faulkner has Bayard explain: "I thought how the War had tried to stamp all the women of her [Drusilla's] generation and class in the South into a type and how it had failed—the suffering, the identical experience (hers and Aunt Jenny's had been almost the same except that Aunt Jenny had spent a few nights with her husband before they brought him back home in an ammunition wagon while Gavin Breckbridge was just Drusilla's fiancé) was there in the eyes, yet beyond that was the incorrigibly individual woman: not like so many men who return from wars . . . almost interchangeable save for the old habit of answering to a given name" (263). Thus the controlled and realistic Aunt Jenny sees Drusilla as "a poor hysterical young woman," whose romantic urge is to make Bayard kill Redmond with a dueling pistol. Having elicited a promise from Bayard that he will see her in the morning before he goes to town, she has the means at a crucial moment to inject her brief story in such vivid terms that when its meaning comes to Bayard, he cannot doubt the course of facing Redmond unarmed. If the men become interchangeable through suffering, not so with Jenny and Drusilla. If anything can be said in Drusilla's defense, although no chaste Diana, moon-goddess of the hunt, and although never like Aunt Jenny, it is that she had lived honestly as a soldier and chastely as a companion to John Sartoris, until compelled to marry and be confined to skirts by her mother and pressures of the community, thus being forced into a kind of life which warped and thwarted her nature and made her turn to Bayard as an agent of the killing in which she now gloried. Aunt Jenny, who has suffered as much, however, gets in the last word to reinforce Bayard's resistance to the serpent's bloody enticement.

In the Victorian imagination, according to Elisabeth Gitter, woman's long, blond hair provided her power. When she was an angel, "her shining hair was her aureole or bower; when she was demonic, it became a glittering snare, web, or noose. . . . She used her hair at times to shelter her lovers, at times to strangle them."[7] The coils of the hair of the Victorian *femme fatale* had the mythic power to be braided into or to take the shape of serpents. In the age of modernism, however, Faulkner gives Drusilla no long golden locks whereby to seduce Bayard to her will, but only short, jagged hair, never described otherwise, whose color Bayard apparently never notices, although Drusilla herself says her hair is black. How she keeps sprigs of verbena— verbena it should be noted grown by Aunt Jenny, for Drusilla cares nothing for gardening—in such short hair is a mystery, but it is certain that the verbena weaves as magic a spell as if Drusilla had the long flowing hair of a mermaid or enchantress of legend.

At the end with Bayard safe and tears of relief literally streaming down her face, Aunt Jenny exclaims, "Oh, damn you Sartorises! . . . Damn you! Damn you!" (292). The suffering she has gone through and will go through because of the Sartoris men is recounted in other stories. In "An Odor of Verbena" she remem-

bers or dreams up a blockade-runner, who, like other fron-
tiersmen and lone rangers, had sworn off women. She thus
effectively warns Bayard that Drusilla's "ideal" of killing for glory
is not viable. As David Williams concludes: "Woman is thus
defeated and her order overturned, this time by a male principle
of intellect devoted to finding a code of existence apart from the
feminine element of blood."[8] It should also be noted, however,
that it is Aunt Jenny, an unusual female, who enables the "male
principle of intellect" to prevail.

If in examining the structure of the story one is to get Freudian, and there is hardly any other way one can get, considering
the five phallic pistols at hand or offered for Bayard's use by
Professor Wilkins, Drusilla, George Wyatt, and Ringo, besides
the one which Redmond discharges, which afterwards Bayard
sits at his desk holding, one notes Bayard's frequent mention of
what he calls "panting" or "it," a breathlessness caused by facing
real death, but also associated with orgasmic death. As soon as
Bayard has arrived home and Drusilla has ushered him into the
house, he puts off looking at his father's corpse, for, he says, "I
knew that when I did I would begin to pant" (270). When she
forces him toward the casket, he hesitates: "I knew that in a
minute I would begin to pant" (272). Later after Drusilla has
kissed his hand, collapsed, and been half carried upstairs by
black Louvinia, Bayard feels even more breathless. "I knew soon
that I would begin to pant. I could feel it beginning like you feel
regurgitation beginning, as though there were not enough air in
the room" (276). When he tells Aunt Jenny that regardless of
what others think about his actions of the morrow, he must live
with himself, he barely contains his panting. "It almost began
again then; I stopped it just in time" (276). As Bayard finally lays
down the pistols which Drusilla has placed in his hands, he is, he
says, "still keeping the panting from getting too loud too soon"
(277). It is a controlled orgasmic experience which Bayard is
undergoing. But as he looks from the window at his father's
casket, he can no longer hold it back. "It had begun by that time;
I panted, standing there" (278).

The next morning, after currying his father's horse, Jupiter, and returning to the house, he remarks, "I had not had to pant in some time now but it was there, waiting, a part of the alteration, as though by being dead and no longer needing air he [the Colonel] had taken all of it" (279). As Bayard mounts the stairs to see Drusilla (Freud equates the breathlessness of mounting stairs to that of sex), he fears, "If I had gone fast the panting would have started again" (280). And as he leaves Drusilla in hysterical laughter once more, he says, "Again I walked slowly and steadily so it would not start yet" (281). When he refuses George Wyatt's offer of a pistol, he remarks, "Now it was not panting," soon after which, he exclaims, "No bloody moon" (284, 285). Remembering the phrase helps to still the panting, which has made it hard to breathe, but afterwards he walks steadily through the hot sun, the male element, and although "enclosed in the now fierce odor of the verbena sprig" in his lapel, he charges in upon Redmond after one knock and walks steadily toward him, to find that it is now Redmond, who after two shots above Bayard's head, is breathless. He at this point knows what Bayard had felt. Redmond knew, says Bayard, "what it was to want air when there was nothing in the circumambience for the lungs" (287).

After Bayard leaves the town, he rides to the creek bottom beyond the house, lies on his back and thinks, "*Now it can begin again if it wants to.* But it did not. I went to sleep . . . for almost five hours" (290). After his climactic love-death encounter with Redmond, his breath returns, the panting has ceased, and he sleeps beyond the grasp of a bloody woman in the arms of Mother Nature.

The natural world in the story corresponds to the human world. The moon, which is woman, appears as a sickle at the start of the story and at the end. When he first sets out with Ringo from Oxford, Bayard has noted "there was a thin sickle of moon like the heel print of a boot in wet sand" (250), one phase of the monthly cycle. After the "bloody moons" which punctuate its climaxes, the story closes with Bayard noting, "and again the moon like the rim print of a heel in wet sand" appeared as a mockingbird sang its "drowsy moony" night song (291). The story is also structured around the time of the fall equinox. As Faulkner tells us in *Sanctuary*, "Nature is a she; because of that conspiracy between female flesh and female season" (Modern Library, 13), and hence in "An Odor of Verbena" the fall equinox, which was "overdue," since it was already October, is "like a laboring delayed woman" (246). (Faulkner would never name a hurricane *he*.) With no frost yet on the land, Bayard feels after Drusilla's first burst of hysterical laughter that there is "not enough air anywhere under the heavy hot low sky where the equinox couldn't seem to accomplish, nothing in the air for breathing, for the lungs" (276). His breathlessness comes, therefore, not only from the tension of his confrontation with Drusilla but because of the undelivered equinox as well.

After his sleep in the dark creek bottom, Bayard can breathe again. And now the equinox can occur. Nature has been through a bloody labor and produced the change of seasons and now the land itself can breathe again. Bayard has triumphed over the blood of killing, as if he had ground the sickle of moon beneath the heel which it resembled. When one considers the bloody trail of killings which Temple Drake left in her wake, after she herself was brought bleeding to the Memphis whorehouse, including besides the deaths of Tommy, Goodwin, Red, and even Popeye indirectly, as well as the moral destruction of Horace Benbow, it is certain that Bayard needed all the support which Aunt Jenny gave him, who even in his innocence knew what he should do, but was not sure he could do it and likely could not have done it without Jenny's "No bloody moon" to fortify his resolve.

Horace, who mixes up Temple and little Belle in his mind, sees his step-daughter as a part of "the wild grape itself," the blossoms of which seem to him "a wild and waxlike bleeding less of bloom than leaf" (14). He associates her with the odor of honeysuckle, as Quentin does Caddy, and is as destroyed by womankind (who, Mr. Compson claims, "are never virgins") as

Quentin is by his love for Caddy. Bayard, unlike these men, although surrounded by Drusilla's "odor of verbena," feels he might have moved "in a cloud of smoke from a cigar," an escape from female domination (283). Bayard is more successful also than Rupert Birkin in D. H. Lawrence's *Women in Love*, who tries in the chapter titled "Moony" to triumph over woman by stoning the moon's reflection in the pond. When he seems to have fragmented it to the point of destruction, however, the "inviolable moon" recreates herself on the water. In spite of Birkin's curse upon the nature goddess Cybele, he cannot escape the moon as woman. She is the great Magna Mater to whom obeisance must be made.

Perhaps the most explicitly bloody woman in Faulkner is, surprisingly, Addie Bundren. "The wild blood boiling along the earth" is almost her motto. She could relate to the school-children only by beating them. "When the switch fell I could feel it upon my flesh; when it wetted and ridged it was my blood that ran." She rejoiced to have "marked your blood with my own," she thought, "for ever and ever" (Vintage, 167, 162). According to David Williams, "Addie's blood-element is really the central symbol of the feminine transformation mysteries; from menstruation through pregnancy to feeding and death, woman reveals her numinous power to create and destroy in this her element. Lifeblood is then both emblem and essence of her awesome domination in the human world."[9] Although Drusilla might hardly seem to play the part of the Great Mother, she partakes of the mystery that is moon and woman, and as such has resources of power unknown to man.

Although Faulkner's claim of having a keen sense of smell is evidenced in many instances in his work, he seems more affected by honeysuckle, jasmine, and wisteria than by verbena, except in the story which carries its name, and Drusilla is never mentioned as devoted to the plant in any other story in *The Unvanquished*. One is led to speculate that it was not his sense of the odor of verbena, the blooms of which florists tell me have very little fragrance, but the "wealth of symbolic meanings" of the plant which influenced Faulkner. According to William Walker in his discussion of the story, verbena was held in veneration by the ancient Greeks and Romans, as well as in Gaul and Britain, as an emblem at the signing of peace treaties and at weddings. Romans also wore crowns of verbena when challenging an enemy; "it was the Herb of Venus as well as Mars . . . was used in love potions . . . and to promote fertility and facilitate childbirth."[10] Walker points out that, in Faulkner's story, verbena for Drusilla stands for the god of war as well as for the goddess of love when she makes Bayard kiss her, while for Bayard, it is a symbol of peace when he visits Redmond, and for birth, since he serves as midwife to the equinox.

Whatever the significations of verbena there is no doubt that the moon as woman goes far back beyond recorded history. According to mythologists Henderson and Oakes, in Babylonian legend the goddess Inanna in her cycle of death, rebirth, and resurrection goes through seven stages of descent according to the phases of the moon: "Through its waning (death) and waxing (rebirth) it completes a cycle, which then recurs indefinitely." The myths of Adonis, Attis, and Persephone, which follow the cycle of the agricultural year from autumn and winter (death) to spring and summer (rebirth), are of much later origin. Thus Inanna, following the phases of the moon, is linked "with a feminine awareness which penetrates more deeply into the unconscious world of prehistory than anything associated with agriculturally-oriented goddesses."[11]

Since we know that Faulkner was also interested in tree magic, to the extent of calling his home Rowan Oak, he may have known of the ancient Irish calendar of thirteen lunar months, named according to the tree alphabet and described by Robert Graves in *The White Goddess:* "Twenty-eight is a true lunar month not only in the astronomical sense of the moon's revolution in relation to the sun, but in the mystic sense that the moon, being a woman, has a woman's normal menstrual period of twenty-eight days." Although we hardly need so esoteric a critic as Robert Graves to describe so obvious a phenomenon, we are convinced by his hundreds of pages of anthropological and literary evidence that the white goddess, sepulchral in the light of the moon, to which she is closely related, is the bane of man's existence—his inspiration but also the cause of his bloody destruction. In the course of lengthy observations, Graves cites Pliny's *Natural History* for a list of the powers for good and bad that a menstruating woman possesses: her touch can blast vines, ivy, and rue, tarnish copper, make bees desert their hives, and cause abortions in mares, as well as turn wine to vinegar, blight crops, kill seedlings, and blunt razors; but she can also rid a field of pests by walking around it naked before sunrise, calm a storm at sea by exposing her genitals, and cure boils. Graves also cites the Talmud for the warning that if a menstruating woman passes between two men, one of them will die.[12]

Robert Graves himself claims to pay obeisance to the moon, "for," he says, "the moon moves the tides, influences growth, rules the festal calendar of Judaism, Islam and Christianity, and possesses other unaccountable magic properties, known to every lover and poet." His complaint is that "the avowed purpose of science is to banish all lunar superstitions and bask in the pure light of solar reason."[13] Such might indeed be said to be Faulkner's aim in "An Odor of Verbena." Faulkner, however, was also aware of the white goddess, whose symbol, according to Graves, "is the double-axe—consisting of two moonlike blades, one crescent, one decrescent, set back to back and fitted with a haft."[14] Although Faulkner's two crescent moons occur on succeeding nights, so much happens in between, including a change of seasons, that they might well be the two blades of the white goddess. In discussing Faulkner's early poetry, Judith Sensibar remarks how often the poems concern "woman as perverse and fatal temptress." In "The Lilacs" "a white woman, a white wanton . . ./ A rising whiteness mirrored in a lake" is a precursor of the poet's death. In *The Marble Faun*, writes Sensibar, "As the moon caresses the Faun, she seems . . . to imprison his mind and body with her powerful hands and feet: 'Like a mad woman in the sky . . ./ Plunging white hands in the

glade/ . . . Her hands also caress me:/ . . . Her white feet mirrored in my eyes/ Weave a snare about my brain/ . . . for the
moon is mad. . . .'" In "Nocturne," continues Sensibar, "building upon an earlier image of the Marble Faun's moon-mad
mother, Faulkner creates another deadly female, a 'spider' moon
[his mother] who becomes Pierrot's 'cage,' 'weaving her icy silver
across his heart.' "[15]

Faulkner is not the priest of a matriarchal God, like Graves,
who has even suggested that the Palestinian icon of the goddess
presiding with her crescent blade over the death of the waning
year was interpreted by the male story tellers of Genesis as Eve
being created from the rib of Adam. Faulkner, nevertheless, in
"An Odor of Verbena" explains the supremacy of woman: "Because they are wise, women are—a touch, lips or fingers, and
the knowledge, even clairvoyance, goes straight to the heart
without bothering the laggard brain at all" (274). He senses that
woman is filled with magic power, malevolent in the case of
Drusilla, benevolent in the case of Aunt Jenny, but always related to the universe through moon mysteries beyond the ken of
man.[16]

NOTES

1. Page numbers cited in the text following quotations from *The Unvanquished* refer
to the Random House (1938) edition. Pagination is the same in the Vintage paperback
edition.

2. Hyatt H. Waggoner, *William Faulkner: From Jefferson to the World* (Lexington:
University of Kentucky Press, 1959), 172.

3. David Williams, *Faulkner's Women: The Myth and the Muse* (Montreal: McGill-
Queens University Press, 1977), 212–13.

4. William E. Walker, "*The Unvanquished*—The Restoration of Tradition," in *Reality and Myth: Essays in American Literature*, ed. William E. Walker and Robert R.
Welker (Nashville: Vanderbilt University Press, 1964), 294.

5. John Ciardi, in *A Browser's Dictionary and Native's Guide to the Unknown
American Language* (New York: Harper and Row, 1980), gives the usual explication of
"bloody": "Brit. taboo intensive; common only in Am. when one is affecting an English
air. Said to be a contraction of *sblood*, His (Christ's) blood; all bodily references to sacred
personages having once functioned as profanity. Also said to be a contraction of *by our
lady, b'lady, bloody;* but both origins are in doubt and this second hardly qualifies as
taboo." In contrast to Ciardi, I believe the second *does* qualify as taboo if it refers to
Mary's bloodiness.

6. Virginia Hlavsa, "The Mirror, the Lamp, and the Bed: Faulkner and the Modern-
ists," *American Literature*, 57, 1 (March 1985), 25.

7. Elisabeth G. Gitter, "The Power of Women's Hair in the Victorian Imagination," *PMLA*, 99, 5 (October 1984), 936.

8. Williams, 213.

9. Ibid., 108.

10. Walker, 292. Since Faulkner was interested in the mythical rather than the botanical significance of verbena, it is perhaps not strange that he seems to assign characteristics to the plant which no one variety appears to possess. The very low, little pastel-flowered border plant called verbena is an annual, of which neither the leaves nor the flowers have any noticeable fragrance. The lemon verbena *(Lippia citri odora)*, a cultivated bush which grows several feet tall, has no observable blooms, but leaves which have a lasting, pungent, lemon odor, dried sometimes to give a pleasant fragrance to a lady's handkerchief drawer. The blue vervain or simpler's joy *(Verbena hastata)* is a wild bush some five feet tall which grows along roadsides and waste places. Although neither the insignificant blossoms nor the leaves are said to have fragrance, the vervain's slender spires were gathered as a magic herb by the Druids of England and by the ancient Greeks, as well as to have been found, according to Christian legend, on the Mount of Calvary. The plant cultivated by Aunt Jenny, with its blossoms which Drusilla at one point crushes, would seem to be the low border plant. The plant of which the leaves have a distinctive odor is the so-called lemon verbena, a cultivated bush of which the blooms are an insignificant part, but which suggestively, although not of the verbena genus, does contain the Latin word for odor in its botanical name. The wild bush with mythological connotations is the blue vervain. Thus combining the blooms of the first, the odor of the second, and the availability on the battlefields of the third, Faulkner has a plant to suit his story.

11. Joseph Henderson and Maud Oakes, *The Wisdom of the Serpent: The Myths of Death, Rebirth and Resurrection* (New York: Braziller, 1963), 99, 29.

12. Robert Graves, *The White Goddess: A Historical Grammar of Poetic Myth* (New York: Vintage, 1948), 169, 170, 170n.

13. Robert Graves, "The White Goddess," *New Republic*, 136, 25 (June 24, 1957), 11.

14. Ibid., 13.

15. Judith L. Sensibar, *The Origins of Faulkner's Art* (Austin: University of Texas Press, 1984), 65, 30–31, 145.

16. An interesting contemporary use of "bloody" is found in Richard Burton's dying admonition: "Remember, now, no bloody flowers." In view of the fact that he had shortly before his stroke in 1984 spoken of the death of his coal miner father, who hated funerals, and of Dylan Thomas's "Do not go gentle . . ." and in view of the close association of women with flowers, Burton seems to be saying, "no bloody women" at my death.

Woman and the Feminine in *A Fable*

NOEL POLK

Almost at the exact dead center of *A Fable* occurs one of those curious Faulknerian scenes which abrupt into the narrative, encounter one or more of the plot's central characters or elements, then ricochet off seemingly into nothing of any moment. The scene occurs on Wednesday evening, and so as precisely at the center of this "Passion Week" as at the center of the novel, following the dispersal of the crowd that had gathered to watch the arrival of the mutinous troops.

In the almost empty road the corporal's wife, who for some unknown reason has been separated from the corporal's sisters, her travelling companions, encounters "an old man and three women, one of them carrying a child."[1] Two of the women are the corporal's sisters, Marya and Marthe. Marthe is carrying a child which is not hers: this fact has such significance that seventeen times within the four pages of the scene she is identified as "the woman carrying the child" and she is only once in these four pages identified otherwise. The second woman is Marya, Marthe's gentle but "witless" sister. The third, apparently though not certainly the mother of the child, is blind; the man is a cripple. They approach, "an old man on a single crutch and carrying a small cloth-knotted bundle and leaning on the arm of an old woman who appeared to be blind." Though blind, the woman sees everything; she anticipates movements; she knows before anybody else when the old man drops his knotted bundle; she strikes down a hand that Marthe reaches to touch her with; she reaches out and grabs the crippled man with "sightless unerring aim" (217).

Thus at the center of the novel is a blind woman leading a crippled man and allowing someone else to "carry" her child. She pushes and pulls the man, "dragg[ing]" him, "holding [him] up," and "jerking him" after her when she departs (214–17). He is obviously crippled in more ways than physically since the one time he speaks he does so in a "thin quavering disused voice," and the blind woman pays no attention to him (216). Her name, which the old man utters once in pathetic remonstance to her harshness, is grimly ironic: Angélique, *like an angel* (216). Angélique, unlike the angels of our dreams and our theology, is bitter, excoriatingly moralistic and contemptuous; she condemns both the "anarchist" corporal for causing the deaths of so many and the woman they have just encountered, whom Marthe has identified as the corporal's wife: "'His whore, maybe you mean,'" she says. "'Maybe you can fool them that don't have anything but eyes, and nothing to do but believe everything they look at. But not me'" (216). At the conclusion of the encounter Angélique moves "unerring as light" toward the child Marthe is carrying and "snatche[s]" it away from her. She then leads the old crippled man away from the three women and out of the book; they are never referred to again. This scene has little or nothing to do with the novel's central narrative, but it is a significant scene, and by no means pointless: in it are sounded several chords that resonate throughout the work, and it stands, I believe, as an emblem for the entire novel, perhaps even, in some ways, for Faulkner's entire fictional oeuvre: a contemptuous, condemning, domineering blind woman leading a crippled man, a woman who "carries" another woman's child, and a child victimized by the harsh caprices of its mother.

A Fable is thus not so far distant from Yoknapatawpha County as most readers have thought, nor are its thematic concerns so very far removed from Faulkner's better-known fiction. I would in fact suggest that underlying *A Fable*'s overt historical and theological scaffolding is a structure which is directly related to Faulkner's earlier work; it is in an important sense but one link in a long series of novels exploring parent-child relationships—in particular Oedipal relationships—and the pressures and anxieties that are the heritage of those victims of too-strong or too-weak or absent parents. Three of the major male characters in *A Fable* are orphans, all are fatherless for most of their lives, nearly all are wifeless and childless, and over and over again men in *A Fable* respond to the present reality of World War I in the terms of their problematic relationships with their parents: over and over again soldiers, even—and in particular, the old marshal—are described as, are treated like, or act like children.

Not just women characters, but images of women, of sexuality and the feminine, occur regularly throughout this novel about men at war, imbuing the narrative with a sexual presence that is as fierce and as fundamental to its various meanings as that in *The Sound and the Fury, As I Lay Dying, Light in August,* and *Absalom, Absalom!* The feminine in *A Fable* is a dark ferocious quantity which resolutely insists, on page after page, that the battlegrounds of *A Fable* are far larger than the fields of northern France and that the casualty lists include those maimed and destroyed by other than howitzers: two of the major battles of World War I occurred at the Chemin des Dames (the women's way), a large area just northeast of Paris along the Aisne River. The second battle there was a resounding defeat for the Germans in the late spring of 1918, approximately the time of the events of *A Fable*, and a bloody confrontation for both sides.[2] They who lost, General Gragnon thinks, lost because they "'thought the Chemin des Dames would be vulnerable, having a female name'" (30). The boche underestimates the strength of the feminine; that is an error few of the Allies are capable of making.

It is doubtless too much to argue that World War I is in *A Fable* merely a metaphor for sexual conflict, but we may glean some sense of the relationship between war and sex in the novel by noting one of the images used by the unillusioned old marshal in his attempt to convince his corporal son that martyrdom is futile and pointless. The war will end soon anyway, he argues, whether he dies or not: the Germans, "the best soldiers on earth today or in two thousand years," have not stopped since they crossed the Belgian border. They will "win perhaps two or even three more [battles]," he says,

> and then will have to surrender because the phenomenon of war is its hermaphroditism: the principles of victory and defeat inhabit the same body and the necessary opponent, enemy, is merely the bed they self-exhaust each other on: a vice only the more terrible and fatal because there is no intervening breast or division between to frustrate them into health by simple normal distance and lack of opportunity for the copulation from which even orgasm cannot free them. (344)

Of the war his meaning is reasonably clear: war is the human condition; peace is not an alternative between victory and defeat, and neither victory nor defeat can stop war permanently. Of the sexual basis for the old marshal's figure, however, the meaning is perhaps not quite so clear, but it does seem to derive from a sensibility very like that of the schoolteacher Labove, in *The Hamlet*, for whom sex is clearly some sort of savage battlefield: "That's it," he tells Eula, when she resists his advances:

> Fight it. Fight it. That's what it is: a man and a woman fighting each other. The hating. To kill, only to do it in such a way that the other will have to know forever afterward he or she is dead. Not even to lie quiet dead because forever afterward there will have to be two in that grave and those two can never again lie quiet anywhere together and neither can ever lie anywhere alone and be quiet until he or she is dead.[3]

The marshal's principle of hermaphroditism is at work throughout the novel in a variety of figures which constantly define war and sex in terms of each other. The Air Force David Levine joins, for example, is not the old Royal Flying Corps of his dreams, his uniform "not the universal tunic with RFC badges superposed on the remnants of old regimental insigne which veteran transfers wore" (87), but rather a newer and to his eyes sissified uniform "not only unmartial but even a little epicene." It looks to him like "the coat of the adult leader of a neo-Christian boys' club" (87–88) and on the hat are "modest dull gold pin[s that look like] lingerie-clips" (88). His flight commander is Major Bridesman, whose succinctly hermaphroditic name is appropriate for one who can herd his military children through all the particularly masculine pursuits of military life— battle and drinking and whoring—and then mother them back into sobriety and responsibility: "he could carry the whole squadron through a binge night, through exuberance and pandemonium and then, with none realising it until afterward, back into sufficient sobriety to cope with the morrow's work" (90). Several times Levine is referred to as a "child" and at least once their squadron is called "the nursery" (93). Levine is not only a "child" here, however; he is also, in the metaphor of hermaphroditism, the bride-to-be: his training consists of three weeks at the aerodrome and "one carefully chaperoned trip" to the front line with Bridesman. The flight he is assigned on this Monday, Levine thinks, might well be called "the valedictory of his maidenhood" (89); on this assignment he does indeed lose his innocence, when he discovers that his guns have been loaded with blanks and that the entire maneuver is a ruse to get the German general past the Allied lines. His suicide follows hard upon his disillusionment.

At home Levine has obviously been a mama's boy: for ten years his mother has been a widow and he her only child. We extrapolate some sense of their relationship from her continual presence in his thoughts and from the fragments of the letter he has written to her (102). In fact, we may gather a great deal from his desire to write these letters at all. At one level, his need to have a "last letter" for his mother to find among his effects after he is killed in battle is merely Levine's sophomoric aping of a sentimental cliché of popular war stories. Just beneath the surface of this cliché, however, seems to lie Oedipal attractions and antagonisms that stem from her ten-year widowhood and from what we readily see is her overprotection, her overnurturing, of her only child. She has, we are told, used her "mother's unrational frantic heart fiercely and irrevocably immune to glory" (88) to make him promise not to enlist until he was eighteen: he is thus a year late, and too late for the glory—since the war, he thinks, is over—because of his "inability to say no to a woman's tears" (88).

Part of why he, like other men in the novel, goes to war is, then, simply to escape his mother, to escape the obviously suffocating security and domesticity she forces upon him. Like the men in the infantry, Levine goes to war seeking "unsafeness" (120); he deliberately flouts his mother's proffered security and, at some psychological level, I think clearly hopes through his own death to hurt her somehow. He "asked only that the need for the unsafeness . . . be held by the nations . . . immune and unchallengeable above all save brave victory itself and as brave defeat" (120). He asks of his government, which he significantly calls the "motherland," that it continue wars so as to continue to supply the necessary opportunities for "unsafeness"—freedom, that is, from those mother's tears even if it is only the freedom to die. But the tears prevail, and just as mother has betrayed him into impotence, so has motherland betrayed him right back into the security he has been hell-bent upon escaping, by putting him into Bridesman's nursery, by sending him on a phony mission, and by rendering his bullets hollow: "those who had invented for him the lingerie pins" (88–89) have filled his guns with blanks.

David Levine's story is complemented by that of Charles Gragnon, the commander of the mutinous regiment, whose life has significant parallels with Levine's, particularly from the Monday of this Passion Week when both at nearly the same time become disillusioned with and betrayed by their respective governments, through the Thursday evening when both die— Levine at his own hands, Gragnon at the hands of the three American soldiers, but a suicide all the same. The similarities between them are instructive, the differences no less so. Both men are equally betrayed by their countries, by their dreams, and by the feminine. Levine's mother and motherland betray him, keep him safe in spite of himself; Gragnon's lack of parents and of any sort of political or military connections get him equally betrayed, in spite of his long years of loyal, dedicated,

military service. Levine kills himself in despair, a gesture of
spite toward his mother; Gragnon is executed by the military
hierarchy he has served all his life precisely because he insists
upon enforcing the very rules that hierarchy itself has taught
him: he goes to his death likewise spiting mother, refusing from
first to last to participate in the sham Mama Bidet and the
military want him to cooperate with.

Gragnon is an orphan, reared at a Pyrenean orphanage run by
Catholic nuns. This is a fact of no little importance to him for,
partly making a virtue out of a fact, he believes his orphanhood
makes him the perfect soldier, since he is therefore "pastless,
unhampered, and complete" (21)—that is, free of the emotional
baggage that others have, free of folks back home to worry about,
and free to live his life, or give it, as he wants. He has no
mother's tears to keep him from enlisting. Until now he has
appeared splendidly competent and tough, perfectly in control
of a career he has nurtured without any of the familial or political
connections that have made military careers easier for others. To
the crisis around which *A Fable* turns, Gragnon responds with
characteristic bull-headed rigidity; lacking other resources, he
falls back on what he knows best. He walks through the scene of
defeat as he always has: "chop-striding, bull-chested, virile, in
appearance impervious and indestructible, starred and exalted
and, within this particular eye-range of earth, supreme and
omnipotent" (37).

But his apparent strength is, we know, a façade. The sisters at
the orphanage try to comfort him by telling him that "the
Mother of Christ, the Mother of all, is your mother." But this is
not enough for the orphan, "because he didn't want the mother
of all nor the mother of Christ either: he wanted the mother of
One" (42). At two very poignant moments in the novel Gragnon
recreates some memories from his Pyrenean childhood by sitting
in the grass of northern France, nestling close to the earth,
whispering "the one word"—obviously "mother"—to the "noon-
fierce stone under his face," and listening for the northern sister
of the Pyrenean cicada, which gives him his only comfort: that

sound is for him "a purring sound such as he imagined might be made by the sleeping untoothed mouth itself around the sleeping nipple" (42–43). He thus longs for the very comfort, the very security, the womb, if you will, that Levine has rejected.

Gragnon's story, too, is rendered in the metaphoric language of sexuality. But if Levine's air force is a "nursery" wherein the children are "chaperoned" by a loving Major Bridesman and their childhood dreams of pleasing mama are nurtured and encouraged, Gragnon's infantry is a grimly adult world composed of men who accept the muck and ooze of the trenches as a fair price to pay for the chance to escape the dull routine of domesticity. It is a military world which not only seeks to escape the feminine but also actively fights back, if not at the feminine itself, then at least at certain symbols of femininity which linger around the battlefield.

Levine has his Major Bridesman, Gragnon has a group commander whom the troops, not with affection, have nicknamed "Mama Bidet." Like "Bridesman," "Mama Bidet" is also a hermaphroditic epithet.[4] Like other officers, Mama Bidet has taken over an abandoned chateau for his field headquarters. When Gragnon goes directly from the battlefield to demand that the troops be executed, he first of all must step over a conspicuous "pile of horse-droppings" which desecrate "the terrace beside the door" (49), and he must pass through a "shabby cluttered cubicle" which has been "notched" into the château, we are told, like a "rusted spur in a bride's cake" (31).

But if the feminine in A *Fable* is in some ways under attack, it is by no means powerless to defend itself. Even though war deliberately upsets and disrupts the domestic, violates the feminine, as symbolized by the military's conversion of several châteaux to its own use, the men who inhabit these domestic settings are invariably drawn to and are in important ways defined by the symbols of femininity, the symbols of their own impotence. Gragnon's headquarters are also in an abandoned château, one built by a self-made millionaire specifically for an "Argentine mistress" (43). Gragnon's bedroom—of choice, apparently—is the millionaire's "gunroom . . . containing a shotgun which had never been fired and a mounted stag's head (not a very good one) and a stuffed trout, both bought in the same shop with the gun" (43–44). More pertinently, when Gragnon goes to Mama Bidet for the second time, he is ushered by candlelight into Bidet's bedroom, where he is received by the group commander, who remains in bed. Faulkner thus depicts Mama Bidet in this scene in terms which connect him unmistakably with the gray-headed bespectacled women—mothers, grandmothers, sisters, lovers, and aunts—whom I have identified as being at the epicenter of nearly all of Faulkner's fiction between *Flags in the Dust* and *Light in August*—who recur in various avatars as a decidedly feminine punitive superego watching over the activities of such emasculates as Quentin Compson and Horace Benbow. In her most condemnatory, Medusa-like avatar, this woman is seen in bed, her graying hair splayed out against the pillow, sitting in judgment on her children.[5]

Gragnon's meeting with Mama Bidet, then, reenacts a classic Faulknerian tableau: the condemning maternal fury, in bed, the son at the foot of the bed, hopelessly yet respectfully suppliant. Levine, who has a similar scene at the foot of Bridesman's bed (97 ff.), despairs that his motherland has failed him: *"What had I done for motherland's glory,"* he thinks, *"had motherland but matched me with her need"* (89). Mama Bidet tells Gragnon that one could stop wars by effacing from man's memory a single word. When Gragnon admits that he does not know what that word is, Mama Bidet sneers, "fatherland" (54). This may merely be Mama's contempt for father; however, if Bidet is correct in assuming the love of *"father*land" to be the main cause of war, the sexual implications of his contempt may be large indeed.

*   *   *

Levine, Gragnon, and Mama Bidet are relatively minor characters in *A Fable*, but the terms in which their stories are told help us to understand something of what is at stake in the central conflict between the old marshal and the Christ-corporal, his illegitimate son, since so much of what is at stake in their confrontation is likewise shaped by their attempts to deal with the feminine in their lives.

The old marshal's and the corporal's stories are not just shaped by the feminine, large parts of them are actually narrated by Marthe; Marthe is herself the epitome of the avenging fury, who has dragged the corporal and her older, witless sister from their Tibetan home to Beirut and thence eastward to France for the sole purpose of confronting the marshal with the fruit of his mountaintop dalliance. In her lifelong hatred of the old marshal for what she calls his betrayal of their mother, she bears many resemblances to Rosa Coldfield, and her narrative of the marshal's abrupt advent into their lives in that remote Tibetan village makes him into a twentieth-century Thomas Sutpen; she even refers numerous times in her story to his "design."

She is so full of hatred, however, that we quickly realize we cannot accept her story completely any more than we now accept Rosa's interpretation of Sutpen as the complete truth. Like Rosa, Marthe tells the tale of a monster; but as in *Absalom, Absalom!*, Faulkner in *A Fable* gives us enough other information about the old marshal's career to suggest that the story is much more complex than Marthe's maniacal recital allows it to be.

Like Gragnon, the old marshal is an orphan; unlike Gragnon, however, who is reared in a rural orphanage, the marshal is reared by an aunt and uncle in Paris: he has through them fabulous social and political and military and financial connections which, combined with his own talent, promise to make him the most fabulous of the fabulous; which not only guarantee that his military career can be pursued with relative ease in Paris, but that Paris itself can be his for the taking. To the astonishment of his classmates at St. Cyr, however—both his supporters, like the quartermaster general-to-be, who believe that he will save mankind, and his critics, who believe that his success is guaranteed merely by his political connections—to their complete astonishment and consternation, upon graduation the old marshal heads not for Paris but for the most remote and primitive outpost he can find, in desert Africa: "a place really remote, not even passively isolate but actively and even aggressively private . . . a small outpost not only five hundred kilometres from anything resembling a civilised stronghold, but sixty and more from its nearest supply port" (253). His critics believe that this is merely a gesture, that he is just doing some obligatory time in the ranks before accepting all the splendor of his heritage; the quarter-master general, the marshal's John the Baptist, sees it as his desert trial before returning to save mankind. But the old marshal foils them all yet again when he leaves that African outpost to go to an area of the world even more remote; he heads to the top of the Himalayan Mountains to a Tibetan lamasery—where, of course, he meets the corporal's mother—and spends an unspecified amount of time there before coming back to Paris, to accept the marshal's baton.

The curious orbit of his career is strange, indeed, but not, I think, completely inexplicable, for his life, too, is described in terms which reflect the peculiarly feminine nature of his experience. We don't know much about his childhood with his aunt and uncle in Paris or what, if anything, he knows of his parents. We do know that when he enters St. Cyr he wears a locket containing two pictures, one a picture of his mother, and that he wears this locket "on a chain about his neck *like a crucifix*" (245, my emphasis); the connection between mother and crucifix is provocative. We know that he had a "secluded and guarded childhood"; that he was "an orphan, an only child" (246). We are told numerous times that he is a small, fragile creature, like a child, *and* like a girl; he is "still girlish-looking, even after two years of African sun and solitude, still frail and fragile in the same way that adolescent girls appear incredibly delicate yet at the same time durable" (252). At dinner during the week of the mutiny, the old marshal, the supreme high commander of the Allied armies in Europe and so one of the most powerful men on earth, sits in a chair whose high carven back topped him like the back of a throne, his hands hidden below the rich tremendous table which concealed most of the rest of him too and apparently not only immobile but immobilised beneath the mass and glitter of his braid and stars and buttons, he resembled a boy, a child, crouching amid the golden debris of the tomb not of a knight or bishop ravished in darkness but (perhaps the mummy itself) of a sultan or pharaoh violated by Christians in broad afternoon. (236–37)

His own headquarters is a château which had been "a boudoir back in the time of its dead duchess or marquise" (228); he employs a "handsome young personal aide" (230), a batman who was "hardly larger than a child . . . rosy and blemishless . . . pink as an infant" (244–45); more ominously, he employs as his chauffeur a "six-and-a-half-foot Basque with the face of a murderer of female children" (230). Though it is hardly possible to say with complete certainty what can be inferred about him from these associates, from the kind of men he surrounds himself with, they do, collectively, suggest the degree to which he is not so very different from other men in the novel, especially in his relation to the feminine.

I propose that the marshal's career takes the direction it does because he is running to escape Paris, the Paris of his powerful aunt and uncle, and all that Paris symbolizes, which is here, as always in Faulkner, a rich, foul, rank, fecund, feminine presence which all men in the novel *except the old marshal* aspire to—the eternal symbol of power, of opulence, and of satiation: "of all cities it was supreme, dreamed after and adored by all men" (247). Paris is "the desired, the civilised world's inviolate and forever unchaste, virgin barren and insatiable: the mistress who renewed her barren virginity in the very act of each barren recordless promiscuity, Eve and Lilith both to every man in his youth so fortunate and blessed as to be permitted within her omnivorous insatiable orbit" (248). Levine wants to lay his glory before his mother and his motherland; the French want otherwise: Paris is "barren"; it "had no sons: they were her lovers, and when they went to war, it was for glory to lay before the altar of that unchaste unstale bed" (248–49). That Paris has no sons, but only lovers, is part of its attraction.

This Paris and its heritage are the old marshal's, if he wants them; yet he, unlike every other man in the novel, runs as far away from Paris as he can possibly get. Why? We can only suppose from what the novel tells us that he is running from something in his opulent, lonely childhood that has made the feminine repellent: he joins the army, a peculiarly male institution, and takes his first commission as far into the heart of desert Africa as he can manage, to a post of foreign legionnaires "recruited from the gutter-sweepings of all Europe and South America and the Levant"; it is a post where "troops were sent as punishment or, incorrigibles, for segregation until heat and monotony on top of their natural and acquired vices divorces them permanently from mankind" (253). Even in this remote, preternaturally unwomanned spot, however, he finds his life complicated by the sexual, by a crime involving the disappearance of a girl and a camel from a tribe of natives in the neighborhood: he coldbloodedly sacrifices the man of his regiment who is responsible, a man indeed who is at that post because he had eighteen years earlier "corrupted and diseased and then betrayed into prostitution and at last murdered" (256) a Marseilles woman. He deals professionally with the situation, but he responds personally to it by retreating even further into what he thinks is an even more impenetrable masculine world: he goes to Tibet, to a lamasery.

Marthe narrates the rest of the story, recounting it to the old marshal himself as a reproach. What emerges from her recital, however, is a story as much about herself as about the old marshal, and as much about the corporal as about either.

Not only can the marshal not escape the feminine in this mountain retreat: if we are to believe Marthe he indeed runs headlong into femininity's quintessence, for there he encounters a mountain Eula Varner, a woman, Marthe says, "who had something in her . . . which did not belong in that village—that village? in all our mountains, all that country" (286). Marthe's story is, to be brief, that her mother was a "weak and vulnerable [and] beautiful" woman (286) and that the stranger came to their peaceful mountain village "just to destroy her home, her husband's faith, her children's peace, and at last her life—to drive her husband to repudiate her just to leave her children fatherless, then her to die in childbirth in a cow-byre behind a roadside inn just to leave them orphans" (286–87). According to Marthe, this mountain Eula has the decency to spare her cuckolded husband as much shame as possible, so she leaves, taking her two daughters and her swollen belly with her; as she dies in childbirth she gives Marthe the locket that Marthe brings to the old marshal and extracts from Marthe the promise that she will take care of her new brother and her older, idiot sister, a promise much like that Ellen Sutpen extracts from Rosa Coldfield when she dies.

As Marthe would have it, the old marshal seduces and abandons her mother and family; he believes, she thinks, "that people are to be bought and used empty and then thrown away" (291). But her hatred is so intense and so long sustained that we cannot simply accept her story as the whole truth; besides, as a nine year old at the time, she surely could not have known or understood all that happened between her father and mother and between her mother and the marshal, or even the limitations and perhaps frustrations of her mother's life in that small village, which we may imagine to be not so different from lives such as hers in the Southern small towns of Faulkner's Yoknapatawpha fiction. Loyal to her father, she has no imagination, no sufficient experience of life, to wonder whether her mother, far from being a victim of the old marshal's cynical manipulations, may rather have embraced this outland stranger as her way out of a lonely and frustrated life in that isolated mountain Eden, her release, perhaps, from an unsatisfying marriage. We who have watched the marshal run in undeviating retreat from the feminine may also wonder whether he is the aggressor. She, at any rate, the corporal's mother, seems to be the strong one in the relationships with the men in her life, and it is at least possible that she has seduced and abandoned him, rather than as Marthe would have it. Tucked away in an earlier conversation between the old marshal and an American officer is a curious exchange. As he explains some detail of his experience with the corporal, the American stumbles into an awkward moment: "I just happened to have found out by accident the last night before we left because a girl had stood me up and I thought I knew why," the American says. "I mean, who it was, who the guy was. And you know how it is: you think of all the things to do to get even, make her sorry; you lying dead right there where she's got to step over you to pass, and it's too late now and boy, wont that fix her—." He stops suddenly as the old marshal interrupts: "Yes," he says. "I know." "Sir?" the captain repeats, and the general reiterates: "I know that too" (277–78). It is a very quick exchange, but Faulkner doesn't want us to miss it, I think, or to believe that the general is lying or simply being nice so the American will get on with the story. Though this conversation occurs in the book several pages before we learn of his relationship with the corporal's mother, it of course occurs chronologically years after his time in Tibet, and I believe it is to that episode that he refers when he interrupts the captain; his comment, then, seems to be an admission that that mountain girl somehow had hurt him deeply and that he, like other men in the novel, had responded to that hurt with that impulse to do himself harm just to spite the offending woman. Unlike Levine, however, he refrains. Like L. Q. C. McCaslin, he leaves the child a legacy of money—a stake if it is a boy, a dowry if it is a girl—which Marthe uses to bring herself and her sister and the boy to Beirut and then to France. The old marshal has kept up with them; without interfering in their lives more than he already has, he has never allowed himself to forget what he has done, though whether from fear or simple guilt we are never told.

At the conclusion of her appeal to the old marshal, Marthe throws at him a locket her dying mother had given her: it contains two miniature portraits on ivory: one is identified as his mother. This is obviously the locket his St. Cyr coevals had noticed so many years ago, the one he wore around his neck "like a crucifix." We do not know whose is the second portrait, but he has apparently given the locket to his mountain lover, as some sort of token, gesture, of despair or love. When Marthe throws it back to him, the "crucifix" indeed comes home to roost; in one important sense, at least, it has never left his neck.

We must be careful to be sympathetic with Marthe. She is herself a victim: at nine years old, hoicked by her pregnant mother out of her home, taken away from her father and forced to wander, homeless and for all she knew destinationless, accepting handouts of food and shelter, to watch her mother die in childbirth in the straw of a dark stable:

> I remember only the straw, the dark stable and the cold, nor whether it was Marya or I who ran back through the snow to beat on the closed kitchen door until someone came—only the light at last, the lantern, the strange and alien faces crowding downward above us, then the blood and lymph and wet: I, a child of nine and an eleven-year-old idiot sister trying to hide into what privacy we could that outraged betrayed abandon[ed] and forsaken nakedness. (290)

On top of this traumatic experience, and as a result of it, she, at nine years old, must accept her mother's charge to care for her sister and her new brother: an innocent child herself, like so many children in Faulkner, she is forced to suffer for sins she is not guilty of, forced to assume burdens not of her own making. As Rosa Coldfield is consumed with hatred of Thomas Sutpen, so is Marthe consumed by hatred of the old marshal.

We can extrapolate something of the corporal's life during this time from her narrative; as she tells it, she assumes that he is as outraged by his father's defection as she is, and no doubt over the years she has filled him as full of his father's faults as Rosa Coldfield fills Quentin full of Thomas Sutpen's. But what clearly emerges from her monologue is the extent to which he, like Levine, wants only to escape his "mother's" clutches. By her own unwitting testimony, Marthe is very like blind Angélique, with whom she is associated at her first appearance in the book, bullying and driving the men in her life, with no concern for what they need or want or think. The matter of his marriage, for example, is instructive in a number of ways: "We had long ago designed marriage for him," Marthe tells the marshal; "he was free, grown, a man. . . . Except that he refused twice, declined twice the candidates virtuous and solvent and suitable which we picked for him." She claims she does not know whether "it was the girl he said no to or the institution": "Perhaps [he said no to] both," she charges the marshal, "being your son. . . . The repudiation of the institution since his own origin had done without it" (298). She thus claims that the corporal rejected marriage and solvency just to spite the marshal; but his subsequent marriage to a girl of his own choice, a Marseilles whore who has neither money nor respectability, is so direct a contravention of *her* preferences that it seems obviously a match made to spite Marthe herself rather than his absent father. When the war begins he—like Levine, like Gragnon, like the old marshal— goes into the military, she says, "almost eagerly" (297): "A stranger," she says, "might have guessed it to be a young bachelor accepting even war as a last desperate cast to escape matrimony" (299). She cannot know either how completely right or completely wrong she is in this judgment. The appalling irony of her narrative, as she admits, is that in her singlemindedness she herself has brought the corporal to France where he could join the French army in the first place and so be at this moment a candidate for execution. We can only speculate how much of his martyrdom, his desire to die, can be attributed to Marthe.

In the Marthe-marshal-corporal family relationships, then, with all its surrogates and substitutes, is yet another enactment of the classic Faulkner triangle: a ferocious, dominating mother; a father absent or on the periphery of the family's life, and having problematic relationships with women, yet potent nevertheless to doom or save; and a gentle and idealistic son burdened with such parents and so, like Quentin Compson, capable only of loving death. It may be worth remembering that Faulkner wrote the Compson Appendix, in which he described Quentin as being in love with death, in late 1945, barely two years after he had begun work on *A Fable*, and so it may not be surprising to find vestiges of his rethinking of that earlier work in the newer one. At least one reading of *A Fable*, then, offers the corporal as yet another of Faulkner's crucified children: the corporal is, I would suggest, the ultimate apotheosis of all outraged abandoned violated and crucified children in all of Faulkner's work, his "crucifixion" but the literal acting out of what has so often, so profoundly, appeared in Faulkner as metaphor.

Under the circumstances, we cannot help but recall that awesome moment in *The Sound and the Fury* when Reverend Shegog invokes the Virgin Mary, sitting in the door with her baby on her lap. "Breddren!" Reverend Shegog says:

> Look at dem little chillen settin dar. Jesus wus like dat once. He mammy suffered de glory en de pangs. Sometime maybe she helt him at de nightfall, whilst de angels singin him to sleep; maybe she look out de do' en see de Roman po-lice passin. . . . Listen, breddren! I sees de day. Ma'y setting in de do' wid Jesus on her lap, de little Jesus. Like dem chillen dar, de little Jesus. I hears de angels singin de peaceful songs en de glory; I sees de closin eyes; sees Mary jump up, sees de sojer face: We gwine to kill! We gwine to kill! We gwine to kill yo little Jesus![6]

In *A Fable*, of course, the "Roman sojers" fulfill Reverend Shegog's promise.

The image, in *The Sound and the Fury*, of that virgin mother and son may be the only actual portrait in Faulkner of something approximating an ideal mother/son relationship; but it is a relationship sealed and perfected into one transient moment. It exists on the edge of destruction and, indeed, for Faulkner's and Shegog's dramatic purposes, exists precisely to be destroyed, by some agent of the "Roman po-lice." But the idea of that tableau, so conspicuously absent from *A Fable*'s elaborate even if ironic reconstruction of Christ's life, of the virgin who is a mother without the need of a man, of the son who is a son outside the need for a father—motherhood and childhood existing complete, outside the complications of time and sex and death—has tantalizing reverberations throughout Faulkner's fictional world.

Marthe drags her family to a small village in France named Vienne-la-Pucelle; it is a name significant enough for Faulkner to have retyped a line of the typescript in order to call it that. *Vienne* is the present subjunctive of the French verb *venir, to come; la Pucelle* means *the virgin,* so that, translated literally, the village's name means *if the virgin comes* or *should the virgin come.* This is the village of the corporal's youth and adolescence: "If the virgin comes," he might therefore think, "if we could have that ideal, then we could have peace." The complex strands of the novel's "meanings" would appear to confirm him in this idea, but only, I think, in the sense that the image of madonna and child represents a regression, a removal from the present difficult world to the complete safety and security of mother's arms.

The village's name cuts quite another direction, however, for of course *la Pucelle* was what Joan of Arc called herself, and since it is Marthe who chooses the place where they settle, she may in some way identify herself with that warrior girl who made kings and slew men. In this case, perhaps, if the virgin comes, she would right all wrongs, conquer all enemies, and restore peace not through motherly love but through military power. The Virgin Mary, the virgin Joan: perhaps herein lies the hermaphroditism of war that the old marshal speaks of—two opposing poles, of regression and aggression, between which poor impotent man ceaselessly moves, opposites which inhabit man's breast and exhaust and renew themselves there in endless conflict. Or perhaps they are not opposed at all, really, in that they offer man the same thing: peace; the one through death—or, since she wields a sword, through castration—the other through regression to the near unconsciousness of that simple relationship, the eternal mouth at the eternal nipple. Recall once again how General Gragnon, early in the novel, in the midst of his troubles, in a rush of loneliness and frustration, regresses to the mother he never had; lying on the ground of the scarred and torn battlefield of his life on which he has just failed, he listens to the cicadas, which are for him "a purring sound such as he imagined might be made by the sleeping untoothed mouth itself around the sleeping nipple" (42–43). Breast and sword, then, equally bring desire's cessation: peace: death. *"[I]f I'd just had a mother,"* Quentin Compson pines, *"so I could say Mother Mother."*[7]

*   *   *

Earlier in the war the British battallion runner, fatigued with the complexities of war, goes to Paris on a deliberate search for his "lost youth dead fifteen years now" (148); it is for him a "pilgrimage back to when and where the lost free spirit of man once existed" (148). As he wanders through his—and, perhaps not incidentally, Faulkner's—old haunts around the Left Bank looking for his garret home—also, like Faulkner's home in Paris, in the rue Servandoni[8]—he stumbles by accident upon the sign announcing the offices of the Reverend Tobe Sutterfield's organization: *Les Amis Myriades et Anonymes à la France de Tout le Monde*. That title, Faulkner tells us, is a designation "so embracing, so richly sonorous with grandeur and faith, as to have freed itself completely from man and his agonies, majestic in its empyrean capacity, as weightless and palpless upon the anguished earth as the adumbration of a cloud" (146). The office he enters seems to him "like a dream" (149), and he climbs the stairs to Sutterfield's office, "mounting to the uttermost airy nepenthelene pinnacle: a small chamber like a duchess's boudoir in heaven" (150).

Gone, then, to seek "the lost free spirit of man," regressed to his youth in Paris, he in fact finds not that spirit itself, but rather an acceptable and inspirational symbol for it, in a dreamlike maternal chamber profoundly removed from the concerns of earth, profoundly removed even from the present moment. From this maternal nest, the runner hears from Sutterfield the story of the fabulous three-legged racehorse that he, Sutterfield, and the English groom and the Negro boy had, four years

earlier, in the Edenic American backwoods, raced throughout
the lower Mississippi Valley. As the runner listens to Sutterfield
tell the story, it is "like listening to a dream" (153). Given the
setting for the story's telling, it is not difficult to understand the
relationship of the "horsethief" episode to the rest of the novel.
To be brief, the story itself is a fable about a crippled male horse
which is nevertheless faster than all four-legged, completely
healthy horses. The horse and Sutterfield and the two attendants
become so famous throughout the area that all men in the area
conspire to protect them from the law that pursues them. The
runner's thrilled imagination responds to the story by roman-
ticizing the chase in curiously sexual terms; he sees it as "a
passion, an immolation, an apotheosis . . . the immortal pag-
eant-piece of the tender legend which was the crowning glory of
man's own legend beginning when his first paired children lost
well the world and from which paired prototypes they still
challenged paradise, still paired and still immortal against the
chronicle's grimed and bloodstained pages" (153). The pairs he
calls up are legend's tragic lovers: Adam and Lilith, Paris and
Helen, Pyramus and Thisbe, and Romeo and Juliet, lovers who
scorned the safe and domestic, who gave their lives to their
passions (153). More violently, he associates the groom with
"earth's splendid rapers" (154).

Of course the law finally catches up with the crew, only to find
that the groom has killed the magnificent racehorse. The ex-
deputy who has followed them around believes he knows why:

> The reason was so that it could run, keep on running, keep on losing
> races at least, finish races at least even if it did have to run them on
> three legs. . . . While they [its owners] would have taken it back to
> the Kentucky farm and shut it up in a whorehouse where it wouldn't
> need any legs at all. . . . Fathering colts forever more; they would
> have used its ballocks to geld its heart with for the rest of its life,
> except that you saved it because any man can be a father, but only
> the best, the brave——— (163)

He doesn't finish the sentence, but clearly in his analysis of the
killing of the horse is the same bitter rejection of both sexuality

and domesticity we have seen in the rest of the novel: *They would have used its ballocks to geld his heart with for the rest of its life*. The horse, then, represents to these Americans the same thing that those wild, untameable, spotted ponies of *The Hamlet* represent to the men of Frenchman's Bend: some edge of passion, uncontrolled and potent, which they do not have—some freedom from the constrictions of the feminine. The men of *The Hamlet* find haven from their women at Varner's store; the men of this episode of *A Fable* retreat to the masculine exclusivity of their Masonic lodges.

That horse, then, is a powerful symbol of masculine resistance to the feminine, and we need only remind ourselves of Mama Bidet's château, into which the army has "notched" an entrance cubicle like a "rusted spur in a bride's cake" (31), and of the "pile of horse-droppings" on the terrace by the door (49) to get some sense of the intensity with which the men of *A Fable* so completely despise the feminine, and to understand how puny their attempts to desecrate it, how impotent their efforts to violate it, how futile their efforts to escape it. They run from it at the moment of birth, they run to it at the moment of death.

Executed with the corporal are two malefactors who like most men in the book are trying to get to Paris and who in the process of trying to steal some money break into a house and confront an old woman in bed: "all she had to do," Lapin says, "was just tell us where the money was hidden and then behave herself, keep her mouth shut. Instead she had to lay there in the bed yelling her head off until we had to choke her or we never would have got to Paris——" (359). *Casse-Tête* is the name of the drooling idiot who kills this screaming mother/woman: literally, *casse-tête* means "break-head" or something done with great difficulty; it is also a club used by primitive peoples. Casse-Tête's nickname, however, gives us the final clue to the meaning of this episode: Lapin, his partner, simply calls him Horse. Both names are significant: Horse is thus identified as the masculine who kills the feminine, out of some primitive, uncontrollable, unrational, impulse.

Horse wants to get to Paris. He is almost totally libidinous about it: "Paris" is the one word he knows and he repeats it over and over again whenever he is spoken to. Lapin, the worldly rabbit, says to Horse, in his joking reassuring manner: "You found out you were going to have to go to Paris before you even found out you were going to have to have a woman, hey, Horse?" (359). It is a complicated statement which Horse can surely not understand: Lapin is referring specifically to the old woman Horse has killed, but the sexual meanings of "to have a woman" are unmistakable, and so is the connection between sex and death, and among sex and death and Paris.

As they are about to be shot, "Paris" is still all Horse can say. "Say something to him," Lapin calls to the corporal, who responds with Faulkner's version of Christ's *This day shalt thou be with me in Paradise:* "It's all right," he tells Horse. "We're going to wait. We wont go without you" (385). Thus if Paris, the world's courtesan, the feminine, is, in Horse's meaning, heaven, it is in the corporal's meaning, death. It is where the corporal goes when he dies, where the old marshal, his father, is laid to rest.

As "articulations" of "two inimical conditions" (345), the father and son are one of the novel's many hermaphroditic pairs. At the close of the novel they are laid together, the two "inimical conditions" they represent no longer inimical but self-exhausted on their deathbeds, the body they now inhabit that of mother earth, the Arc de Triomphe's symbolic masculine bulk rising high above them. There are two piétas at the end of the novel— one, implied, is the martyred corporal safe and comforted at last at mother earth's breast; the other, more potent, that of the crippled and scarred batallion runner receiving the masculine comfort of the quartermaster general—masculine idealism, or fantasy, sucking yet again at the dry breast of the military.

*   *   *

I do not know whether it is possible to generalize from *A Fable,* or from any single book or combination of books, or from any biographical circumstance, about Faulkner and women, to determine whether he is or is not a misogynist or gynophobe or simply a male chauvinist pig. It is all well and good to say, to remind ourselves, that antifeminine and misogynistic sentiments are nearly always dictated by the peculiar requirements of the work in which they occur. Yet there is throughout Faulkner something disturbing about the comprehensiveness with which women in his work are associated with blood and excrement and filth and death. I know enough about Faulkner's manuscripts and typescripts to know that these images are not accidental; yet they are in some ways too compulsive, too upsetting, too regularly intrusive, and too genuinely basic to his fiction for anybody to conclude with certainty that they are for Faulkner merely literary devices of which he was always consciously in control; they burst upward time and time again like sour bubbles out of some sour primal marsh, and it seems to me that some conclusions about Faulkner and women may be inescapable, though I shall leave the biographical implications of such conclusions to others.

I have in this essay barely touched the full extent of the feminine presence in *A Fable,* or of its significance to the novel, though I dare hope that an approach to Faulkner's most misunderstood work such as I have here suggested may open up the novel to studies which will not dismiss it, as most studies do, as a pious aberration from Faulkner's other work. *A Fable* is not at all a simple-minded reenactment of Christ's passion. It is rather a tough-minded and artistically perilous attempt to invest that hollow fable of sacrifice and salvation with meanings more profoundly tied to the people of the Waste Land of the twentieth century, whose anxieties are not so easily laid to rest by any hope of ultimate peace, or dissolved so completely at any martyr's feet.

NOTES

1. *A Fable* (New York: Random House, 1954), 214. Further citations in parentheses.
2. C. R. M. F. Cruttwell, *A History of the Great War 1914–1918*, 2nd ed. (Oxford: Clarendon Press, 1936), 522 ff.

3. *The Hamlet* (New York: Random House, 1940), 138.

4. The *OED* suggests that a "bidet" was, in slightly archaic French, a small horse. Apparently the lavatory was so named because of the riding position astraddle it one must assume in order to use it.

5. "'The Dungeon Was Mother Herself': William Faulkner: 1927–1931," in Doreen Fowler and Ann J. Abadie, eds., *New Directions in Faulkner Studies* (Jackson: University Press of Mississippi, 1984), 61–93. See also my "The Space between *Sanctuary*," in Michel Gresset and Noel Polk, eds., *Intertextuality in Faulkner* (Jackson: University Press of Mississippi, 1985), 16–35.

6. *The Sound and the Fury*, new, rev. ed. (New York: Random House, 1984), 296.

7. Ibid., 172.

8. Joseph Blotner, *Faulkner: A Biography*, 1-vol. ed. (New York: Random House, 1984), 158 ff.

Woman and the Making of the New World: Faulkner's Short Stories

ALEXANDRE VASHCHENKO

The unique world of William Faulkner's short stories still has not received sufficient critical attention. In many individual studies the stories are considered as somewhat subordinate to the novels, and the examination of the short fiction has certainly lacked a detailed, systematic approach. Too often one finds merely brief commentaries instead of lengthy discussion.[1] Yet many of Faulkner's short stories constitute perfectly developed and self-contained narratives, which provide broad historical or mythological perspectives and involve heroes and types no less monumental and powerful than those that appear in his novels. This is equally true of the most elusive of Faulkner's personalities—his women characters, and so their study should attract a special interest.

An impressive gallery of women is presented in Faulkner's short stories. Still, even this limited body of work, comprising only a small part of the writer's legacy, would appear too difficult to plow within a short essay like this one, providing that one aims at some unity and system. But suppose that from among these many texts there emerges a group of stories distinguishable by the particular intensity of their content, possessing some strong similarities of genre, narrative technique, and symbolic structure, and aimed at outlining broad historical experiences in American history and culture? Such a group is easily singled out. In particular, I have selected for my analysis the following three stories: "A Courtship," "Mountain Victory," and "Delta Autumn." In many ways they really seem to stand apart from all the other short prose forms created by Faulkner. Indeed, I would argue, they compare with any of the major Yoknapatawpha works, for they undoubtedly concentrate in themselves some of the deepest and most universal aspects of the whole saga's design.

First, these stories deal with culminating points in the history of the American South and, by extension, the history of North America in general. Thus, "A Courtship" elaborates on the pre-colonial and colonial past; "Mountain Victory" has to do with the immediate aftermath of the Civil War; "Delta Autumn" is concerned with the most crucial conflicts of modern times and attempts to define some hope for the future. Yet, each of the stories is much more universal in meaning, for each one scrutinizes the intricate paradoxes of human nature, not the least of which are the meaningful differences between man and woman.

Second, it is worth noting that each of the three stories is significant because it is not what we might call literally "a twice-told tale"; rather each presents a separate, self-contained treatise on some aspect of the Yoknapatawpha saga never incorporated or repeated in any of Faulkner's other fictions. In other words, these stories are comparable in artistic merit to such works as *Absalom, Absalom!*, or "The Bear," or *Light in August*.

Third, and this is certainly an extraordinary feature which is characteristic of these three narratives: the stories are particularly interesting because of the women characters who appear in them. Indeed, once acquainted with the Yoknapatawpha imaginary population, and particularly the females who constitute the most beautiful part of it, we think that we know each of these individuals by portrait characterization or by some distinctive actions. Sometimes Faulkner lavishes extensive commentaries on these characters. Sometimes, in fact, Faulkner even becomes overinsistent, sharpening this or that feature in his description, as he does in the case of Eula or Linda Snopes. Nevertheless, we know these people intimately, and almost always we know them by their names.

Notable exceptions to this rule are the three women characters who appear in the previously mentioned stories. However
different these women are, they have something in common:
they are described sketchily; they remain in the background;
and, above all, they are nameless. As the stories unfold, it
becomes evident that one of these women is an American Indian
("A Courtship"), another is white ("Mountain Victory"), and the
last is black ("Delta Autumn"). Thus, from the point of view of
their ethnicity and the cultural tradition they represent, these
characters embody three cultures that have come together to
shape the history of the New World.

From their somewhat episodic appearance in the plot one
might hastily conclude that these characters are of minor importance; yet this is not the case. In fact, I would argue that these
three nameless heroines, perhaps the least characterized of all
their kind throughout all the Yoknapatawpha saga, are crucially
important because of the heavy load of meaning that they bear.
Besides, a correction is in order: the women of "A Courtship,"
"Mountain Victory," and "Delta Autumn" are not the "least
characterized"; rather, within the structure of the story, it is
more correct to say that they are characterized by indirect
means; although with Faulkner, it seems, it is not uncommon to
encounter a heroine who is described indirectly. As a matter of
fact, close study of the texts in question creates the impression
that Faulkner is deliberately creating a subtle vacuum around
the personality of his female characters so that the reader might
delicately (for one is expected to move delicately within
Faulkner's narrative space) fill in the empty spaces according to
one's own perception of the plot and design.

The symbolic aspects and the universal significance of these
stories are enhanced by a pronounced folk effect characteristic of
each of these fictions. This folk quality becomes especially evident at the plot level. From this standpoint, "A Courtship" deals
with the epic rivalry of two knights/culture heroes in the heroic
age; "Mountain Victory" uses the folk motif of Ulysses, or any
soldier/traveller interminably returning home from the war, for

with each new step that he makes homeward he is again delayed by a new adventure which leads him farther away from his destination. "Delta Autumn," in this respect, resembles an etiological human-animal parable in the guise of a hunting tale. In sum, it is natural to conclude that in narratives like these the dramatis personae are intended to serve some larger philosophical purpose. The Biblical layer of meaning, plainly manifested in all three stories, in combination with the pagan symbolism, produces a clear-cut type of parable/fiction. Now, following not so much the chronology of publication dates as the chronology of history, as well as fictional time of Yoknapatawpha, let us probe these narratives, starting with the earliest, the "colonial" story.

1. "There is just one wisdom for all men . . ."

The female character in "A Courtship" is identified only as "Herman Basket's sister," a name which is changed towards the end of the story to "the wife of Log-in-the-Creek." The narrator tells amazingly little about her; the one brief passage dedicated to the girl deals with the effect she produces on all the male population in her vicinity. And as many scholars have observed, the words Faulkner uses to characterize her are almost identical to those which describe Eula Varner in *The Mansion*.[2] (Faulkner's propensity to this kind of image-construction, evident in these two narratives, which are separated by both genre and time of publication, might be in itself an interesting point to consider in analyzing Faulkner's skill in creating his women characters.) In any event, the girl in "A Courtship" draws men toward her unintentionally, and both her beauty and her passivity are described in this characteristic roundabout way: "Anyone who looks as Herman Basket's sister did at seventeen and eighteen and nineteen does not need to wash."[3] Indeed, this woman's distinguishing characteristic seems to be her laziness, which, by the way, is strikingly shared by her unworthy suitor, Log-in-the-Creek. Through the entire story Herman Basket's sister remains sitting, merely a presence, and thus resembling a dramatic mute character on stage, who is no less important than the others, albeit speechless.

It soon becomes evident that what Faulkner wants to produce here is a figure of monumental static shape, as universal in its significance as the land and the earth itself. Parallels between the girl and the earth are clearly stated from the beginning of the narrative, for the rivalry is connected with the ownership of the earth, as has been pointed out by Lewis M. Dabney.[4] In fact, once in the course of the story Faulkner even implies that this epic female character may be really something more than just a human being—perhaps a force of nature, the law of earth's existence: "and besides, because of that damned sister of Herman Basket's, there had been no light nor heat either in that sun for moons and moons" (376–77).

On the other hand, the individual female character is also depicted here by means of the generic categories associated with womankind, as perceived by the narrator and as stated in the final verdict of the main characters. She is seen as unpredictable, passive (or patient), and eventually inevitably prevailing—as the earth usually does in Faulkner's fiction, as in the case of Sam Fathers, Mink Snopes, or, in fact, any other male character— frustrating all man's efforts to transform it according to his plans.

In relation to Herman Basket's sister, the figure of Log-in-the-Creek is ambivalent. On the one hand, he is unequal to all men's activities, which is reflected even in his name, a reference to an obstacle in the course of the stream. On the other hand, his laziness is as symbolic as his marriage is superficial (or, more accurately, we might call it nominal). For he seems to be not so much a husband as a tool in the hands of a woman who, in a symbolic way, transforms the obstacle in the Yoknapatawpha "creek" into an allegorical bridge to the future.

The story contains a subplot: Ikkemotubbe's pony is hidden by the conspiring aunt of the girl. First, the pony, a wedding present, is rejected, then hidden, thus introducing the theme of woman's treachery. The reader is challenged to wonder why, on the functional level, this motif has been employed. One guess might be that Ikkemotubbe is to be deprived first of his horse (a symbol of his manhood) before he is deceived in love and disposed of by time and history. Of course, this subplot also functions to prolong Ikkemotubbe's rivalry with David Hogganbeck, thus helping "the dark horse" to win the race.

The girl in "A Courtship" clearly becomes the symbol of a rite of passage—man's initiation into his mournful earthly destiny (as is suggested by Ikkemotubbe's new name, "Doom"). In the course of their epic rivalry, the two participants, Ikkemotubbe and Hogganbeck, make discoveries that henceforth will define their behavior and will leave traces on the history of the country and, as it is implied, on mankind. The rivals become aware of many truths they never before bothered to take into account: comradeship transcending race, prejudice, and enmity; and, even more importantly, the limits of their potential resources, both physical and spiritual. Because of this new sad knowledge, tears come into Ikkemotubbe's eyes, who sheds them not for the lost girl, but for himself, or, more accurately, for the lost universe of his innocent self. A concrete illustration of this loss is the acknowledgement of defeat by both rivals at the conclusion of the story. This ending asserts the ever enigmatic nature of woman as well as woman's unpredictability—a constant theme in Faulkner's works. The effect of the narrative is such that in the end much remains between the lines. But then, if the girl is the land, no special direct or detailed characterization is necessary, for she/it can be seen best through the aftermath of her actions—as Faulkner seems to say.

Finally, "A Courtship" appears to be especially meaningful and universal in its appeal, because it relates to so many epic variations on the American Dream. Certainly, the first "courtship" to become a significant part of the American letters took place in the sixteenth century and, by a meaningful coincidence, in the South: the legendary story of Captain Smith and Pocahontas. And later, the analytical study of a "courtship" evolved through Cooper's and Longfellow's versions (one might add others) and was inherited by the major American writers of the twentieth century, reverberating throughout the works of London, Hemingway, and Fitzgerald. And, in each of its reincarnations, the courtship story added new dimensions as, in time more illusions were lost and Americans were initiated into a deeper knowledge of "doom."

2. ". . . the power to be afraid."

Although "Mountain Victory" does not seem to focus on a woman character, it is the story of two conflicting forces: hatred and love, both of which play a crucial role in the life of the central character, a major in the Confederate army, Saucier Weddel. Even more importantly, the relationship between Saucier Weddel and the unnamed white girl is the key which unlocks the meaning of the story, and the conflict between these two characters articulates the theme of the story. Of the three stories, this one is the most concrete in its depiction of circumstances, although it is no less symbolic than the others.

In "Mountain Victory" the female name is more than simple— it is generic: she is merely called "a girl." An analysis of the plot reveals the girl's narrative function: she is needed for the characterization of Saucier Weddel, because at certain important turns in the story, she contributes significant comments which direct the reader's attention to certain of Weddel's qualities—his personal charm, bravery, nobility, and humanism. Much of what we know about his character is relayed through this sincere witness. It is she who introduces the concept of "the unvanquished" (one of the most relevant to Faulkner's works) and the notion of "victory in defeat," the only condition which permits people to reveal to the utmost their personal resourcefulness and humanism (the girl simply says: "You can whip me, but you cant whip him"). Still more important is her total acceptance or acknowledgement of the personal qualities of the Confederate major, and this acknowledgement, which is also the author's to some extent, is related through the penetrating and foreknowing eyes of a woman.

In her character and in the boy, Hule, one can easily recognize Faulkner's favorite pair, a woman and a boy, who, in their sensitivity to truth, attempt to save the world; who understand and perceive so much, while others are not merely blind, but possessed by evil. In *Intruder in the Dust* a somewhat similar pair saves the life of a condemned black man. In "Mountain Victory" the two point to the truth, which is embodied in their ragged defeated guest. They are the only persons who choose Weddel's side and remain with him to the very end.[5]

The story very powerfully evokes the subject of social and class difference. The girl, who apparently falls in love with the defeated and invalid major, belongs to the poorest segment of the white population in the South. The major, on the other hand, is a member of the Southern aristocracy, and so the class barriers between them at first seem to be impenetrable. The girl well understands this difference. But Weddel embodies for her not only the world of material wealth (which is at the present time more than problematic), but also the revelation of the possibility of a humanness and a civility that she has never been exposed to in her home environment, where she has known only hatred, narrowness of mind, and violence.

The girl's immediate surroundings create the impression of prison, without any possible escape. Naturally enough, she is shocked by the discovery of humane treatment: for example, Weddel's treatment of his servant is contradicted by the facts of Civil War history; but what Faulkner means to show is that the conflicts caused by racial hate, social inequality, violence, or uncontrolled passion are not exclusively the province of the American South—in fact, they may be manifested almost anywhere.

As is so often his practice, Faulkner prefers here an indirect method of portraying the female character; and, as in "A Courtship," his description is laconic. There is almost no physical description of the girl, and the narrator observes only three general traits: her immobility, her enigmatic expression, and her femaleness. So, unlike her counterpart in "A Courtship," the girl in "Mountain Victory" is characterized both in terms of general symbolism and concrete realism, for she is the person craving freedom and happiness who is being kept in bondage. In fact, Faulkner contrasts the girl with Weddel's black servant, who is not only free but even despotic.

It is not easy to establish the major's attitude towards the girl. On the surface it appears that he is not interested in her and that his only ambition is to return safely to his home country. But then his consciousness is tormented by war experiences, and he admits, " 'But it's hard to keep on feeling any way for four years. Even feeling at all' " (758). During the entire story, he does not address a single word to the girl. At the same time, the more we read, the more we become aware of Weddel's almost subconscious concern about her. Perhaps he simply will not allow himself to be concerned—and he almost inadvertently states as much. This much is certain: it is at least in part because of the girl that his spirit and his feelings, frozen at the time of war, begin to reawaken, after he experiences hatred and love and hope. As Weddel expresses it: " 'I am still alive. Still alive, since I still know fear and desire. Since life is an affirmation of the past and a promise to the future. So I am still alive' " (772–73).

Does Weddel reject the girl because of the intellectual, social, and cultural distance between them? Or because she is alienated from him by his present state of spiritual exhaustion? Or for both these reasons taken together? "Mountain Victory" does not provide a direct answer to the question; but like many of Faulkner's stories, it presupposes a multitude of keys with which to approach the complexities of the human soul.

The girl, without doubt, symbolizes "the road not taken" by the Confederate major from Mississippi. Does she also symbolize the possibility of harmony between the North and the South, the prospect of spiritual union between the warring parties, shaping American history at the second half of the nineteenth century? It would be tempting to say so, even though the characters themselves do not seem to be aware of their potential impact upon each other. For instance, Faulkner describes the girl's first reaction to Weddel's appearance: "Then she saw the stranger for the first time and then she was holding her breath quietly, not even aware that she had ceased to breathe" (749). In a parallel to this, the hero's reaction is rendered thus: "Again the father called that name [the girl's] which Weddel had not caught; again he did not catch it and was not aware again that he had not" (762).

In interpreting the conflict of "Mountain Victory," one is tempted to conclude that the two characters—Weddel and the girl—are in many ways opposed to the rest of the dramatis personae, and even, to some extent, to the logic of the historic circumstances. What the author seems to imply is their deep internal similarity, a similarity which may seem to be greater than the social, economic, racial, or any other limitations imposed by society, which, by necessity, defines their behavior—and the course of history.

3. "The ruined woods I used to know . . ."

"Delta Autumn," another example of a very intense short fiction, investigates the many complex, interrelated problems of contemporary time and mind. This close and vital interrelationship between the individual and historical cataclysms, which Faulkner observes in this story, marks the unmistakable reality of our time. Indeed, although written in the forties, the issues raised in the story, as we can plainly see, have only become more deep and meaningful as well as urgent with the passing of time. In this sense, this is the most all-embracing story of all of Faulkner's short fiction. In this story Faulkner explores the conflict between despotism and an individual's love of his native land. Parallel to this, Faulkner also formulates an eloquent warning against man's irresponsible behavior towards his fellowman and his environment.

At first, the plot of the story seems to involve no female character, as she appears only on the final pages of the narrative. But her arrival is foreshadowed by many intricate devices. This time the young woman is black, and she is the subject of a masculine/feminine dichotomy which is introduced early in the story not only in abstract terms—for example, man against wilderness/nature—but also, as the story develops, in terms of does and bucks. Thus, the problem of the ethics of the hunt is related to the threat of destruction, either by war or by militant individualism. Hence the protection of game raises the issue of the protection of country, women, and children. And the young black woman, who appears at the story's conclusion, serves to reinforce all that has been said earlier. So, when the young woman finally appears on the scene, the generally circular movement of the story from abstract towards the concrete and back again nears completion; and Ike McCaslin's last phrase, "It was a doe," completes the movement, returning it to the universal level: the problem of man and the land and the drama that is constantly repeated between "does" and "bucks."

This central analogy is further developed by Ike's reminiscences of his married life, which are colored by bitterness. As we recall, among the Yoknapatawpha characters Ike McCaslin is a distinctive figure, or, at least, he is very important for the narrator, who seems to put some of his own ideas and feelings into Ike's mouth and mind. And in this connection it would be appropriate to note a specific feature of Faulkner's narrative technique. At times the author voices his deepest concerns through Gavin Stevens, and at other times V. K. Ratliff or Ike McCaslin is used as his mouthpiece. While endowing these and other characters with his own sympathies, Faulkner often mocks or disparages them, sometimes in a very pronounced way: instances of this attitude are many.

The same phenomenon can be observed in the portrayal of Ike in "Delta Autumn," although it is manifested, as is usual with Faulkner, indirectly. And in this connection it is significant that the only direct severe judgment of Ike is voiced by the young nameless black woman, who sweeps aside all the individual abstract theories and puts before Ike some of the most concrete truths. Quite simply, the black woman of "Delta Autumn" says,

"'Old man, have you lived so long and forgotten so much that you don't remember anything you ever knew or felt or even heard about love?'"[6] Several crucial moments of his past flow through Ike's mind, during which he dwells for some time on his family life, formulating general conclusions on the differences between men and women. Somewhat cryptically, he observes that he "lost his wife because she loved him," concluding the statement with a key phrase, penetrating far beyond the story: "But women hope for so much. They never live too long to still believe that anything within the scope of their passionate wanting is likewise within the range of their passionate hope" (352). Are we to understand that this aphorism is a part of Faulkner's wisdom, too? In any event, the narrator carefully poises the comment between himself and his protagonist. The tone of the Ike's axiom is not very joyful, and it is interesting to note in passing that some of the formulaic expressions that appear in "Delta Autumn" anticipate Hemingway's *The Old Man and the Sea*, with its tragic stoicism: for example, the statement that because of the merciless laws of nature one has to "kill" his loved ones.

One other slight but definite foreshadowing of the arrival of the female visitor occurs at night, when for a moment Ike mistakes Edmonds's outline for one of the Negroes. In light of what follows later, one is compelled to think that this is not a chance episode.

When the black woman finally does arrive, she is introduced by the same device as in "Mountain Victory," by her eyes. At first, we are told, Ike "became aware of her eyes, and not the eyes so much as the look, the regard fixed now on his face with that immersed contemplation, that bottomless and intent candor, of a child" (357). Later, she looks at him with "that unwinking and heatless fixity" (359) and with "the dark and tragic and foreknowing eyes" (361).

With the Negress appears the motif of the cold, which torments old Ike, corresponding to some of his deepest, hidden, and most troubling thoughts. And although their conversation seems not to go beyond personal and racial matters, nevertheless it concerns the tragedy of black women and their status in society and so it summarizes the problems that the narrative is dealing with. As the black woman departs, Ike formulates his second, general dictum: "No wonder the ruined woods I used to know dont cry for retribution! he thought. The people who have destroyed it will accomplish its revenge" (364).

John Longley, in his brief analysis of this story, comments on Ike's reaction: "When the woman arrives with the baby, Ike is impressed by her quiet dignity and her obvious moral superiority to the spineless father of the child."[7] I would argue that Ike's emotions are even more complicated and conflicting. The Negress disturbs him by confronting him with some of the basic questions that remain unsolved for him throughout his life. Outwardly, Ike turns her away; inwardly, he tries to avoid the compassion and fear that she stirs in him. He hastens to send her away because he is really afraid that his views of the Southern social norms, albeit real, are to be discarded, if not in life, then in principle. His last phrase, "It was a doe," comes as an acknowledgement of his defeat and of the impossibility of change.

This undoubtedly is one of the strongest ideas of Faulkner's realism—that is, his ability to allow himself to criticize his protagonists through a minor character, thus demonstrating the limitations of the protagonist's world view, as well as the writer's lofty objectivity. But in this story Faulkner does not think of black and white relations only in concrete terms: for him, what transpires between the Negress and her lover as well as between Ike and his wife, bucks and does, man and the land (in Faulkner it is always men who are responsible for the violation of the land) are manifestations of a universal life-drama. The parallel between woman and the land, as two evasive but desirable objects, neither of which is being well treated, is recurrent in Faulkner, and it sounds loudly in "Delta Autumn."

Some general conclusions can be drawn from this discussion. First, all of these stories appear to be tales of defeat; and although each one treats a different aspect of a male/female dialectic, be it philosophical, racial, or social, in each case the fiction also dramatizes, either explicitly or implicitly, individual human relationships. Faulkner's purpose is to test man's capacity for nobler thoughts and behavior under the most tragic and pitiful conditions, circumstances that appeal for him "to prevail."

Next, in each of the stories considered, the crucial conflict deals with a characteristic American phenomena. And it is deeply significant that while analyzing the colonial era, or the Civil War, or modern times, an inner logic requires Faulkner to solve the mysteries and paradoxes of human existence not merely through the investigation of economic, historical, or social conflicts, but through the investigation of the fragile harmony between a man and a woman, which seems for him to be inseparable from any historical situation.

One must also observe the unusual manner in which Faulkner presents his female protagonists. He chooses to introduce them not by direct portrayal or even indirectly by peripheral characteristics, which is one of his typical devices (as, for example, in this description: "Log-in-the-Creek's wife shelled corn or peas into old Dave Colbert's wife's grand-nieces's second cousin by marriage's wine pitcher" [379]). Rather he chooses to characterize these women by recurrent symbolic motifs.

Finally, it is apparent from the comparison of the male and female characters presented in these three stories that in shaping his plots and endings Faulkner achieves an equilibrium. For insofar as his male heroes fail in what they hope to do, the women, suffering from harsh treatment, through an intricate system of understatements or indirect characterizations, critique their male counterparts and take their final revenge, which is accomplished not through their own will or intention, but through the logic of history or the law of natural life.

NOTES

1. For example, Walter K. Everett, *Faulkner's Art and Characters* (Woodbury, N.Y.: Barron's, 1969). 155.

2. For example, Lewis M. Dabney, *The Indians of Yoknapatawpha: A Study in Literature and History* (Baton Rouge: Louisiana State University Press, 1974), 61.

3. "A Courtship," in *Collected Stories of William Faulkner* (New York: Vintage Books, 1977), 362. References to "A Courtship" and "Mountain Victory" are from this edition and appear parenthetically in the text.

4. Dabney, 61.

5. Everett, 155.

6. "Delta Autumn," in *Go Down, Moses* (New York: Vintage Books, 1973), 363. Subsequent references are cited parenthetically in the text.

7. John L. Longley, *The Tragic Mask: A Study of Faulkner's Heroes* (Chapel Hill: University of North Carolina Press, 1963), 100.

Double Murder:
The Women of Faulkner's "Elly"

ALICE HALL PETRY

Faulkner and women: the books and essays devoted to this issue—not to mention this very conference—bear eloquent testimony to the fact that William Faulkner created some of the most appealing, appalling, but ultimately unforgettable female characters in fiction. And something more: in much the same fashion that the history of Yoknapatawpha County parallels and encapsulates the history of the South, so too the shifting fortunes of Faulkner's women, their individual resistance or capitulation to the hard facts of social and economic change, embody the Southern experience. This special function of Faulkner's women is particularly evident in the fiction set between the wars—a phase which is generally characterized, as Linda Wagner points out, by a high degree of violence and death usually directed towards male characters;[1] but nowhere, perhaps, is it more blatant—and tragic—than in the short story "Elly," written in 1929 and twice published in 1934 (in the February issue of *Story* magazine, then collected in *Doctor Martino and Other Stories*).[2] "Elly" is one of Faulkner's least-known works; and yet it offers something—a key perhaps—to help us understand more completely Faulkner's ambivalent attitudes towards the women of the Old South and the New.

"Elly" is both the title of the story and the name of the protagonist. The use of the character's name as the one-word title suggests that the story owes much to the literary naturalists' "case study" approach to fiction (cf. *McTeague, Nana*), and indeed Faulkner offers an atypically cold and objective narrative style: glaringly absent is the comforting sense of Faulkner-as-Narrator hovering over his creation. Such coldness jars at first with the superficial warmth of the name "Elly": it sounds so feminine and infantile (elle-y / she-y / girlie) that the reader tends to resist the portrait Faulkner presents of an eighteen-year-old vixen who has a fling in the family shrubbery with a visiting mulatto and who initiates his defloration of her in a forest after a ride in his roadster. The obligingly amoral Paul de Montigny is not to blame: honest from the outset ("'I don't marry them'" [212][3]), he has apparently left a string of sexual conquests throughout the South and has no reservations or regrets about relieving Elly of her virginity. Paul is an agent, nothing more; although he frequently appears in the story, he barely materializes as a character. As a result, Faulkner's focus is firmly on his titular antiheroine—or, more precisely, on the curious relationship between Elly and her grandmother.

Clearly the grandmother embodies the Old South. In public, she wears an "archaic black bonnet," her profile looking as if it were "cut from parchment" (222). And as the product of an era when miscegenation (between Caucasian women and black men) was taboo, she has a sort of built-in radar for detecting Negro blood. She instinctively recognizes Paul as a mulatto the moment she meets him, and reacts dramatically: "without moving below the hips," she starts "violently backward as a snake does to strike" (211). Further, she lays down edicts of her own Code Noir: "'That man must not sleep under this roof'"; "'He shall not drive me to Jefferson'"; "'No blood of mine shall ride with him again'" (218). In fine, the grandmother of the Old South stands in stark contrast to the "painted" granddaughter of the New,[4] and it is the tension, the struggle between them over Elly's "modern" lifestyle (of which Paul is symptomatic) which constitutes the story.

That struggle is underscored by the paucity of characters. As noted, Paul scarcely materializes, and the same may be said of Elly's parents, with whom she and the grandmother live in a large house in Jefferson. Indeed, when the grandmother travels to Mills City to visit an equally noncorporeal son and daughter-in-law, Elly remarks how the house seemed "bigger and emptier than it had ever been, as if the grandmother had been the only other actually living person in it" (214). The seeming physical isolation of the old woman and her teenaged granddaughter, and the tension which it engenders, acquires a new dimension when one considers their names: the grandmother's given name is Ailanthia (212)—as, indeed, is Elly's. Of course, there was nothing that unusual about utilizing the same name across generations (witness Faulkner's naming his daughter "Alabama" after his favorite great-aunt[5]); and thus M. E. Bradford, one of the few scholars to comment at length on this story, sees nothing noteworthy in both women being named Ailanthia.[6] But as Kelsie Harder justly points out, Faulkner "structures, allegorizes, even symbolizes through names" in his fiction.[7] The shared name "Ailanthia" is as significant, as complex, as the shared name "Quentin" in *The Sound and the Fury* or the three-way shared name "Bayard Sartoris" in *Sartoris*. For it confirms what Faulkner not-so-subtly suggests throughout the story: that the grandmother (Ailanthia I) and the granddaughter (Ailanthia II) are *Doppelgängers*: doubles.[8]

As with most literary doubles, they share much: the same name,[9] the same home, even the same capacity to fix each other visually: "they glared eye to eye" (e.g., 217) is one of the commonest phrases in the story. Not surprisingly, their identities often blur: the grandmother rides in the same car with Paul as did Elly to her defloration; and Elly, once arriving upstairs (the special domain of Ailanthia I), would "change completely. Wearily now, with the tread almost of an old woman" (208), she would go to her room, usually after looking into the grandmother's room. Faulkner is even careful to situate them closely physically: they sit together on the veranda (210), and the dance-card which Elly uses to write notes to her "join[s] them like a queer umbilical cord" (218). And as occasionally happens with literary doubles—as in Poe's "William Wilson"—one of the characters serves as a sort of guardian angel "seeking to annul the evil" of his double.[10] This is the role assumed by the grandmother, what with her ophidian reaction to Paul, her settling herself between him and Elly in the car, and her literally walking in on Elly and Paul during their initial rendezvous in the shrubbery: "The grandmother stood just behind and above them. When she had arrived, how long she had been there, they did not know. But there she stood, saying nothing, in the long anti-climax while Paul departed without haste and Elly stood, thinking stupidly, 'I am caught in sin'" (211). But such protectiveness on the part of a double is far from welcomed; for as Robert Rogers observes in *The Double in Literature*, "the double is always, in some basic way, an opposing self": as a result, "disharmony invariably exists between doubles"—a disharmony that "may be portrayed as outright hostility on the narrative level, or as a mixture of friend-liness and antipathy ranging all the way from moderate philo-sophical disagreement to physical violence."[11] William Wilson I fears and hates William Wilson II, and there is no love lost between Ailanthia I and Ailanthia II. For all her aforementioned efforts to "protect" Elly from the mulatto Paul, the grandmother comes across less as a sweet, cookie-baking granny than as (to quote Elly) an "old bitch" (209). Faulkner is insistent that the old woman has "inescapable cold eyes" (208); that seeming sixth sense she possesses for sniffing out mulattoes in bushes is com-plemented by what Elly perceives as her capacity to detect evidence of kissing: "tomorrow she must face the old woman again with the mark of last night upon her mouth like bruises" (209). The palpable fear and hatred that Elly feels towards her grandmother result in her deliberately antagonizing her. Part of Paul's attraction for Elly, of course, is that he is "'a nigger. I wonder what she would say if she knew about that'" (210); and as they tussle in the shrubbery Elly exults, "'I wish she were here to see!'" (211)—a wish that eerily comes true as the all-seeing grandmother instantly materializes to prevent the consumma-tion. But at the same time that Elly seeks to antagonize the grandmother, she also blames her: "'She drove me to [fornication], then prevented me at the last moment'" (211). "Drove" her? Elly's patent incapacity to assume the responsibility for her own actions, even when those actions are evidently deliberate and conscious, results in her seeming out of control. Her necking sessions on the shadowy veranda before the advent of Paul— sessions with "youths and young men of the town at first, but later with almost anyone, any transient" (208)—are clearly not something she truly wants: "'My God. Why do I do it? What is the matter with me?'" (209). Likewise, her engagement to Philip, a milquetoast bank cashier, seems to consist of two months of somnabulism shattered by a painfully abrupt awakening: "'God,' she thought, 'what was I about to do? *What was I about to do?*'" (214, Faulkner's emphasis). Significantly, both of these jolts to reality occur in front of a mirror—and as Otto Rank observes in his classic *The Double: A Psychoanalytic Study*, the "mirror-motif" points to "the inner significance of the double."[12] The mirror is a "reflector," as indeed is the double.

Claire Rosenfield encapsulates this inner significance thusly: one of the doubles "represent[s] the socially acceptable or conventional personality," while "the other externalize[s] the free, uninhibited, often criminal self."[13] In Freudian terminology, one character represents the *id*, the "appetitive nature of man," while the other represents the *superego* which acts as a "censor dictating abstinence" and imposing "honorable duties and noble standards of conduct."[14] Ideally, of course, the two should be in balance—or, more precisely, the superego should keep id in check. But the id seeks to thwart the superego's efforts, and as a result there arises a struggle between the two for the mastery of the psyche. Approaching Faulkner's allegory of the clash between the Old and New South in psychoanalytical terms, then, Elly represents the id and her grandmother the superego, with the story itself recording not what Sally R. Page terms Elly's "revenge"[15]—revenge for what?—but rather the perennial struggle between id and superego. "Freud I'm not familiar with," claimed Faulkner.[16] Believe it if you will; but as John T. Irwin wryly notes in *Doubling and Incest/Repetition and Re-*

venge, even if Faulkner did not know Freud, his characters in *Mosquitoes* certainly did.[17] And Faulkner did go so far as to admit that a writer does not "have to know Freud to have written things which anyone who does know Freud can divine and reduce into symbols. And so when the critic finds those symbols, they are of course there."[18] Where (or if) Faulkner acquired knowledge of the Freudian concepts of id and superego is a moot point. The fact is, as Noel Polk points out, that Faulkner did create "doubled" characters who functioned as ids and super-egos, the most dramatic example being that of Popeye and Horace in *Sanctuary;* and Polk notes further that the "gray-haired bespectacled old lady" was an ubiquitous character in Faulkner's writings of 1927 to 1931—a character who often (Polk cites the case of Elly's grandmother) functioned as the con-science of another individual.[19] In the particular case of "Elly," it would appear that Faulkner is drawing upon these Freudian notions to dramatize the clash between the Old South and the New.

Caught in the throes of that clash is the New Woman, Elly. For all the nasty adjectives usually applied to her—Dorothy Tuck summarizes them as "self-pitying, selfish, and hateful, a sexual tease, utterly cold and amoral"[20]—the truth of the matter is that she is one of the most confused women ever depicted in liter-ature. As noted earlier, she often seems out of control, alternat-ing between a catatonic lethargy and manic motion (item: she was "leaning forward and taut with urgency and flight like an animal" [216]). Abrupt gaps in the narrative ("Then she was in her room"; "Then she was lying with the sun in her eyes still fully dressed" [211]) confirm she is unaware of much that she does, and at one point she does not even realize her eyes are closed (220). She cries throughout the story, repeatedly says she is afraid, and becomes engaged to dreary Philip (in part a pa-thetic attempt to emulate the "proper" behavior of a Southern belle) in large measure to impose some order on her inner chaos. The bid is doomed from the start on both counts, as Faulkner brilliantly conveys by the ironic repetition of "quiet" in the description of the newly engaged Elly: "Sometimes at night she cried a little, though not often; now and then she examined her mouth in the glass and cried quietly, with quiet despair and resignation. 'Anyway I can live quietly now,' she thought. 'At least I can live out the rest of my dead life as quietly as if I were already dead'" (213). Critics have repeatedly termed Elly a Southern "flapper"; but if that is the case, then she is far from being a successful one. In light of her palpable guilt and distress, she is much worse off than the flappers depicted in Fitzgerald's Tarleton trilogy, who at least derive a modicum of enjoyment from their riotous lifestyle.[21] True, Elly wears make-up, associates with a young woman who smokes cigarettes hidden in her dress (!), entertains the notion of getting a job,[22] and heads with Paul to the seclusion of the nearest clothes closet moments after meeting him. But her motives are confused: although she is clearly to be associated with the id, she is no nymphomaniac. Before she met Paul, "she *half* lay *almost* nightly with a different man"; true, she would neck freely, but only "with *almost* any-one"—"provided his appearance was decent"; also true, she would drive with them—but "*never* . . . at night"; and, like Cinderella, she dallied with them only "until the courthouse clock struck eleven" (208, emphases added). One receives the strong impression that Elly's status as a "sexual tease" is not all deserved: it is as if she knows that the New Woman of the 1920s is supposed to be sexually liberated, but she cannot determine how that fact is to be translated into her own behavior. Stated simply, Elly's crisis is this: How (if at all) can the nationwide call for sexual freedom accommodate the persistent myth of the virginal Southern belle—let alone the personal situation of one Elly, age eighteen, of Jefferson? Hence her erratic behavior, especially in regard to sexual matters; hence also the confusion over her relationship with Paul. Part of his attraction, as noted, is that he is mulatto; even to date him would be "sexual liberation" with a vengeance. And yet Elly wants desperately to marry him—so desperately that she begs him repeatedly, deliberately loses her virginity to him, even threatens him with scenarios of unwanted pregnancy. No dice. So she does the next best thing: becomes engaged to Philip, dark Paul's pale double. Characteristically, she illogically attributes that doomed engagement not to herself but, once again, to her grandmother: "'All right!' Elly cried. "'I'll get married then! Will you be satisfied then?'" (212). Since the grandmother had not even mentioned marriage, the act of getting engaged to dreary Philip illustrates how complete is the old woman's control over her granddaughter: true to the subconscious nature of the superego, she need not even speak to get her way, as Elly tries to behave—contrary to her personality and era—like a sensible Southern belle. And yet the superego/grandmother's victory is short-lived, for the id reasserts itself; the engagement is broken.

The limited power of the superego is an eloquent symbol of the limited relevance of the standards of the Old South. Consider the grandmother's edicts, alluded to earlier. She insists that Paul "must not" sleep in the same house as her son in Mills City—but sleep there he does; he "shall not" drive her and Elly home to Jefferson—but drive them he does (218). And Faulkner's refusal to depict the scenes wherein the grandmother backed down from her Code Noir implies that there were no such scenes. The grandmother's edicts, which would have been law in the Old South, are just so much hot air in the 1920s.

Neither the Old South nor the New offers anything permanent and meaningful in the way of guidelines for the woman of the 1920s: the grandmother is deaf—but Elly is equally blind (219). The happy medium, a healthy balance between Old South/ superego and New South/id, is nowhere to be found. The generation of Elly's parents *should* have acted as a buffer between the Old and the New—should have offered some behavioral and attitudinal guidelines which would draw the best from both worlds. But caught up in the stresses of the postbellum period and World War I, the transitional generation never came into its own, as is graphically conveyed by Faulkner's refusal to flesh

Elly's parents into characters. They are mere shades, scarcely mentioned. Small wonder that Elly perceives her family home as eerily containing only herself and her grandmother.

And small wonder too that the confused Elly, trapped between the meaningless, suffocating strictures of the Old and the equally meaningless chaos of the New, vows to destroy what she perceives as the source of her stress: she will have Paul fake a car accident, thereby killing the grandmother. The decision comes after a major confrontation with the old woman in front of a mirror, that blatant symbol of their doubleness. Elly's confusion and illogic peak as she denies that Paul has black blood (218)—another momentary capitulation to superego. Then id prevails, as Elly taunts the old woman with the details of her defloration: "'Tell [my father]! Tell him we went into a clump of trees this morning and stayed there two hours. Tell him!'" (218). Of course, both Elly and her grandmother realize fully that the threat to tell Elly's father is an idle one: the battle is strictly between the two women, and so Elly's determination to "'keep [the grandmother] from telling daddy'" (220) rings false. It is one last excuse for her to beg Paul to marry her, but more importantly it is the proverbial last straw for which she has been waiting for so long—a concrete motive for murder. But they are doubles, remember; and as Otto Rank states, "The frequent slaying of the double, through which the hero seeks to protect himself permanently from the pursuits of his self, is really a suicidal act."[23] In killing the grandmother, Elly will be killing herself. This is foreshadowed in her repeated self-destructive acts: her misguided engagement to Philip, her insistence upon semipublic sexual encounters (in the woods, at the drugstore, in the bank), her giving the grandmother information to use against her. And it helps to explain how although she had initially planned to take the train home to Jefferson, she finally rides in the death car with Paul and the grandmother—a change of plans so compulsive, so clearly dictated by the subconscious, that Faulkner omits the scene depicting it. For Elly *must* ride in that car:

anyone can kill an old woman, but only a double can kill a double.

And if indeed Faulkner is following the murder/suicide pattern so common in the literature of the double, then a case could be made that the grandmother realizes Elly plans to kill her. She watches Elly's erratic movements in her car quite carefully (her "sight nothing escaped" [223]), and before the crash she gives her granddaughter one last stare-down "for a profound instant of despairing ultimatum and implacable refusal" (223). She makes no attempt to save herself and neither, significantly, does Elly: having screamed "'die!'" *twice* (223), Elly grabs the steering wheel (cf. the mad Nicole Diver's attempt at vehicular murder/suicide in *Tender Is the Night*); Paul strikes Elly, the car goes out of control, and then—apparently by accident—she falls out: "When the car struck the railing it flung her free" (223). Paul, the grandmother, and the crushed car merge "in an inextricable and indistinguishable mass" (223) against the trunk of a tree. True to Elly's confused world view, she has killed the one thing she most loves (Paul) in the process of killing what she most hates (the grandmother). No wonder the final scene shows her whimpering pathetically (the word "whimper" appears in some form five times in the last paragraph). However much the reader may react against Elly for committing "double murder"—(a) she kills two people; (b) she kills her double—Faulkner leaves us with an impression of her as a childlike, and hence fundamentally innocent, creature. When the grandmother was alive, Elly was able to flesh out her personality to a certain extent: she may have been selfish and confused, but the battles with her grandmother certainly drew forth the reserves of power in her character, plus her considerable (albeit misdirected) sexuality. Conversely, Elly served as the grandmother's raison d'être, for we have no sense of her life being directed at anything but Elly. True doubles, each complemented the other. With the grandmother out of the picture, however, the stronger, sexual side of Elly's personality has disappeared: it died with the death of the double, leaving her "digging stupidly" at her palm full of glass—clearly the symbol of a shattered looking glass—and wondering at the blatantly sexual image of "warm blood stain[ing] slowly down upon her skirt" (224). The girl who once had the physical and emotional strength to kill two people waits helplessly to be rescued—a true death-in-life.

Faulkner's story of "Elly" may help to qualify some of the most persistent assumptions about his attitude towards women. It is a virtual *donnée* of Faulkner criticism, for example, that he "especially admired older women—and most particularly women born well before the turn of the century. His young women, if they are 'modern,' rarely come out well."[24] This is applicable to "Elly": the grandmother does—to a certain extent—come across as a protector, an upholder of virtue, of past values; and Elly does—to a certain extent—come across as a cold, sexually obsessed "flapper." But there are far more gray areas. As Robert Penn Warren once observed,

> If Faulkner feels the past as the repository of great images of human effort and integrity, he also sees it as the source of a dynamic evil. If he is aware of the romantic pull of the past, he is also aware that submission to the romance of the past is a form of death. If he finds in modernity a violation of the dream of the "communal anonymity of brotherhood," of nature, and of honor, he does not see it as the barred end of history; it is also the instant in which action is possible, with a choice between action as "doom" from the past and action as affirmation.[25]

Faulkner's awareness of the evil lurking in the romantic Old South, as well as of the potential for positive action embodied in the New, is subtly conveyed in the very name he gives to Elly and her grandmother: Ailanthia. As David Williams remarks in *Faulkner's Women*, Faulkner was quite deliberate in his choice of character names, being especially sensitive to the capacity of names to indicate—sometimes subtly, sometimes transparently—the mythic dimensions of the characters he created. In effect, a *personal* given name in Faulkner can be simultaneously the key to a character's *im*personal status as an archetypal symbol. This technique is particuarly evident in Faulkner's fondness for associating young women "with tree images in a conscious and allusive manner": for example, "the coy and insincere" Cecily Saunders of *Soldiers' Pay* is linked "to Hamadryads and to poplars" in an attempt to "convey an arboreal image of the voluptuous and eternal Virgin."[26] In light of this, it seems quite possible that the given name "Ailanthia" is derived from *Ailanthus altissima*. The ailanthus is a lovely shade tree, well deserving of its nickname "the tree of heaven." But its flowers, alas, are remarkably foul-smelling: hence its equally well-deserved other nickname, "stinkweed."[27] The double nature of the ailanthus—both attractive and repulsive—comprises its identity. Were it lacking either characteristic, it would not be a true ailanthus. By the same token, both admirable and regrettable elements coexist in *both* the Old and the New South, as well as in the grandmother and granddaughter who symbolize those eras. The Old South may well have been overly restrictive, especially in regard to the sexual activities of young women; but it also had redeeming qualities—including a sense of order, dignity, and self-worth—which *needed* to be retained to counterbalance and channel the great energy, independence, and spirit of adventure of the New South. For young Elly to attempt to destroy all that the Old South embodies is therefore doubly foolish: it is self-defeating, in that her misdirected energies have left her life in chaos; and it is unachievable, simply because she is a Southern woman: the Old South is a part of her being, just as surely as the grandmother's blood runs through her veins. Far from murdering the Old South, she must accept the best that it has to offer if she is to survive in the New.

"Elly" is an extraordinarily complex story. Its two female characters are intended simultaneously to be flesh-and-blood individuals, doubles, manifestations of id and superego, and symbols of the Old South and the New; and this complexity increases geometrically as these four roles shift and interact constantly, thereby mutually enriching and illuminating one another. Clearly this story is not simply the uncompromising attack on the "flapper" to which it has generally been reduced. It is a modern-day allegory or parable which calls for positive and constructive behavior by utilizing a negative and destructive "worst case" scenario. Much as the old fable of "The Little Boy Who Cried 'Wolf'" encourages honesty by demonstrating the damaging effects of falsehood, so too "Elly" uses the tragedy of murder to exhort the New South to be receptive to the best of the Old. Despite its tragic ending, therefore, "Elly" is ultimately a hopeful story; as the romantic glow of the Old South dims considerably in its pages, so too Faulkner's insistence upon doubleness holds out at least the possibility of hope for the New.

NOTES

1. Linda Welshimer Wagner, "Faulkner and (Southern) Women," in Evans Harrington and Ann J. Abadie, eds., The South and Faulkner's Yoknapatawpha: The Actual and the Apocryphal (Jackson: University Press of Mississippi, 1977), 133.

2. Hans H. Skei briefly discusses the composition and publication of "Elly" in William Faulkner: The Short Story Career (Oslo, Norway: Universitetsforlaget; dist. Columbia University Press, 1981), 30; 117, note 5. With the title of "Salvage" (and/or "Selvage") it had been rejected by Scribner's in a letter dated 23 February 1929 (see Skei, 117, note 5; and Joseph Blotner, ed., Selected Letters of William Faulkner [New York: Random House, 1977], 42). I find no basis for Olga W. Vickery's calling the story "Miss Elly" (The Novels of William Faulkner: A Critical Interpretation [Baton Rouge: Louisiana State University Press, 1964], 304). There is some evidence that Estelle Oldham Franklin, whom Faulkner married on 20 June 1929, had written an early draft of "Elly" (see Skei and Blotner). The inclusion of "Elly" in the 1934 collection Doctor Martino did not enhance its reputation; as Michael Millgate remarks, that volume is "much inferior" to These 13 (The Achievement of William Faulkner [London: Constable and Company, Ltd., 1966], 265).

3. "Elly" in Collected Stories of William Faulkner (New York: Random House, 1950). All page references are to this edition.

4. Faulkner's use of two blood-related characters to dramatize the radical differences between generations in the South may well owe something to George W. Cable's short story "Madame Délicieuse," from Old Creole Days (1879).

5. See David Minter, William Faulkner: His Life and Work (Baltimore: The Johns Hopkins University Press, 1980), 127.

6. M. E. Bradford, "Faulkner's 'Elly': An Exposé," Mississippi Quarterly, 21 (Summer 1968), 182.

7. Kelsie B. Harder, "Charactonyms in Faulkner's Novels," Bucknell Review, 8 (May 1959), 189.

8. Faulkner's interest in doubles is evident in many of his writings. Claire Rosenfield, for example, points out that Sartoris and Go Down, Moses "both explore the idea of the psychic unity of twins and, therefore, reveal Faulkner's fascination with bodily Doubles" ("The Shadow Within: The Conscious and Unconscious Use of the Double," Daedalus [Spring 1967]; repr. in Albert J. Guerard, ed., Stories of the Double [Philadelphia: J. B. Lippincott Company, 1967], 327). Faulkner might have learned of literary

doubles from any number of writers with whom he is known to have been familiar, including Conrad *(Secret Sharer)*, Dickens *(The Mystery of Edwin Drood)*, Poe ("William Wilson"), Dostoevsky *(The Double)*, James ("The Jolly Corner," "The Private Life"), and Clemens *(Pudd'nhead Wilson)*. For an overview of Faulkner's reading, see Richard P. Adams, "The Apprenticeship of William Faulkner," *Tulane Studies in English*, 12 (1962), 113–56.

9. Faulkner does not indicate which of Elly's parents is the child of the grandmother. If it is the father, then Elly and her grandmother also share the same surname.

10. Rosenfield (see note 8), 321.

11. Robert Rogers, *The Double in Literature* (Detroit: Wayne State University Press, 1970), 62, 61.

12. Otto Rank, *The Double: A Psychoanalytic Study*, trans. Harry Tucker, Jr. (Chapel Hill: The University of North Carolina Press, 1971), 17.

13. Rosenfield, 314.

14. Rogers's remarks specifically refer to the doubles Sancho Panza and Don Quixote—two of Faulkner's favorite characters (see the interview with Jean Stein in Malcolm Cowley, ed., *Writers at Work: The Paris Review Interviews* [New York: The Viking Press, 1959], 137).

15. Sally R. Page, *Faulkner's Women: Characterization and Meaning* (Deland, Fla.: Everett/Edwards, Inc., 1972), 95.

16. Frederick L. Gwynn and Joseph L. Blotner, eds., *Faulkner in the University: Class Conferences at the University of Virginia, 1957–1958* (Charlottesville: University of Virginia Press, 1959), 268.

17. John T. Irwin, *Doubling and Incest/Repetition and Revenge: A Speculative Reading of Faulkner* (Baltimore: Johns Hopkins University Press, 1975), 5.

18. Gwynn and Blotner, *Faulkner in the University*, 147.

19. Noel Polk, " 'The Dungeon Was Mother Herself': William Faulkner: 1927–1931," in Doreen Fowler and Ann J. Abadie, eds., *New Directions in Faulkner Studies: Faulkner and Yoknapatawpha, 1983* (Jackson: University Press of Mississippi, 1983), 70, 77, 84. I find that Polk has anticipated some of my remarks about the Freudian dimensions of the two Ailanthias in "Elly." Our arguments diverge somewhat in my belief that, in the final analysis, Faulkner's primary concern was less psychology per se than the clash between the Old South and the New.

20. Dorothy Tuck, *Apollo Handbook of Faulkner* (New York: Thomas Y. Crowell Company, 1964), 166.

21. For discussions of Fitzgerald's Tarleton flappers, see C. Hugh Holman, "Fitzgerald's Changes on the Southern Belle: The Tarleton Trilogy," in Jackson R. Bryer, ed., *The Short Stories of F. Scott Fitzgerald: New Approaches in Criticism* (Madison: University of Wisconsin Press, 1982), 53–64; Scott Donaldson's "Scott Fitzgerald's Romance with the South," *Southern Literary Journal*, 5 (Spring 1973), 3–17; and Alice Hall Petry, "Love Story: Mock Courtship in F. Scott Fitzgerald's 'The Jelly-Bean,' " *Arizona Quarterly*, 39 (Autumn 1983), 251–60. "The Jelly-Bean," like "Elly," focuses on young people caught between the Old and New South.

22. Elly's desire to have a job seems much more half-hearted than Elizabeth M. Kerr implies in "William Faulkner and the Southern Concept of Woman." One of the least of his concerns in "Elly" is what Kerr terms "the problem of the career girl in the South" *(Mississippi Quarterly*, 15 [Winter 1961–1962], 6).

23. Rank (see note 12), 79.

24. Melvin E. A. Bradford, "Certain Ladies of Quality: Faulkner's View of Women and the Evidence of 'There Was a Queen,' " *Arlington Quarterly*, 1 (Winter 1967–1968), 108.

25. Robert Penn Warren, "Faulkner: The South and the Negro," *Southern Review*, 1 N.S. (July 1965), 526.

26. David Williams, *Faulkner's Women: The Myth and The Muse* (Montreal: McGill-Queen's University Press, 1977), 74.

27. *Random House Dictionary of the English Language* (New York: Randon House,

1967), 30 ("ailanthus"), 1509 ("tree of heaven"). Faulkner's interest in the odors of trees and plants, and in particular the associative and symbolic aspects of those odors, is evident throughout his work (e.g., "Caddy smelled like trees" in *The Sound and the Fury*; Drusilla and verbena in "An Odor of Verbena" from *The Unvanquished*). Faulkner's interest in plant odors may well have been heightened by his reading of Havelock Ellis's *Studies in the Psychology of Sex*, vol. 4: *Sexual Selection in Man* (Philadelphia: F. A. Davis Company, 1928), which frankly discusses the close relationships between human and plant odors (44 ff.). Faulkner's knowledge of Ellis's pioneering work in human sexuality is discussed by Ilse Dusoir Lind in "Faulkner's Women," in Evans Harrington and Ann J. Abadie, eds., *The Maker and The Myth: Faulkner and Yoknapatawpha, 1977* (Jackson: University Press of Mississippi, 1978), 97 ff.

Faulkner's Hen-House: Woman as Bounded Text

MYRIAM DÍAZ-DIOCARETZ

Beware, now Her cackling is an endless verbal interaction

The Writer, Women, and Hens

William Faulkner was no poultry litterateur, nor a member of the American Poultry Association, nor did he fuse the chicken business with writing. However, both as an Oxfordian and a Mississippian, more than once he called himself a farmer and expressed himself from the inner voice of a countryman. It is no surprise then, that when asked about the symbolic meaning of the dates used in *The Sound and the Fury*, he replied: "Now there's a matter of hunting around in the carpenter's shop to find a tool that will make a better chicken house. And probably—I'm sure it was quite instinctive that I picked out Easter, that I wasn't writing any symbolism of the Passion week at all. I just—that was a tool that was good enough for the particular corner I was going to turn in my chicken house and so I used it."[1] Faulkner's metaphors of the chicken house to refer to his own writing and of the tools to build it as equivalent for artistic components stimulate discussion on craft and creation as well as on the question of writing from a particular point of view with an objective that precedes the creative production itself. The chicken house rises as the result of a plan (both in *topos* and utility); in a parallel code, Faulkner's discourse emerges from an arrangement conceived by a strategic consciousness orienting the literary text towards a trajectory of prescribed meaning.

When we delve into the subject of women and Faulkner we

limit ourselves to the writer's relationship to about half—or a little more—of the human world, and, if we follow the chicken-house metaphor, we have to veer our attention from the universal chicken to the more specific figure of the hen as the sum of the female enclave among his characters. Yet still this remains too general a notion. Within the large area of the presence of women in Faulkner's written discourse, including his auto-biographical, biographical, and creative material, I will concentrate on an area of his fiction, the short-stories "Episode" and "Jealousy" from the *New Orleans Sketches*, "Nympholepsy," "Frankie and Johnny," "The Priest," all written in 1925, "Two Dollar Wife," "Adolescence," also from the 1920s, "Miss Zilphia Gant" (1928), "Idyll in the Desert" (1930), and "Evangeline."[2] Although I will not be able to cover the two works on this occasion, I will suggest there are structural concomitants between the above mentioned stories and *Sanctuary* and *Requiem for a Nun* in the trajectory of the narrative conception of Temple Drake. My selection is motivated by a general proposition, namely, that Faulkner's artistic design for woman—here called program—can be traced from the beginning of his writing and that this program remained for him a crucial artistic dilemma.

While it is true that Faulkner is not to be confused with his characters, or with his creations in general, there is a critical problem that we must confront concerning the fact that the writer is not absent from the utterance he has constructed. Yet, these two entities, producer and production, are not independent from one another, even though they are moved by very different forces.[3] Neither of them nor the horizons of prospective readers are devoid of sociality. Thus, one way of understanding more fully the social orientation of Faulkner's discourse is to study woman in order to analyze how she exists, which elements surround her with meaning, through which strategies she is given verbal life, what kind of symbolic function rules woman as text, as verbal construct embedded in the writer's plan. The work of art, being a finite text where woman is reflected as a particular and as a universal, has boundaries demarcating its

artistic vision that need to be distinguished for a better understanding of its form. [4] Above all, it is important to locate and draw
what evaluations these factors place upon her as a social being,
given that Faulkner's existence is a textuality distributed in the
very organization of its discourse, in the modes of composition.
In this sense a text is a territory of ideological reality, since every
text is not only a point of view but also the vehicle for an
evaluating point of view. What is taken as the author's truth are
texts built and sustained by underlying strategies that convey
value judgments subsequently absorbed by the reader. [5] It is
those strategies that reveal, within the general scope of
Faulkner's fictional discourse, how the figuration known as
"woman" is made coherent, given content and representation.

By reading Faulkner from this stance we find a recurrence of
consistent patterns uncovering the two worlds: of the male, of
the female, with different spatial, situational, and social conditions. This difference does not originate in my own imposition of
this idea into my reading of the author's discourse, but in a
perception of an asymmetrical correspondence. That is to say,
the "total environment or circumstances of a given event" differs
for each of the two groups. [6] I would like to suggest that
Faulkner's narrative construction of woman proceeds from an
ideological function that exists *a priori,* previous to the writing of
his utterance, from cultural assumptions of collective beliefs
assimilated and incorporated into his individual ideology, transformed by the writer's strategic consciousness into his conception of the represented world. [7] The result of this
transformation is a program for woman's life in the text-given
world. As a preliminary example, we can keep in mind the image
of Caddy's "muddy drawers" in which the function of mud for the
female being is to announce the girl's beginning and her supposedly promiscuous end; or, we may remember the phrase
"once a bitch, always a bitch." [8]

The major bound is the question of "doom," marking from the
beginning a woman's fate within a context of conceptual as well
as narrative constraints creating the circumstances that bring

together a modeling of the writer's artistic design. This is not to be understood as a feature of inflexibility, even less of predictability, but as an indication that "woman" as fictional construct exists by virtue of the words chosen, of sentence structures selected and arranged by the writer who determines the *viewing position*, the angle from which woman as object of representation is to be seen.[9] A consideration of woman as represented content, as dominant discursive units (image, theme, symbol, metaphor, anthroponymy, description, utterance in speaker/addressee interaction), helps us to delineate the composition of her societal and artistic design. From *definition* to *the defined*, woman, in the interaction of those elements, is a multistructural notion given signification not only in the form of "character"; she is, above all, the product of an ideological reality.

The connection between women and hens is neither new nor original. It is evident in the many popular expressions in several languages, expressions lexically referring to hens and semantically describing women, or in the interchangeable swing of images in metaphoric language. Since ancient times both have been linked, discussed, and named as subject of philosophical debates, and also in numerous treatises of anatomy and of moods and character, all instances that have provided open field for the making of stereotypes. Aristotle was a keen observer of and an authority on chickens. So was Plato, and we can also recall the Roman Julius Alexandrinus, the Latin Collumella, Varro (another Roman, 100 B.C.), Pliny the Elder, and many others.

> It was said of Socrates that when Alcibiades asked him why he did not turn out his shrewish wife (the same wife whose naggings were reputed after all to have made him philosophical about life), Socrates replied, "why don't you drive out hens that are noisy with their wings?" When Alcibiades answered, "Because they lay eggs," Socrates replied, "A wife bears children for me."[10]

I do not wish to imply that Faulkner used those terms or practised those beliefs in the empirical world; but I would like to associate the metaphor of his discourse with the subject of women and the allusions to hens. To complete my framework, we need to recall what a hen-house is. I have not relied on the *Oxford English Dictionary* or the *Webster's New Twentieth Century Unabridged Dictionary;* instead, I have followed the definition of Calvin Brown's *A Glossary of Faulkner's South:*

> **hen-house. 1.** (*Ham.* 83; *Reiv.* 203; *WP* 244): a small house, 8'–10' square, in which hens roost. It usually has nest-boxes for laying, though hens often ignore them and lay in various hideouts around the barn instead. A hen-house is often entirely enclosed by wire and the chickens are shut into it at night, in an attempt to protect them from possums and other vermin. **2.** (*Sanc.* 187; *GDM* 23): any place where women live, or are available.[11]

A symbolic relation will be presented to suggest that women exist, in Faulkner's discourse, as hens, protected, surrounded by boundaries that act as fence and restrictions, creating confinement and shelter (as protection and in the Victorian sense). I would like to stress the connotation of the hen-house as an enclosure, as a concrete structure with a difficult access and exit. Its overtones of imprisonment or protectiveness should also be borne in mind. The nest-boxes indicate yet another feature: hens are expected to perform a function for which they are assigned a place (the nest-boxes) and it is known that they are inclined to disobey this rule. So are women. When the bounds are respected, the expectations dutifully followed, we speak of a "henly behavior." If a hen runs away, *she* may never return, for she has been domesticated to the point that she is unable to cope with the outside world on her own. If a woman leaves her assigned world, she becomes *lost* if she never returns. There seems to be no place for the wandering hen in the texts being discussed here, for she who leaves the hen-house is doomed.

Let me use the wire enclosure as symbolic boundary to indicate the discursive territory where woman exists and to envision the outermost limits allowed to her by Faulkner's strategic consciousness. Women, in the sense previously defined, are allowed mobility; yet, there are limits to their freedom. As in any verbal event in the poetics of fiction, "woman" as text is constrained, by definition, by two discoursive situations: that of the writer and his readers, and that of the speaking subjects and the addressees. Furthermore, in the text-given world, they are bounded by social conventions, assumptions, and expectations about their nature and what they are supposed to do. Their existence is framed, narratively speaking, by the microstories summarizing their fortunes and misfortunes (e.g., Judith Sutpen's in "Evangeline," Minnie's in *Sanctuary*, and Temple Drake's as recurrent motif in *Requiem for a Nun*).

Thus, I shall adopt the term *hen-house* as the *hypothetical place* in Faulkner's discourse where he, as creator and generator of textural structures, has control over the writing and the meaning of "woman" and "women" in his aesthetic production. Women, as characters, symbols, images, or metaphors, constitute social subjects that seem to be defined first of all by gender. *Male* and *female* designate the natural, *feminine* and *masculine* call for the expectations and conventions that apply to each function. Given this segregating principle, women are constructed within the *semantic coherence of closed spaces*. One could affirm, metaphorically, that they are circumscribed the way hens are allowed to go along their chicken-runs. Their walkway is limited. Following the system of the hen-house, I dare say that Faulkner the writer is the guardian, caretaker, foster father of them all. To conclude this preliminary mapping, I would like to clarify that I do not pretend to propose a method— the chicken-house method, so to speak—but that I do hope to contribute a reading of Faulkner that stands away from the position placing him either in favor or against women, or as an explorer of human nature, yet maintaining a focus on a critique of the discursive handling of women by a male strategic consciousness. My interest will be to follow an exploratory path leading to some central paradigms that help us to demarcate what structures belong to woman in Faulkner's artistic texts, and, by implication, which ones belong to the nonartistic world, to the universe of reality in general. Having said this, I now proceed with my chicken scratches.[12]

A Room of the Hen's Own: A Hen's Place Is in Her Home

I begin with the concrete aspect of the territory where women are allowed to exist, where they are to be found, where they are "available"; in other words, with the spatial demarcation of people in a place that defines their sociality, expressed through semantic fields referring to locations inhabited by women, and the places from which and to which they circulate.

In "Jealousy" a Sicilian wife must help her husband at his restaurant, in spite of his constant nagging because he imagines, quite obsessively, that she has an affair with a young waiter. The details describing her converge on the wife's submission. Even when she complains to her husband about her situation—even in her cackling—she is tied to further enclosures: she would rather be knitting in her little red room. For six months she stays where she has not chosen to be until she rebels and threatens her husband to abandon him if he does not stop this unjustified pestering. Where will she go? The narrator tells us she will return to her people, where he took her from, to her father's house. Her walkway goes from her little red room to the cashier's counter in the restaurant and, if she frees herself, to her father's house.

"Episode" provides another example in which a single sentence contains the sixty-year-old woman's realm of experience, her fenced-in runway: "Talking in a steady stream, gesturing with her knotty hand, she leads him daily to the cathedral to beg; at sunset she returns for him and takes him home" (Ep., 7). As readers we must assume that she remains at home all day, or that whatever she does until it is time for her to go out to perform her duty is not relevant. The semantics of space are closely related to the asymmetry in roles and expectations for husband and wife, man and woman respectively. "Jealousy" contains already a behavioral bound:

> Of what do you accuse me? Have I not been a good wife to you? Have I not at all times observed your wishes? You know well that I do not sit here night after night of my own wishes, of my own desires. (J, 2)

Both the spatial and situational spheres are central in "Miss Zilphia Gant":

> Mrs. Gant and the two-year old girl lived alone in the small house while Gant was away, which was most of the time. He would be at home perhaps a week out of each eight. Mrs. Gant would never know just what day or hour he would return. (ZG, 369).

One day Mr. Gant decides to announce he will never return. After that, "they told in the town how she and her daughter, Zilphia, lived in a single room twelve feet square for twenty-three years" (ZG, 371). The place of habitation becomes part of the confinement suffered by Zilphia, who has no other diversion except what her mother allows. She must walk from the playground straight to her mother who watches her while she plays, "until the bell rang again and Zilphia returned to her books and Mrs. Gant to the shop and the seam which she had laid aside." Zilphia's early life consists of "going to and from school at her mother's side, behind her small tragic mask of a face" (ZG, 372). The child becomes ill—a progression of anemia, nervousness, loneliness, and actual despair—so Mrs. Gant has to yield to provide her with some companionship (the doctor's prescription) and encourages her daughter to bring her girl friends *in* rather than letting her go out: "Won't that be nicer than visiting?" she asks Zilphia (ZG, 372–73).[13]

In addition to those aspects, Zilphia is reiteratively described as returning to the barred room above the lot. Her potential freedom is her mother's constant threat and obsession. One day Mrs. Gant finds her daughter with a boy lying beneath some blankets, engaged in sexual games: "It was in a ditch in the woods on the outskirts of town, within hailing distance of the highroad" (ZG, 374). On the verge of promiscuity—to her mother's eyes—Zilphia is placed by the narrator on the physical borders of the town, almost out of bounds. She is also at the very limits of her protected world. After this transgression, Mrs. Gant forbids her daughter to go to school. Subsequently, for twelve years, Zilphia "[sits] beside the window" (ZG, 374) observing how her former playmates grow and become adults and get married, until a young man comes to paint the shop. Mrs. Gant acts immediately:

> She moved Zilphia into the back room . . . it was now a fitting room; for two years now they had been living in a frame bungalow bleak as a calendar picture, on an obscure street . . . and when he came inside to paint the walls Mrs. Gant closed the shop and she and Zilphia went home. For eight days Zilphia had a holiday, the first in twelve years. (ZG, 375).

Further attempts to protect the daughter "from possum and other vermin" occur:

> After eight days Mrs. Gant fell ill; idleness brought her to bed. One night they had the doctor. The next morning Mrs. Gant rose and dressed and locked Zilphia into the house and went to town. Zilphia watched from the window her mother's black-shawled figure toil slowly down the street, pausing now and then to hold itself erect by the fence. An hour later she returned, in a hired cab, and locked the door and took the key to bed with her. (ZG, 375–76)

Zilphia finds the key and leaves the house, but she does not run away. Instead, she goes to the shop to see her friend the painter; they get married without her mother's consent and Alas! Zilphia insists she must go to inform her mother. Her husband begs her not to do it. She ignores his request and throws away the chance of liberating herself. Mrs. Gant is at the door with a shotgun; the only words uttered are Mrs. Gant's commands: "Go in the house," then, "Go on," then "Shut the door," and finally, "Shut it." So "Zilphia shut the door carefully, fumbling a little at the knob" (ZG, 377–78). She is locked in again; her husband gets tired of waiting. It is only at her mother's death that Zilphia is really free, yet her husband has vanished. She wants to believe he will come back. The voluntary immobility represented by her choice to wait is a restriction she accepts almost as self-imposed burden: "She realized how terrible the waiting and believing had been, the *having to* believe" (ZG, 378, my emphasis). Two narrative moments in this story unfold the question of choice, free-will, and determinism; in the first one the reader may wonder, why does she go back to her mother after her wedding? The second instance is her hopeless determination to live in the stasis of her husband's unlikely return. Because Zilphia is deeply distressed, but not crazy, soon she sees her reality:[14] "now that she was free she dared not even put into thinking the reasons why she should wait for him. Her husband had left her. For that reason she left the shop half finished, as he had left it, for a symbol of fidelity" (ZG, 378). After an absence of three years, she returns to the town—as a "good" Faulknerian woman should do—with a daughter, and explaining to her townspeople that her mourning was caused by her widowhood. This last detail justifies the fact that Zilphia is not rejected by the community. The final image of the story is not only an echo of a replay, but a parody of Zilphia's own childhood and the anticipation of little Zilphia's life. That is, a fated repetition that must ground every descendant of a woman who has not complied with social expectations. As mother and daughter are on their way to the girl's school, we witness the Faulknerian determinism territorialized on women at its best. The program of duplication of the mother's life—without a man—perpetuating her fate points to the doom and the strong conditioning framing women's lives. Furthermore, this binding is an implicit assertion from the point of view of the narrator who suggests that under certain circumstances women cannot change their fate. Faulkner's view, on the other hand, is not necessarily negative, because in this story he clearly questions that determinism by way of emphasis.

In "Idyll in the Desert" the woman is abandoned by her lover after two years of her nursing him. Her waiting lasts for eight years. During this time she is alone and ill; she would never come to the door and would only speak from the house. Her illness is not what confines her in a remote and desolate place in the South, but it is her hope that the lover will return. Her choice of illusion rather than reality (one that includes a well-to-do husband in the North) binds her to her tragic ending of utter loneliness and eventual death. But it is *her* choice not to go back to her husband. The crucial question here is, why doesn't she? Not only has she left her home and abandoned her husband, but she has behaved like an unnatural hen by abandoning her offspring. As the saying goes, "It's a bad hen that lays away from the farm."[15]

The Sutpen descendants in "Evangeline" have a hen-house of their own: "They live in a cabin about a half mile from the house—two rooms and an open hall full of children and grandchildren and greatgrandchildren, all women. Not a man over eleven years old in the house" (E, 585). While Colonel Sutpen, Henry Sutpen, and Charles Bon go to the war, Judith and her mother stay home "never doing anything":

> "'Jes hid the silver in de back gyarden, an et whut dey could git."
> (E, 587)

Judith's life is recapitulated later in a micronarrative within the story, in a single sentence:

> and so when she told how Henry and Charles had gone away to the war in seeming amity and Judith with her hour old wedding ring had taken care of the place and buried her mother and kept the house ready for her husband's return, and how they heard that the war was over and that Charles Bon was safe and how two days later Henry brought Charles' body in the wagon, dead, killed by the last shot of the war. (E, 600–601)

Then we are told,

> they carried him up to the room which Judith had kept ready for him, and how she sent them all away and locked the door upon herself and her dead husband and the picture. (E, 601)

These are but a few examples of semantic features related to the woman's space. Her habitat and the socially restricted life correspond to the traditional beliefs and expectations toward women prevalent in the North American South of the 1920s—hopefully, obsolete in the 1980s. These expectations, suppositions that the hen will lay her eggs in the assigned nest-boxes, are also correlated with the traditional bourgeois novel of the nineteenth century in which women are economically dependent or inactive beings, whose main asset of prestige is the bearing of legitimate children as expected social norm. The duty of motherhood predominates as the tangible bond between the woman and her community. In Faulkner these roles are also socioculturally inset: a given behavior and the corresponding value judgment operate within the prescriptive modes encircling woman as wife, widow, mother (with or without a husband in the house), servant, prostitute, mistress, all societal vestibules that lead to archetypal or to stereotypical figurations. Each one of these compartments is directly linked with the woman's relationship to her assigned living space. Around these external boundaries for women, Faulkner develops, in a society of transition between postcolonialism and preindustrialization, a number of attitudes shaping as a totality a network of what we might call *themes of the female self*. Among the major *nuclea* in the stories under scrutiny is the theme of "waiting" to which semantic features of fidelity, patience, obedience, passivity, protection, and resignation are closely attached and serve as the structural forces of the narration as well as for the bases of characterization of women.[16]

Waiting is a passive activity, the way female passion is—or is expected to be—lived through as the unquestionable expression of feminine loyalty; in the Faulknerian enclave, waiting is as tragic an act as any done by a hero of Greek drama; inscrutable, yet deceiving, because appearance suggests that the very act may change events on one level, while it perpetuates the condition of the one who waits on the other. An additional aspect is the asymmetry of the situation. In Faulkner's text waiting, inactivity, and idleness are feminine "occupations," just as abandoning the spouse or lover is a forgivable event in a man—a man's business, or going away from home, is a necessary social act except for women. When transgression of those codes is done by a woman, she stops being feminine, regresses, or is made to resemble a man (I shall return to this point in the pages that follow).

The early sketches and stories offer a kind of blueprint of woman's territory and of the limits they must not cross. It is a question of *leaving* or *staying;* she may choose to remain in a given place, for better or for worse, in spite of her awareness that what she decides will provoke her confinement. Or, she may be unaware of the sequels to her decision. She may refuse to accept an alternative exit as means of salvation, and then her doom will be her own doing. Underneath the recurrent feature of the female figure returning home or never coming back lies the writer's program as well as the deceiving network surrounding her fate spread on her as her own responsibility.[17] Yet, I would like to emphasize that it is an illusion that the doom "is her own." It is in her apparent freedom that we are to scrutinize the deeper recesses of her feminine entrapment. Therefore, let us ask ourselves the question once more: to what extent can women in Faulkner's discourse change their fate? If the answer is in the negative, what enmeshes their being? What does "a woman's fate" mean?

The Frame, The Word

I shall refer now to two patterns of restrictions encoded in Faulkner to define women: one of objects (pictures, portraits as representation) and the other, of verbal enclosures concerning woman as inscribed thought, in addition to her framing/framed situation in written texts as two emblematic modes of discourse.

"Evangeline" is quite suggestive in the use of objects as symbolic semantic frames. Charles Bon's departure is summarized as follows: "he took with him Judith's picture in a metal case that closed like a book and locked with a key, and left behind him a ring" (E, 588). The representation of the beloved's image (the picture) enclosed (the metal case) and guarded (the key) is also a sign of the static condition that will surround Judith in her relationship with Charles. The ring is more than the traditional symbol of engagement: Judith's insistence on wearing it (E, 589) serves as the center for yet several units that are functional to the theme of "waiting." As the token of Charles's promise of engagement, it makes more salient Colonel Sutpen's reluctance to announce it officially, and it is a challenge to Henry's opposition and to his silence around the situation (silence itself being another frame). The ring also stands out as a constant reminder that Charles will eventually return to marry her. After four years he comes back, they get married, and on the same day he must leave again. A new stage begins for Judith, from waiting as a bride to waiting as a wife. The only real contact she ever has with her husband is through his letters.

Women's dependence on the outside sphere, such as on the reception of news through letters, telegrams, newspapers, is another semantic nucleus that illustrates another fence, so to speak, of their inhabited area in closed spaces. By way of example, in her unfulfilled wish to be with her husband, Zilphia Gant feeds her anxiety by "reading," interpreting texts that constitute the possibility of inscription of her desires, to make them come true. A search for clues as evidence of her own existence leads her to an initial substitution of names: "She took three or four newspapers, thinking that she might some day see his name in print. After a while she was writing guarded significant letters to agony columns, mentioning incidents which only he could recognize. She began to read all the wedding notices, substituting her name for the bride's and his for that of the groom. Then she would undress and go to bed" (ZG, 378–79). She makes this her habit as she also begins to perform a ritual that culminates in masturbation in order to purge the frustration out of her being with fantasies of conceiving a child like Christ, not from religious fervor or maternal impulse, but for the belief that she would then be able to transcend her desire and be liberated, since "Mary did it without a man. She did it." (ZG, 379). In addition to this, when her husband's wedding announcement actually appears in the newspaper, she hires a private detective agency that keeps her informed with weekly reports of every detail of how the couple lives. The agency becomes the substitute lover, to a certain extent, on a discoursive level. Parallel to the substitution

of inscribed names in the newspapers, her sexual desire is transformed further as she identifies in such a way that a doubling of
her self occurs, becoming "the other" in her dreams; yet this
doubling acquires a wider dimension when Zilphia splits her self
interchangeably, that is, she becomes husband, or his actual wife
in her desire, creating thus in her fantasies *l'amour à trois:*

> By means of the letters she knew how they lived. She knew more
> about each than the other did. She knew when they quarrelled and
> felt exultation; she knew when they were reconciled and felt raging
> and impotent despair. Sometimes at night she would become one of
> the two of them, entering their bodies in turn and crucified anew by
> her ubiquity, participating in ecstasies the more racking for being
> vicarious and transcendant of the actual flesh. (ZG, 379–80)

The texts from the agency become the narration of her own life;
in her act of reading them she appropriates those alien events
and transforms them into the fulfillment of her desire. The
search for written evidence is not motivated by external factors
or circumstances but by her own failure and unwillingness to
forget her husband. Gradually this reading act becomes her way
of subsistance, which, simultaneously, as fidelity or obsession,
traps her from within.

It is a telegram that calls the woman to join her lover in "Idyll
in the Desert." During the eight years before her death, she
receives periodically and unknowingly an envelope with money
sent from her husband. It had a "fake number and [a] fake
postmark and all" (ID, 408). Quite significantly, "The only thing
she seemed to mistrust about it was the only thing that was
authentic. 'There's no letter.'" She suspected the message had
been stolen.

The above-mentioned instances of dependence on messages
from the outside world reveal the women's willingness to accept
their roles, to cling to the pretence allowed to them by their
"feminine nature" and to the belief that change in the course of
events must come from the external sphere, from the one in
which they do not participate as agents, as it is evident in the
pattern of resignation at the departure of the fiancé, lover, hus-

band. It is the possibility of good news that safeguards their existence and provides a basis for their belief in man—not in the generic sense—as the center of the world, the cock as the principle of order in the barnyard.[18] The one who crosses over this restriction is no longer feminine.

One of the earliest exercises in articulating "woman" appears in "Episode" in two modes of representation that are intertwined. Our vision of the woman is dual: that of the narrator as he observes Spratling, the painter, sketching her portrait, and on a symbolic level, that of the portrait itself, described in the process of its creation. In the following passage, the dialogue is balanced by the painter's instructions to the woman, and by her own objections:

> "No, no," Spratling told her, "not like that." Her face fell. "Turn toward him, look at him," he added quickly.
> She obeyed, still facing us.
> "Turn your head too; look at him."
> "But you can't see my face then," she objected.
> "Yes, I can. Besides, I'll draw your face later."
> Appeased, her smile broke her face into a million tiny wrinkles, like an etching, and she took the position he wanted.
> At once she became maternal. (Ep., 8)

Malleability, obedience, passivity, and being maternal are set in progression to define the feminine. In this early sketch the roles are already divided between what is supposed to be feminine and masculine. The phrase "One knew immediately that they had been photographed so on their wedding day" (Ep., 8) qualifies the narrator as authority and prepares the reader to interpret the bride image as the woman's own daydream, as if it were her own inner vision. Yet it is actually the narrator who sees her under that light and who projects his own stereotype of the female on the sixty-year-old lady:

> She was a bride again; with that ability for fine fabling which death alone can rob us, she was once more dressed in silk (or its equivalent) and jewels, a wreath and a veil, and probably a bouquet. She was a bride again, young and fair, with her trembling hand on young

Joe's shoulder; Joe beside her was once more something to shake her heart with dread and adoration and vanity—something to be a little frightened of. (Ep., 8)

It is not an unrelated instance that because the husband "takes her mood" and is influenced by her in his attitude to pose, he is seen as "no longer the dominating male."

Of equal importance in this story is the question of the woman's identity (how she is seen by others, how she sees herself, how she wants to be seen, who she is). First, the narrator does not give us her name, even though she is the visual interest of the painter and the core of the narrative episode. Yet we know her husband's name is Joe. Her insistence that Spratling draw her face is an appeal to see her individuality represented. But Spratling finds it impossible to capture her singularity—in addition to the fact that he was not really interested in her face—because "something in her face was not her face. It partook of something in time, in the race, ambiguous, enigmatic" (Ep., 9). His sketch results in a portrait not of *the* woman, but of *a* woman. In the conclusion, the narrator's remark moves to the stereotype, then to the woman in the plural:

> And then I knew what I had seen in her face. The full-face sketch had exactly the same expression as the Mona Lisa.
> Ah, women who have but one eternal age! And that is no age. (Ep., 9)

Connecting the individual figure of a particular woman to the common lot of them all, as an abstraction and a plurality, seems to be the only and nearest way of envisioning, of naming her as the depersonalized being, the ungraspable meaning.

"Woman, the nameless feminine"

Let us now turn to another aspect, keeping in mind the peculiar plurality I have just introduced. Woman is yet to be found in another narrative dimension in Faulkner: the discursive domain of male desire.[19] In "The Priest" Faulkner explores the conflict a young man has on the day before the end of his

novitiate. Quite predictably, the priest is torn between the preservation of his chastity and virginity and the satisfaction of his
male desires. Quite predictably also, the modalities of the story
proclaim that women are harmful.

The inner temptation of the priest offers the heretic whisper
that the rejection of women is an imposition. What is interesting
is that the story proposes that women exist in three different
forms: as *act,* as *discourse,* and as *thought,* each of them being
morally qualified by the priest: Woman is at her worst as the
agent of the most harmful act, of the deed itself, because she
causes man to give in to that "hunger of blood and flesh," a not
uncommon Christian and priestly belief. He discards the deed
and reflects on the suspicious origin of the discourse on women
by men: "Surely his companions could not be chaste: no one
could speak of women in that familiar way and be unknown to
them, and yet they would make good churchmen. It was as
though a man were given certain impulses and desires without
being consulted by the donor, and it remained with him to
satisfy them or not" (TP, 350). Eventually he decides that thinking about women is less sinful than talking about them, than
doing anything with them. So, in the second movement of the
narration, he embarks fully on the unpriestly transgression of
thinking about them; woman is enclosed as thought, as a text
produced in the mind. To appease his conscience, once he
decides he will "think thoughts he had long wanted to" the
priest shifts from calling the object of his desire "women" to
"girls" as a rhetorical device to repress his own appetites and to
deprive the female world of sexuality. Furthermore, he does not
allow himself the thought of a particular "girl" but only the
pluralized being is acceptable and harmless, because it comes to
be diffused into the general:

> Girls were everywhere: their thin garments shaped their stride
> along Canal street; girls going home to dinner—thinking food be-
> tween their white teeth, of their physical pleasure in mastication and
> digestion, filled him with fire—to wash dishes; girls planning to
> dress and go out to dance among sultry saxophones and drums and

colored lights, while they were young taking life like a cocktail from a silver salver; girls to sit at home reading books and dreaming of a lover on a white horse with silver trappings. (TP, 350–51)

Even men's attitudes become rigid and limited, and also transformed when the thoughts connect them with women: "At the corner was a cigar store with men buying tobacco, men through with work for the day and going home to comfortable dinners, to wives and children; or to bachelor rooms to prepare for engagements with mistresses or sweethearts—always women" (TP, 351).

"Nympholepsy" also contains the notion of woman in the discourse of male desire, as a choice between mate for copulation or for companionship. Throughout the story, desire fills a man's mind with hopes that "perhaps a girl like defunctive music, moist with heat, in blue gingham, would cross his path fatefully" (N, 331); the articulation of his thoughts is the real protagonist in the story. The male-oriented viewing position surfaces here, as the woman "turns into something alive" (when his desire turns into fear), then it is "that imminent Presence"; the thought clings to him "like importunate sirens, like women"; it is evasive, yet disappearing at his touch, a "troubling Presence." In his own imagination they have been together, yet she leaves him remembering "how like running quicksilver she had looked, how like a flipped coin she has sped from him" (N, 336). Evasive, dangerous, yet woman as thought in male desire is soon forgotten.

From a purely grammatical structure, the center of which is the plural "women" or the unit "a woman" in a reference or a definition, we can extrapolate as part of a general stylistic feature the social orientation of the organizing principles in Faulkner's discourse. As it is evident in his early fiction, Faulkner strives to define woman and the feminine in order to place her in the text-given world that is closest to his vision. Faulkner's dominant strategy of plurality consists of the incorporation of the voice of popular and collective belief into his utterance, which results in the referential movement that goes from a particular woman to the enunciation of the plural, a generalization that takes over, once again, as the voice of authority. This particular technique has been masterfully studied from another perspective as one of the characteristics of the best of Faulkner—called "narration by conjecture"—by Albert J. Guerard.[20] The critic relates ambiguity to the spectrum composed by history, legend, and myth in the author's act of narration and contextualizes all of the above in the Oxford-Jefferson community's love for storytelling. I would not like to part from such analysis, merely to expand it by exploring an aspect that has remained unstudied up to now. I will proceed with several examples to show the recurrence of the stylistic feature of the dichotomy of singular/plural naming of woman.

In "Frankie and Johnny" the girl's thoughts on her own pregnancy are expressed as follows: "Throughout the world hundreds of girls lay like this, thinking of their lovers for a while, then of their babies" (F&J, 344–45). Near the conclusion of the story, Frankie's pregnancy, quite naturally, moves her to reflect on motherhood as center for women's lives in general:

> Frankie lay thinking of all the other girls throughout the world, lying with babies in the dark. Like the center of the world, she thought; wondering how many centers the world had: whether the world was a round thing with peoples' lives like fly-specks on it, or whether each person's life was the center of a world and you couldn't see anybody's world except yours. . . .
> But it was more comforting to believe that she was the center of the world. That the world was centered in her belly. (F&J, 346)

It is quite significant that following this multiplied image of the pregnant woman, Frankie eventually becomes gradually incorporeal, ceasing an awareness of self as woman, thereby integrated in the impressionistic landscape, feeling "as impersonal as the earth itself" (F&J, 347), plural, and a woman only in the abstract as the feminine archetype of motherhood.

Faulkner's strategy of naming may be present in the conspicuous, apparently trivial statement in the middle of a dialogue or description:

> "Only now and then I would make her think that she had found herself some way to get the grub done without burning it or having it taste like throwed-away cinch-leathers. I reckon though women just ain't got time to worry much about what food tastes like." (ID, 407)

Or, in statements such as:

> "you ain't got no more chance than a female in a frat house." (TDW, 418)

Or it may be through the thoughts of a male character's mind, mediated by the narrator:

> Watching her, Benbow did not see her look once at him as she set the platter on the table and stood for a moment with that veiled look with which women make a final survey of a table. (S, 11)

Still a better example is a text by the "objective" narrator himself, in *Sanctuary*, in the episode in which Temple Drake is telling Horace and Miss Reba about the rat, the corn-cobs, and the cottonseeds:

> She went on like that, in one of those bright, chatty monologues which women can carry on when they realise that they have the center of the stage. (S, 208–9)

In these texts, Faulkner's inner speech brings forth assertions about female behavior assuming in turn a dialogue with a listener that does not include women. It is an opinion and, as such, it is an evaluation about women. It originates in the speaking subject striving to assert himself, as if saying, "I am not that way," "we are not that way." A sociohierarchy arises here, between the narrating voice expressing judgment about women and the implied listener and reader, so that women are placed in a less privileged position in this interaction. In such texts, the male writer's voice can be heard in what appears to be a categorically knowledgeable voice to the detriment of women; in them, however, the voice is dual, because it contains the speech flow of two ideologies, two points of view, that of men and that of women. The dialogic nature of Faulkner's narrative is built upon variations of the uses of voices, heterophony, on the same subject. As vehicle for the word of authority, Faulkner also uses the voices of women, with stronger effects. In "Frankie and Johnny" it is the grandmother:

> "God knows I dont want you to go the way I've had to go, but if it's in your blood and you got to do it, I'd rather see you on the street

taking them as they come, than to see you tied down to some damn penny pinching clerk. God, how hard life is on us women." (F&J, 342)

The question of determinism linked with being female is in Faulkner's early stories already a concrete design for women. The grandmother's wisdom is delivered to the reader as an irrevocable truth:

"You'll learn, like me, that men dont never help women like me for nothing; and whenever you have any dealings with 'em you got to look out for yourself, and you got to put up a good front to get 'em and to keep 'em. No man aint never yet helped a woman through pity. And another thing: getting a man aint the half of it. Any woman with sense at all can get one, its keeping him that makes the difference between me and them poor girls you see on the streets. And good or bad, there's one thing any woman will do: she'll try to take him away from you, whether she wants him herself or not." (F&J, 342–43)

Thus, remarks about women ring louder when an evaluation of a certain type of woman is pronounced by one that qualifies within the range of that definition or description, or conjectural allusion:

"And if he is just man enough to call you whore, you'll say Yes Yes and you'll crawl naked in the dirt and the mire for him to call you that." (S, 57)

In *Sanctuary* the female voice of wisdom is echoed in Miss Jenny's in a question about a specific woman, answered by her with a statement relating to any woman:

"Why hasn't she ever married again?" Benbow said.
"I ask you," Miss Jenny said. "A young woman needs a man." (S, 23)

Speaking of Narcissa, she comments:

"Some women wont want a man to marry a certain woman. But all the women will be mad if he ups and leaves her." (S, 25)

Miss Jenny is certainly apt to talk about women:

"What I want to know is, why he left. Did you find a man under the bed, Horace?" (*S*, 104)

Her comments could hardly be called innocent:

"Was that why you left Belle?" Miss Jenny said. . . . . "It took you a long time to learn that if a woman dont make a very good wife for one man, she aint likely to for another, didn't it?" (*S*, 104)

This rhetorical strategy is consistently applied not just to and by certain characters, but also by the narrator as a discoursive framing of women in the semantic bounds I have outlined. In the next example, note the shift in the parenthetical remark, from *her* to *any*, and the framing of wife and mother roles:

He hadn't expected her—any woman—to bother very much over a man she had neither married nor borne. (*S*, 115)

In these patterns of evaluations, the paradigmatic "women are" or "any woman is/does" and similar structures, the value judgment is transferred and communicated and therefore shared between speaker and addressee and between writer and reader in the reception of the text. Woman, when defined in this combinatory form of singular/plural assertion or determinate/ indeterminate reference, is restricted by the writer's knowledge on the subject. Simultaneously, the writer is bringing in the presupposed and collective agreement about "women," an implicitly assumed "truth" gathered from the extratextual world, from the sociocultural community. The plural introduces an apparent general conclusion from the world and the word of empirical reality, so that as readers we are invited to apprehend woman, or women, under those same eyes. The feature women/ woman/girls as semantic nuclea to represent the feminine provides a variation in the intonational quality of the text through the shift from a particular woman to the wider category of womankind in general. In the plural we hear the speaking subject (such as Miss Jenny) transcending the narrative boundaries of the story, reaching the common language where the female gender is evoked in its totality. From the known personal to the unknown impersonal—and, equally valid, the personal known to the impersonal unknown—women are defined and pronounced with the voice of the community and the dominant group of which the writer himself is part, comprising the point of view that orients his utterance: the male-dominated strategic consciousness.[21] The juxtaposition of singular/plural, determinate/indeterminate, does not weaken Faulkner's argument, nor is it contradictory. In this paradigm we perceive an inner dialogue where instead of a clash of perspectives lies an expression of a concrete reality uncovering the constant presence of one speaking ideology (Faulkner's) and, by implication, of the silenced ideology being defined and spoken about (women's).

Faulkner's dialogic word includes also the voice of the other (of his community, of his culture), a voice that preexists his own text. The common belief "women are" antedates the conception of his fictional world. If a character says of women "their brains are as fuzzy as the cotton we grow!" (TDW, 412), it is a gathering of statements from his social milieu (since "cotton" refers not only to the fluffiness of the female brain, but it is made of the stuff produced in the South, Faulkner's South) where woman appears not simply and only as a text that is *repeated* in a new context (each story) but also as a *repeatable* text. In assertions of the type just quoted, woman is ideologically confined to a number of categories built around an implied complicity between Faulkner's strategic consciousness and the voice of popular wisdom and cultural belief from which a given statement apparently originates. This consciousness is also the addresser, and the community is the addressee. It is in this way that the propositions contained in such texts help consolidate the values and the images about women from the male-oriented point of view.

The notion of woman, then, becomes an assimilation of interpreted beliefs, a notion leading to the equation of the positive or negative aspects of the women created by Faulkner, setting them, for example, with the interpretative cooperation of an area of the critics on his work, closer to evil (Caddy, Temple Drake) or to good (Dilsey). I would like to suggest that these polarizations of the female—whatever their nature and the extremes chosen to name her—are central to the dialogic harmony in Faulkner's discourse. I refer to the writer's inner struggle to achieve an aesthetic creation that will approximate his ever ungraspable vision; I refer to his constant interaction of voices and narrative forms that contribute to the variations in the spectrum of woman/women. For William Faulkner, the "imminent Presence" is almost within reach only when viewed as a whole, to be approached merely as the "nameless feminine." Therefore, the integral image and concept of woman in Faulkner can be best apprehended in its own dialectics of approval and disapproval of the concrete behavior and consequent cultural valorization applied to a particular woman. In this sense, woman as text is the product of the writer's own argument in polemic with the judgments imposed on women by his society, as an implicit artistic response provoked in the course of Faulkner's own questioning of the ways of the world to define women; in his aesthetic project we find an interaction between opposition (by creating a character that contradicts a common belief, such as Dilsey to disassemble a racist category that would deny her endurance) and acceptance (by creating a figure that illustrates a given assumption, such as Mrs. Gant and Mrs. Compson).

Underneath Faulkner's aesthetic questioning and the arrangement of his argument centered on women, we must also acknowledge the makings of an alternative vision implying that perhaps women are not what they are said to be; the transcendence of such a rendering reveals Faulkner's testing of his own presuppositional design for women. His dilemma, rooted in the social world of outer reality, is reproduced in his textual world: "'the church aint got no place in politics, and women aint got no place in neither one, let alone the law. Let them stay at home and they'll find plenty to do without upsetting a man's law-suit'" (S, 181). Systematically confined by individual and collective assumptions expressing a glimpse of presupposed "truth," woman is named by a male-oriented ideology that speaks to itself, and in the process the image in which she is to be seen is created. *What she is named she becomes.*

"Half the trouble in this world is caused by women, I always say. Like that girl gittin her paw all stirred up, running off like she done" (S, 181). Implicitly, the other half seems to be caused by men *because* of women. Let us remember, for instance, the question of murder and the women's responsibility in provoking it. The internal logic of women in Faulkner approximates a binary attitudinal function that positions them closer to man as either the *sexual* or the *social* being.[22] From the orientation to either of them, moral, psychological, and ethical values are derived. In the early sketches and stories women bear a significant function on the side of man as a sexual being. In this context, I would like to digress briefly on the very relevant subject of women and their bond with nature.

As a symbological microcosm, nature belongs more with the sexual rather than the social being. Both polarizations—of the social and the sexual in man—are developed in these early texts as ontological forces out of which a male and a female *ethos* originate. If nature is the substance, the inherent and immanent being that from within seems to rule every human act, in Faulkner the link between women and nature—translated as the fusion of "female flesh and female season"—alludes to a radical split of codes for male and female. Nature in the Faulknerian sense is instinct, desires, appetites, drives, while progress and honor imply mastery of those elements. The institution of marriage, for instance, a constant social arena to explore male and female ethos, unsettles centrifugally the text-given world where women are faced with crucial choices pointing, above all, to the sexual being. Ideally, woman must be in harmony between the two; if the design is not followed, by rejection or rebellion, or by sheer indifference and she refuses to consider man as the center of the dichotomy, she becomes unnatural, a "manly woman."

The Roman philosopher Julius Alexandrinus, in agreement with Aristotle, noted "I have myself seen some hens now and then who have taken the spirit of the males,"[23] referring to the phenomenon observed in dominant hens that had masculine characteristics. Those hens were also compared to women who tyrannize their husbands, or who could be without a man. The girl in "Frankie and Johnny" is named Frank at birth because her father expected a boy; she is soon described as someone who does not need a man to marry her (F&J, 347), a remark that anticipates eventual independence from any need a male companion could provide. She behaves with "no ineffectual lady-like jerking" (F&J, 339) and is more than ready to smack a boy. In "Adolescence," a story essentially about relationships among women (daughter/stepmother/grandmother), the girl's name is Juliet when she is born, and, since she proves to be untamable, she is called Jule by her stepmother and soon by everyone. This renaming corresponds to another phase, after she moves to her grandmother's (Ad., 460). At seven, Jule, Joe Bunden's daughter, was "a hoyden who cuffed her duller witted brothers impartially and cursed her parents with shocking fluency" (Ad., 460); she then grows up away from her direct family, purging herself of her "fierce sensitive pride" and, from time to time, freeing an "uncontrolled turbulence." At twelve she could climb faster and surer than a boy and was proud of her flat body, which was a replica of her boyfriend's. When she loses her friend she suffers, yet not for long, and not the feminine way: she is contented without a companion. She is not Juliet, but Jule, alone.

Mrs. Gant, who had a failed marriage, had avenged her defeat by killing her husband and his new wife; she can strike a man with a single blow, beat him many times, lift him bodily and fling him from the porch to the ground. "Well, I reckon Mrs. Gant ain't got a whole lot of use for men-folks no more" (ZG, 371). In "Idyll in the Desert" the narrator tells us that the woman also makes man irrelevant: she "was a durn sight handier with that axe than he was, and sometimes there wouldn't be a thing for [him] to do when [he] got there" (ID, 406). Correspondingly, she is dressed in a "man's flannel shirt" (ID, 407).

We can summarize the situation of those women with the following: Reverend Edmund S. Dixon, in his nineteenth-century treatise on cocks and hens—where he projects in these creatures the virtues and attributes of Victorian husbands and wives—remarks:

> Any one whose Hens have from accident been deprived of a male companion will agree with me saying that they have not done so well till the loss has been supplied. During the interregnum, matters get all wrong. There is nobody to stop their mutual bickering, and inspire an emulation to please and to be pleased. The poor deserted creatures wander about dispirited, like soldiers without a general. It belongs to their very nature to be . . . marshalled by one of the stronger sex.[24]

To please and to be pleased, to be dominated but not to dominate are the modes of acceptable behavior; furthermore, when a woman is too proficient in the practice of her femininity she is a loss to those she should honor and obey. Her social responsibility, and the moral "danger" in the texts we are studying, is that the "lost" woman sweeps away with her the man who would otherwise be dominated by the social being; thus, the potential harm of women is greater to those men who are weak. Faulkner's exploration of the female and the feminine contributes to a more comprehensive understanding of the factors that seem to rule man's life both within and without; in some cases, factors that often lead to a world which destroys him. In the background of a supposed determinism coloring women with a static and unavoidable fate, Faulkner challenges his own design in the creation of Temple Drake.

Textual Bond: From Temple Drake to Mrs. Stevens

When we read *Sanctuary* in the context of the semantic cohesion of closed spaces—in setting, theme, and discourse—we can see that Faulkner has not abandoned the paradigms of his early stories and sketches; we find, in fact, a continuity and a much more complex elaboration of patterns. For reasons of space I merely sketch the basic components. The most obvious one, disseminated throughout the novel, is the application of different aspects of expected roles for women at home, or the male-oriented critique of their confinement, such as the comment on Benbow's sister, whose idleness consists of "living a life of serene vegetation like perpetual corn or wheat *in a sheltered garden instead of a field*" (*S*, 103, my emphasis); the same is suggested for Miss Jenny and Narcissa. Above all, also, a woman defines a man's beginning: "When you marry your own wife, you start off from scratch . . . maybe scratching. When you marry somebody else's wife, you start off maybe ten years behind, from somebody else's scratch and scratching" (*S*, 16). Moreover, the micronarratives of biographical conciseness of Minnie's (202), Ruby's (59, 269), and Popeye's mother's stories (296) confirm woman's servitude to man and the eventual rejection—accompanied by moral and monetary theft—of the latter to a spouse or lover who has sacrificed herself ("slaved for him") vainly.

In terms of setting and surrounding, the contrast of two atmospheres belonging to two divergent world-orders is framed in the realm of the campus, where the university, her studies, family, friends set Temple in the spaces of the social being, and the realm of Miss Reba's house (ho'house/hen-house); the Old Frenchman Place is the transition between both, as we witness Temple toying dangerously between the social and the sexual being: she "would dash out one door and in a minute she'd come running in from the other direction"; finally, the Luxembourg Gardens are a kind of no man's land, appropriate for the spatial circumscription of someone whose morals have no place in the worlds of narrated events.

The physical descriptions of Temple, her "long legs blonde with running" and her "bold painted mouth" (28, 29) are concomitant to her transgression of a rule on campus, for which she is already on probation at the moment of her introduction to the reader, for her violation of the restrictions of her "hen-house" enclosure. Furthermore, in the Old Frenchman Place the confrontations between the social and the sexual worlds, between imminent promiscuity and institutionalized prostitution, are confronted in the speech of "Mrs." Goodwin—called "the woman"—whose warnings about the brutality of *her* world are delivered in the language of sexual codes and also define the class boundaries that separate both women. Before she reaches the Old Frenchman setting, the physical descriptions of Temple's appearance add thematic features focusing on her "skinny legs," her "belly and loins" filtered through the narrator's stress on the lusty look of one of the men, after the accident; then the visual focus changes to "her lifted thigh" (*S*, 40). This fragmentation of Temple's body becomes functionally semanticized later in the car scene with Popeye, not only through the focalization on Temple's legs, but also on her blood (*S*, 133, 134), to be fully developed in the scene of Temple's first hours at Miss Reba's, culminating in Minnie's omen that the young girl's is "the most hardest blood of all to get" (*S*, 142). Thus, Temple as a textual figure develops in a twofold way: there is evidence in the bounded features of setting and theme—mentioned above—that she is already embodying the world of the sexual being much earlier than her cognizance about such change; her situation is permeated by what must surround her according to the writer's program, since the details gathered in progression correspond with what she was meant to become; she was narratively equipped and structured with elements that reaffirm her circumscription.[25]

While Temple's social being disintegrates in Miss Reba's house, she learns that as a woman she is powerless; in one of her most difficult moments, when Popeye is in the room, it is she and not the narrator who refers to an escape that can only be carried out by no longer being a woman (*S*, 210). First through her wish to be a boy, then the certainty that she "ought to be a man," Temple reaches a conclusion that is all the more poignant when it is uttered by a woman's voice: only by being a man could she save herself, a thought that points to a narrative constant in Faulkner related to the presence of woman as an inscription of his reflections on her as a being socially determined because of her biological nature. Faulkner was indeed mystified by the paradox of determinism and the individual will. In this domain women are given the opportunity to choose, or to take a stand that will shape their lives; yet the choice is bounded. It is not by chance that twenty years after *Sanctuary* Faulkner explores in *Requiem for a Nun* Temple as a character responsible for her doom; that is, he gives voice, without the mediation of the narrator, to his creation so that she herself can analyze her own existence, the threefold bound: "the fate, the doom, the past."[26]

The program of shame and guilt for a girl who transgressed the boundaries of the social world is put to test in the two voices, of the speaking first-person singular, Mrs. Stevens—the present, and also the embodiment of the *choice*—in dialogue with the writer, about Temple Drake—talked about as "she" by Temple herself—who is the past, the one who made the choice. When Temple comments on her past life and refers to that stage of her life in the third person—she—she creates a commentary of herself as character. As Mrs. Gowan Stevens and Temple Drake, her *doubling* in order not to be the other—yet still herself—we are given the voices of the commentator and the commentary, with the nucleus of the signifying forces centered on the question of woman's choice. Faulkner's dilemma about why he would give such a program to Temple is given in the discursive strategy allowing the character to speak for herself about herself on the moral nature of the one who chose "the murderer" and on the consequences of such an act, inextricably entangled with her being a woman versus her fate. Besides the internal intertextuality between the two novels, in *Requiem for a Nun* the artistic achievement emerges from the dialogic interaction on the one hand between the two women as created figures and on the other, between the writer and his creation. Temple's choice in the past is interpreted by Mrs. Stevens exactly in the prescribed way in which the latter accuses herself, a fact that clearly attests to an eventually unresolved dilemma for the writer. If Temple was prone to evil and corruption (*RN*, 117), if she was already among the bad and the lost (*RN*, 128), one who was by nature inclined to follow "the wrong world" because "the bad was already waiting" (*RN*, 130), and she admits—as Mrs. Stevens—

she "hadn't ever reformed" (*RN*, 131), the moral burden within the text falls upon woman: concretely, in both novels it is the major restriction of a tainted past and a concealed truth and its effects upon her inner being. The real condemnation is actualized not on Nancy but on Temple; yet the semiotic burden is not merely the character's own progress, because there is another recurrent feature that bears responsibility for the symbolic function of woman in these two works, represented in *Sanctuary* by the inscription of Temple's name written in pencil on a lavatory wall (*S*, 34, 37), later mentioned also by Horace (*S*, 168): "In the lavatory he saw, scrawled on the foul, stained wall, her pencilled name." Once a woman's name is written in a public place—in the domain of the hen-house of Faulkner's discourse— she can hardly see evil or corruption and reject it, since her fate cannot be changed, *for it is written*.

To conclude, in the context of the themes of the female self, the unchanging patterns of choices and the paradoxical fate where free will is useful only to allow a given woman to follow what she was meant to choose, Faulkner also inscribes what in the first and last place woman should not, as a woman, stop wanting to choose.

Space does not allow me to go beyond the applications of the hen-house code on additional areas. I invite you to use your imagination in this semiotic game, by associating, for instance, the Faulknerian women with the roles of hens as indifferent mothers—for other hens must raise the chicks hatched from them—or the hen as symbol of motherhood; or the image of henpecked men—wife-dominated husbands; or the beauty of the cock's crest as symbol of male pride; also, the cock as symbol of virility; without forgetting the utilitarian function of the hen; and the theme of the caponized or castrated cock (Benjy, Popeye), or cockfighting for male games and hunting. In Faulkner's world, the associations are endless. Having said this, I stop my cackling not only because one must not put all of one's eggs in one basket, but because you may have other eggs to fry.

NOTES

1. "Faulkner Discusses *The Sound and the Fury*," in *Twentieth Century Interpretations of the Sound and the Fury*, ed. Michael H., Cowan (Englewood Cliff, N.J.: Prentice-Hall, 1968), 21.

2. "Jealousy" was originally published in the *Times-Picayune* (March 1, 1925), reprinted in the Winter (1954) issue of *Faulkner Studies*; "Episode" appeared first also in the *Times-Picayune* (August 16, 1925), was reprinted in December 1, 1954 in *Eigo Seinen* translated into Japanese by Ichiro Nishizaki, and reissued in *Faulkner Studies* (Winter 1954), as well as in *The New Orleans Sketches*, 104–7. Both stories appeared in book form for the first time in *Jealousy and Episode: Two Stories*, from a reprint of *Faulkner Studies* (Folcroft Library Editions, 1977), 2–6, and 7–9 respectively. All references are to this edition. The texts from all the other stories cited in this study are from Joseph Blotner, ed., *Uncollected Stories of William Faulkner* (New York: Random House, 1979). For a detailed editorial history of each of the stories, I suggest the section "Notes" in this edition, *passim*. Also, Vintage editions of *Sanctuary* and *Requiem for a Nun* are cited in the text of my paper.

3. For this distinction I follow Michail Bakhtin, *Bakhtin School Papers*, ed. Ann Shukman, *Russian Poetics in Translation* (No. 10, 1983).

4. I take this notion from Jurij Lotman, "The Composition of the Verbal Work of Art," in *The Structure of the Artistic Text*, trans. Gail Lenhoff and Ronald Vroon (Ann Arbor: University of Michigan, 1977), 209–84.

5. A *text* is a "network of different messages depending on different codes and working at different levels of signification" (Umberto Eco, *The Role of the Reader: Explorations in the Semiotics of Texts* [Bloomington: Indiana University Press, 1979], 5); on the complex question of *strategies*, the reader is referred to Josué V. Harari, ed., *Textual Strategies: Perspectives in Post-Structuralist Criticism* (Ithaca, N.Y.: Cornell University Press, 1979). See also *Bakhtin School Papers*, 145.

6. V. N. Voloshinov [M.M. Bakhtin], "Literary Stylistics," in *Bakhtin School Papers*, 107.

7. For Julia Kristeva, a "bounded text" has its "initial programming, its arbitrary ending, its dyadic figuration, its deviations and their concatenation" *Desire in Language*, ed. Leon S. Roudiez [New York: Columbia University Press, 1980], 38). I have taken this notion and developed it in quite a different way; rather, to the idea that there is no discourse without strategic consciousness, if we understand the function of discursive strategy in verbal communication as the result of all social interrelations existing among the speakers with their ideological horizons, and the concrete situation of the event in dialogue as well as in literary signification. See Tzvetan Todorov, "Bakhtin's Theory of Utterance," in *Semiotic Themes*, ed. Richard T. De George (Lawrence: University of Kansas Publications, 1981), 165–78.

8. To the already existing interpretative kaleidoscope around the image of "Caddy's muddy drawers" allow me to add yet another one concerning the genderized functionality of certain symbols in Faulkner, such as mud, filth, blood. Applied to women, they are permeated by a moral ideologeme that applies differently to men. Thus, while blood in a male context often signifies the workings of violence by the human condition, in a woman it reveals loss of virginity, or "it has a price"; a man's "muddy shoes" pass unnoticed in *Sanctuary*, as men's clothes may be dirty as a product of work.

9. See Roger Fowler, *Linguistics and the Novel* (London: Methuen, 1977), for this concept in fiction.

10. The author wishes to acknowledge her debt on the subject of hens, chicken-houses, and the like to the inspiring study by Page Smith and Charles Daniel, *The Chicken Book* (Boston: Little, Brown, & Co., 1975), from which this quotation and the relation of chicken to Antiquity have been taken, 16.

11. Calvin S. Brown, *A Glossary of Faulkner's South* (New Haven: Yale University Press, 1976), 102.

12. I am far from proposing that the patterns presented here apply to all of Faulkner's work. I am aware of the dangers of misreading and of interpretative fallacy in Faulkner scholarship rightly explained by James B. Carothers in his "The Myriad Heart: The Evolution of the Faulkner Hero," in *"A Cosmos of My Own": Faulkner and Yoknapatawpha, 1980*, ed. Doreen Fowler and Ann J. Abadie (Jackson: University Press of Mississippi, 1981), 252–83. At the risk of seeming rather restricted, this study will not refer to some specific connections with other texts, but will aim at suggesting them as ground for thought to the reader. Subsequent studies are yet to be done to demonstrate the continuities and discontinuities in Faulkner from this perspective. I would, in any case, support the notion of a dynamics in the writer's designs.

13. This short story illustrates particularly well the analysis proposed by Ilse Dusoir Lind, "Faulkner's Women," in *The Maker and the Myth*, ed. Evans Harrington and Ann J. Abadie (Jackson: University Press of Mississippi, 1978), 89–104, on the relationship between the studies of psychology centered on women as sources of their characterization by Faulkner in his first decade of writing. This is a fruitful area for the feminist critic to study Faulkner's work as a whole.

14. From the symptoms, and from the adjectives used to describe Zilphia, she would be a serious case of *neurosis*, according to the physical and biological studies of the 1930s to describe some psychological "disorders" in women. See n. 13.

15. A Danish proverb. See *The Chicken Book*, 137.

16. It is necessary here to point out that this network of themes is not related to the *the themes of the self* in the discourse of the fantastic as genre ("the transition from mind to matter" that becomes possible in the narrative event). See Tzvetan Todorov, *The Fantastic: A Structural Approach to a Literary Genre*, trans. Richard Howard (Ithaca, N.Y.: Cornell University Press, 1975), 107–23.

17. I would agree with Sally R. Page, *Faulkner's Women: Characterization and Meaning* (Deland Fla.: Everett/Edwards, 1972), 66, for instance, that "had Caddy been allowed to return home to care for Quentin and Benjy and thus to fulfill the destiny of her nature, the Compson history might have been different." On the whole, the question of doom is complex and abundant in its thematic system concerning women: death, promiscuity, inability to procreate, unwanted pregnancy, abortion, surrogate maternal love, and many other related topics, all appear consistently in Faulkner as being closely related in the dilemma of personal choice and family responsibility, which seems to be a burden to be dealt with by women rather than by men.

18. Thus their attitudes are bounded to their relationship with the "absent provider" through the themes of the female self; if refusal occurs, woman approaches Faulkner's notion of the masculine; it can also be "a lack" that prevents the polarization of male and female in these terms: the same can be said of the men who do not follow the organizational code of gender in social and sexual domains, e.g. Benjy and Joe Christmas.

19. Faulkner's most sucessful experiment in this dimension is *The Sound and the Fury*. The different ways in which women exist in Faulkner is a crucial aspect often taken for granted in Faulkner scholarship. One basic distinction concerns the discoursive mode of direct or indirect rendering; naming, description, allusion, dialogic reference by the women themselves, or mediated through the narrator's or other characters' voice (male or female). Caddy, Dilsey, Judith Sutpen, and Temple Drake, as women, belong to the same category, but none of them exists in the same way as the others in the narrative mode of textual production. In this sense, Caddy exists, in *The Sound and the Fury*, essentially in the domain of male desire; therefore, she would not actually be a character—the way her brothers are—but a defocalized figuration given coherence only through the constant variations of viewpoints. From this perspective the novel, with Caddy as central figure, is a quest for the meaning of woman that arises from the consciousness of each perceiver, a quest that proves to be impossible since not even the Appendix suffices; clearly the signifying practice that results from the interaction of

subjective representation seems to propose that Caddy exists only as memory and a cluster of past perceptions, and as a different message to each of the brothers' discourse. Caddy as bounded text illustrates that each woman is a product of interpretation; those critics who condemn Caddy for being evil are actually condemning an interpretation of evil projected on the perception of Caddy. In the novel, Caddy is, structurally speaking, a tale told by a man.

20. Albert J. Guerard, "Faulkner the Innovator," in *The Maker and the Myth*, 84. See also his *The Triumph of the Novel: Dickens, Dostoevsky, Faulkner* (New York: Oxford University Press, 1976).

21. The question of consciousness has barely been touched upon in Faulkner's work beyond the level of conscious/subconscious units of content. One exception is the perceptive study of Arthur F. Kinney, *Faulkner's Narrative Poetics: Style as Vision* (Amherst: University of Massachusetts Press, 1978), esp. 71–119. The first notion presented is the structural consciousness of the reader, who is provided meanings by the writer's narrative consciousness, "the primary function of which is to shape events for us." It is in the readers' constitutive consciousness that the perception of the structure of the work and the perceptions of the characters attain full meaning as Faulkner's narrative poetics. My notion, however, refers to the function of Faulkner's discursive strategies designed to produce dominancies (of compositional principles as well as linguistic constituents) that convey artistic effect and are recaptured and decoded by the reader in the textual cohesion produced by this interaction.

22. My proposition is quite congenial with that of Joseph Blotner who, from another perspective, presents a division of five kinds of women in Faulkner: (1) admirable; (2) virginal young women; (3) voluptuous; (4) the mature temptress, and (5) the matron. See his "Life and Art" in this volume.

23. *The Chicken Book*, 18.

24. Ibid., 225.

25. Miss Reba's remark "us poor girls . . ." (*S*, 141) is the symbolic door (frame) closed behind Temple announcing she has already crossed the threshold because "us" includes her as well.

26. Applying the binary function of the sexual/social beings introduced in the present essay, my reading of *Requiem for a Nun* agrees with Noel Polk's in his proposition that Temple rather than Nancy is the "moral" center of the story. See his excellent work *Faulkner's "Requiem for a Nun": A Critical Study* (Bloomington: Indiana University Press, 1981).

Faulkner and Women Writers

JUDITH BRYANT WITTENBERG

"That writers assimilate and then consciously or unconsciously affirm or deny the achievements of their predecessors is, of course, a central fact of literary history," say the critics Sandra Gilbert and Susan Gubar,[1] and J. Hillis Miller points out that any individual literary work "is inhabited . . . by a long chain of parasitical presences, echoes, allusions, guests, ghosts of previous texts."[2] When I first began thinking about William Faulkner's texts and his female literary predecessors and remembered that Michael Millgate's 1978 essay on Faulkner's indebtedness to male writers such as Conrad, Joyce, and Melville was entitled "Faulkner's Masters,"[3] I realized that I couldn't very well call my study "Faulkner's Mistresses." Somehow the semantic issue of what to title this essay seems to indicate the array of larger problems that present themselves during any effort to discuss the ways in which a male writer like Faulkner may have been influenced by female writers who preceded him.

Certainly there are difficulties in assessing the role of literary influences on any writer. For one thing, the aesthetic genealogy is rarely clear-cut, as I discovered in doing an earlier essay on ways in which Faulkner might have been affected by Eugene O'Neill and was forced to confront the fact that both writers' indebtedness to Joseph Conrad complicated my assessment;[4] mosts texts have multiple literary fathers and mothers. Another difficulty is created by the fact that the writer's unspoken struggle to free himself or herself from a specific ancestor may result in the transformation of the materials in question; rarely does one find such conscious acknowledgment of a predecessor as in, for example, Faulkner's allusions to T. S. Eliot in his poem "Love Song." Finally, there are special problems in the case of a writer like Faulkner, an autodidact who read widely but not in any systematic way, except perhaps for the early years when he functioned under the tutelary eye of Phil Stone. Moreover, Faulkner never kept any sort of reading journal that would provide reliable clues to those of us ferreting about for information about literary ancestry, and his correspondence rarely touched on "literary" subjects; even his public statements about literature, though seemingly candid and sincere, are often incomplete or misleading.

Additional problems present themselves when the topic is the influence on certain male writers by what Gilbert and Gubar call "foremothers." Faulkner tended almost always to cite only males when asked to name those authors who had been important to him—in one telling moment in 1947 he put a woman on a list of the most important American authors and then rephrased his comment to exclude her[5]—and Harold Bloom, in discussing the "anxiety of influence," has provided us with a model that is male, Oedipal, and seems to involve some sort of hand-to-hand (or pen-to-pen) combat. Using almost exclusively pugilistic terms, Bloom describes the "battle between strong equals, father and son as mighty opposites" and talks about poetic influence as a "filial relationship."[6] In speaking about the writing process in his discussion of Faulkner, John Irwin uses a metaphor that, while not specifically on the subject of influence, seems relevant to the discussion here, for he discusses the "phallic generative power of the creative imagination" and goes on to describe writing in terms that evoke rape, "the use of the phallic pen on the 'pure space' of the virgin page."[7] Attempting to position the woman writer in this overwhelmingly phallocentric lineage, Gilbert and Gubar offer a countermodel that presents its own problems, for they see her as a sort of "eunuch," outside the male line, functioning on the margin, experiencing her gender as a "painful obstacle," and searching desperately for "foremothers" to give her a sense of empowerment.[8] Their alternative lineage is almost exclusively female-female, or, in certain "dangerous" cases, male-female.

Few critics or theorists seem to have addressed the complex relationship of a male author to his literary "mothers." In part this may be because men are reluctant to acknowledge such a relationship; certainly Faulkner's public statements evince reluctance in that direction. The seeds of this attitude, according to Nancy Chodorow, lie in the cultural formation of gender identity, during which the male learns to define masculinity as that which is not-feminine and to reject the female within.[9] This process becomes particularly complicated for the male writer because, as Anne Taylor has pointed out, both his vocation and his routine are in some sense "womanly," for the "passivity and retirement" necessitated by artistic activity make his daily life "more like that of a woman in the world than like a man."[10] In a talk here a few years back, Ellen Douglas suggested that Faulkner himself implied that some kinds of authorship were "female" activities with his portrait of Harry Wilbourne in *The Wild Palms;* when Wilbourne writes true confession stories, says Douglas, he is doing "woman's work," which he further feminizes by, "as narrator, transform[ing] himself into a woman, and as writer even us[ing] a female penname."[11] Whatever their ambivalences about acknowledging indebtedness to writers of the female persuasion, that male writers incurred those debts is hardly in question; one needs only to remember F. Scott Fitzgerald throwing himself reverently at Edith Wharton's feet or repeatedly pirating his wife Zelda's ideas.

Assessing influence in general and influence on a male by a woman is thorny enough, but Faulkner's case is also compounded by contextual issues, specifically the fact that he was a Southerner and that he came to artistic maturity during the Depression. Bertram Wyatt-Brown, writing about the powerfully masculine concepts inherent in the idea of "honor" that pervaded the culture of the Old South, points out that males were pressured to be "brave and manly" in all their activities and to choose a career that was validated by the patriarchy, such as law, medicine, planting, banking, or the military; authorship is nowhere to be found on this list.[12] The family figure whom Faulkner always cited as providing his earliest literary inspiration was of course his great-grandfather the Old Colonel, but the first William Falkner was as much a man of action as he was a writer. Judith Sensibar has noted that the Old Colonel was a war hero and successful businessman who only "played" at writing "while aggressively pursuing his real work, amassing a modest fortune."[13] A sense of writing as somehow an "unmanly" occupation for a Southerner seems to have been pervasive; in Ellen Glasgow's 1932 novel a character who wants to become a poet is regarded by his family as "deficient in manliness,"[14] and along with writing, William Alexander Percy struggled to maintain some semblance of a simultaneous "masculine" vocation such as law or public service.[15] Louis Rubin has suggested that Faulkner's fiction reveals an equation of "the artistic sensibility with weakness, lack of physical courage, and sexual awkwardness and virginity."[16] Certainly Faulkner's praise of Keats's poetry as evincing "entrails: masculinity" beneath its "spiritual beauty"[17] implies that he felt some sort of need to find something strongly male in that most lyrical and sensual of poets, and Michael Grimwood has addressed in some detail the problems created by Faulkner's discovering his artistic vocation in a sexually polarized Southern context.[18]

While Faulkner's immersion in the early twentieth-century culture of the South was probably responsible for his ambiguous responses to authorship, causing him at one level to overaffirm its masculine nature and at another to reveal uncertainty about this, the temper of the period during which he began to publish his novels may have affected some of his comments about women who wrote. One critic has assessed what he deems "the cultural and intellectual misogyny" of the Depression era; this resulted in a "literary stance" on the part of many writers and critics that was "self-consciously masculine and antifeminine."[19] Although labeling the literary zeitgeist of an era as misogynistic is hazardous, certainly the openly condescending nature of many of

Faulkner's comments about women writers suggests that something was affecting, or infecting, his attitudes. Unlike Hawthorne, he may not have denounced them as "damned scribbling women," but he managed to follow warm praise for Anita Loos's 1925 novel with the dismissive statement, "I am still rather Victorian in my prejudices regarding the intelligence of women, despite Elinor Wylie and Willa Cather and all the balance of them."[20] One could charitably attribute this comment to Faulkner's relative youth, but a decade and a half later he was revealing comparable attitudes.

In 1940 he told an interviewer who asked what he thought about women novelists that "Evelyn Scott is pretty good, for a woman,"[21] and I understand that after reading a short story by Eudora Welty, Faulkner wrote her a letter in which his certainty about her gender, coupled with an assumption that she was also black, led him to make some rather patronizing statements. Considering that Evelyn Scott was one of the first people to both understand and passionately admire *The Sound and the Fury* and that Eudora Welty became one of the most prominent perpetuators of the "Faulkner tradition," his comments seem ungrateful at the very least. But Faulkner's reluctance to acknowledge the merit of female writers, though not consistent— in a conference at the University of Virginia in 1957 he readily named women who had been important to him, including the Brontës, Glasgow, and Cather[22]—was certainly in evidence at several points over the years. Even when a young woman writer at a crucial point in her own apprenticeship turned to him for advice about what to read, Faulkner failed to suggest any authors of her own sex; Joan Williams said recently, "Bill never mentioned any women writers to me—and I rue that he did not guide me to people who might have been helpful."[23]

Whatever the manifold problems in assessing ways Faulkner was influenced by women writers, the topic is a fruitful one, meriting both general discussion and some consideration of specific parallels, because Faulkner listed several of them among important literary ancestors in his public statements and owned and presumably read works by several others. His library, cata-logued at the time of his death, included, for example, many of the nineteenth-century masterpieces written by women, includ-ing *Sense and Sensibility, Persuasion, Jane Eyre, Wuthering Heights, Mill on the Floss,* and *Silas Marner.*[24] It is provocative to think of Faulkner's depiction of powerful brother-sister bonds, with their component of longing for lost childhood innocence and unity, as having been inspired by the portrait of the rela-tionship between Maggie and Tom Tulliver in *Mill on the Floss,* or to consider Faulkner's male characters who are obsessed with women now dead and eternally unavailable, such as the grief-stricken and passionate Wilbourne at the end of *The Wild Palms,* as partly derived from Emily Brontë's Heathcliff and his titanic mourning for his lost Catherine. Or it is intriguing to imagine the potential effects of a lesser English novel, Margaret Ken-nedy's *The Constant Nymph,* for which Faulkner expressed ad-miration about a year after its 1924 publication, perhaps because it is, says Anita Brookner, a romance for men rather than women and one told mostly from a male point of view.[25] One of the female characters, notable for her beauty, her "placid animal poise," and her almost total indolence, might well have contrib-uted to Faulkner's later depiction of earthy women like Eula Varner, and the qualities of the central male artist figure, with his defensive cynicism, his concern with the "secret of man's eternal pain," and his sense of undergoing a private Calvary, could have inspired the sculptor Gordon of *Mosquitoes,* even as the way Kennedy shows the male point of view as in some sense "creating" the women it perceives might lie behind Faulkner's portrayal of this process in several of his major novels.[26]

One could hypothesize endlessly about the parallels between all fiction and poetry written in English by women and Faulkner's own work, attempting to differentiate between those "who influenced him in the broadest and deepest sense" and those who taught him the "tricks of the trade,"[27] but as Henry James said in another context, the circle has to stop somewhere. Because Faulkner was so profoundly regional and, in crucial

ways, so profoundly American a writer, I have chosen to confine
my explorations and speculations to a selective group of fiction
written by American women during the approximate period
1900–1935 and to consider its potential influence on Faulkner's
novels. I have no illusion that I have covered every possible work
from this grouping that Faulkner might have read, and I am well
aware that I will not be considering the issues raised by his
awareness of later writers such as Eudora Welty or Elizabeth
Spencer. Nor will I be dealing with what someone called the
necessity of including Henry James in any list of women writers,
even though Faulkner's expressed distaste for James seems
somehow to substantiate the claim that he belongs in that group.
My discussion will be limited to the work of American women of
whom Faulkner was likely aware in the years he was coming to
artistic maturity, and it is intended to be suggestive rather than
inclusive. All but one of these writers are now considered minor
and most of them have fallen into total obscurity, out of print and
unread. This may be as much the consequence of their work's
failure to hold up over a half-century or more as it is an indication
of the difficulties women have finding their proper niches in
literary history.

Four women who seem to have in common the fact that they
failed to influence Faulkner in any profound way, although his
exposure to their work has been documented, are Zona Gale,
Elinor Wylie, Djuna Barnes, and Anita Loos. In 1922 Phil Stone
apparently placed a book order for Zona Gale's *Miss Lulu Bett*,
though whether it was the novel or its dramatization that won a
Pulitzer Prize in 1920 is not recorded,[28] and it is difficult to tell
whether Faulkner ever read it, for this story of a spinster who
rebels against her constricted existence as an exploited dependent in a middle-class family seems to have few corollaries in
Faulkner's fiction, save in the broadest possible outlines. Phil
Stone also ordered two works by the poet and novelist Elinor
Wylie, *Nets to Catch the Wind* in 1922 and *The Orphan Angel* in
1927;[29] Faulkner himself owned two volumes of her poetry published in the 1940s and included her in his backhanded tribute of

1926. Wylie's novel *The Orphan Angel* imagines what would have happened if the poet Shelley were rescued from drowning and brought to America, there to confront a series of frontier adventures in the company of a rustic friend; it offers little to the influence-hunter save for the fact that its Huck-Finn-picaresque quality reappears in Faulkner's last novel, as does the idealism about women and sense of cultural dislocation that characterize both its protagonist and Faulkner's Lucius Priest.

A different sort of problem is created by Faulkner's declared indebtedness to the expatriate poet and novelist Djuna Barnes, whose poetry Faulkner supposedly quotes in passages in both *Intruder in the Dust* and *The Town* and whom he mentions in a conference at the University of Virginia.[30] Yet the work of hers published in book form before 1957 includes almost no poetry and nothing I ran across echoes the passages in question; perhaps Faulkner read work of hers published in periodicals, particularly when he was in Paris, where she was a figure of some significance. *Nightwood* is Barnes's most highly regarded novel, but that was not published until 1936 and seems to show few parallels with Faulkner's work, save for techniques that he had been using since the late 1920s; her 1923 collection, entitled simply *A Book*, contains a few suggestive elements, such as the sketch "A Night Among the Horses," whose protagonist, watching horses thunder by and thinking how he would like to make his mark, bears a few similarities to the figure in Faulkner's "Carcassonne," or the postmenopausal spinster of "Indian Summer" who suddenly discovers sensuality, like Joanna Burden; but we do not know whether Faulkner ever saw *A Book*, so these are merely conjectures.

A woman whose life and work were very different from those of Barnes but one whose connection to Faulkner has been more accurately documented is Anita Loos. Faulkner met her in New Orleans in 1925 when she was visiting the Sherwood Andersons and subsequently attempted to see her during his trip to Italy that year; he also wrote her a warmly congratulatory note in early 1926 after reading *Gentlemen Prefer Blondes*, remarking that he was "envious" of her creation of Lorelei's sidekick Dorothy and saying "I wish I had thought of Dorothy first."[31] It is intriguing that Faulkner emphasizes a secondary figure in Loos's fine satiric comedy, for in the depiction of the main character, Lorelei, and in her relationship with Dorothy one sees more that might have influenced him. The work purports to be Lorelei's diary, and both its method, the presentation of a self-deluding first-person narrator, and its protagonist, a grasping, materialistic, un-scrupulous individual, remind one of Jason Compson's interior monologue in the third section of *The Sound and the Fury*. At the same time, Lorelei's dialogues with Dorothy, who provides, with her slangy honesty and principled behavior, a striking contrast to the narrator's false gentility, are vaguely similar to the contrapuntal exchanges one sees in Faulknerian passages such as section 4 of "The Bear." *Gentlemen Prefer Blondes* is full of memorable comic moments, and though it lacks the underlying seriousness that marks Faulknerian comedy, it obviously made a strong impression on him, for more than thirty years later he was telling students that he tended to stop writing "while I'm still looking good, as *Gentlemen Prefer Blondes* put it,"[32] and one can see what may be its traces in a few of Faulkner's major novels.

Two writers with specifically regional roots who may have affected Faulkner rather more significantly than those already mentioned are Elizabeth Madox Roberts and Evelyn Scott. Roberts has already been cited on several occasions as meriting consideration as an important predecessor of Faulkner—Robert Penn Warren says that she is like him in "recogniz[ing] the dignity of the lowliest creature," and Michael Millgate and William Slavick, among others, have cited parallels in their discussions of one or the other[33]—and Faulkner is known to have owned a copy of the first edition of her 1926 novel, *The Time of Man*.[34] Roberts's conception of her fiction as to some degree encompassing the history of a specific region, the Salt River area of her native Kentucky, which she renames the Pigeon River, her depiction of poor whites, her interest in revealing the inner lives of her protagonists, and even some of the names she uses, such as Gowan, Burden, and Horace—all of these have their subsequent parallels in Faulkner's Yoknapatawpha novels. This is not to suggest that Roberts is solely responsible for the inception of Faulkner's region-based vision—Thomas Hardy and Willa Cather are other important precursors in this respect—but she provided a useful American Southern agrarian example.

The Roberts novel that Faulkner owned was a Book-of-the-Month-Club selection and received favorable critical comment when it appeared in 1926; one of those who praised it at the time was Sherwood Anderson, who was also closely involved with Faulkner's own apprentice fiction. Anderson called it a "wonderful performance," with prose he compared to "things growing suddenly on rich land,"[35] and he may well have been responsible for Faulkner's acquisition of the work. *The Time of Man* is the story of Ellen Chesser, daughter of a tenant farmer, and chronicles her progress through life; although it is distinctly un-Faulknerian in remaining exclusively focused on a female character from whose point of view the tale unravels and in having an episodic plot and a simple chronological structure, one can see in it things to which the young Mississippi writer might have been drawn. Roberts stresses the inner life of her character, detailing her thoughts and emotions, and effectively depicts a whole array of poor whites who inhabit her world, as later would Faulkner; moreover, her scenes dramatizing the pulse of daily agrarian life anticipate Bayard Sartoris's brief rural idyll in *Flags in the Dust*. The Yoknapatawpha novel with the most similarities to *The Time of Man* is *Light in August*, which Faulkner said was inspired by his vision of a woman, "a young girl with nothing," and by his "admiration for . . . the courage and determination of women."[36] Both Ellen Chesser and Lena Grove are depicted early in their novels as poor and lonely women painfully coming to maturity, and both have suitors who leave them with a promise to return and marry them, which they fail to keep, impelling the young women to go after the reluctant bridegrooms. Later they become mothers, in the process revealing a good deal of tenacity and a sense of being connected with the fertile world around them. Faulkner might have borrowed from *The Time of Man* not only the situation of his central protagonist but also a crucial structural device, for the novel opens and closes with Ellen's family on the road, commenting on the fact that they are going a "far piece."[37]

Roberts's next novel, *My Heart and My Flesh*, was published in late 1927, just about the time Faulkner was completing the manuscript of *Flags in the Dust*. There are numerous parallels between those two works, ranging from their depiction of several generations of a family confronting a certain sense of decline, their portraits of a well-meaning but ineffectual male, their rather startling suggestions of an incestuous relationship, and their crucial scenes in which pivotal figures confront artifacts from the past in an agonized way. Both even include early scenes of a buggy ride to the ancestral house and of a ladies' party to establish the pulse of local life and also the emblematic description of choking foliage to suggest ways in which the protagonists' lives are stunted. Despite these many parallels, they can be attributed only to coincidence, for Faulkner made few major additions to *Flags in the Dust* after completing it in the fall of 1927; nevertheless they are of interest in showing that the writers' conceptions had some fundamental likenesses. We have no idea whether Faulkner saw Roberts's 1930 novel about eighteenth-century Kentucky pioneers, *The Great Meadow*, but in it Roberts uses two devices that also appear in Faulkner's subsequent fiction, the letters discussing the family patrimony that, like comparable documents in *My Heart and My Flesh*, anticipate the McCaslin ledgers in part 4 of "The Bear," and the central figure often discussed with awe but not seen until late in the novel, with effects like those of Faulkner's similar depiction of Sutpen in *Absalom, Absalom!*, though both writers might well have been indebted to Fitzgerald's 1925 treatment of Jay Gatsby.

While the similarities between Elizabeth Madox Roberts's major fiction and some of Faulkner's are provocative, his exposure to her work has been documented only in a limited way; the reverse case seems to be true of Evelyn Scott, of whom

Faulkner was patently aware but who seems not to have influenced him save in the vaguest possible general sense. Faulkner referred to Scott's fiction as "pretty good, for a woman" and she wrote a laudatory essay on *The Sound and the Fury* published as a pamphlet sent to critics and book dealers along with the novel; she was also a Southerner who revolted against the prevailing literary traditions of the region and published a series of novels that were either ambitious or experimental or both. Some of them appeared before Faulkner's major work and others were more or less contemporaneous with it; comparison of the two corpuses reveals some suggestive parallels. Nevertheless, it is equally likely that Faulkner simply found Scott valuable in an exemplary way, both as a Southerner capable of writing fiction that revealed her regional roots but one who also found many of her most influential antecedents in European literature, and as an American contemporary with an ambitious sense of possibilities. Faulkner may have "gone to school" to Scott for some of the specific things that appear in his own fiction, but, as in the case of Roberts, an awareness of the larger dimensions of her work may be the most important thing he derived from her.

Virtually all of the general statements made by Scott about *The Sound and the Fury* in what began as a letter written after she read the galleys and later expanded into an essay were critically acute—she called it, for example, a "tragedy" with "all the spacious proportions of Greek art" that constituted "the reassertion of humanity in defeat"[38]—and some of her specific comments might well have influenced Faulkner when he came to write his 1946 Appendix to the novel; for example, she describes Jason as "a completely rational being," and Faulkner later called him "logical rational contained."[39] Her comment, however, about Faulkner's "pessimism as to fact, and his acceptance of all the morally inimical possibilities of human nature" and about his novel's "unique" methods of presentation[40] could also apply to her own work, which is mostly bleak and intensely serious and occasionally unusual in its method. Her first three novels, published between 1921 and 1925, treat several members of the Farley family over the years and have as a central theme the failure of love and marriage in a middle-class environment. They are almost unrelentingly bitter, like Faulkner's early work, and evince details that appear in his fiction. One of the novels is entitled *Narcissus,* and the characters in all three constantly look at themselves in mirrors or reflections, while another is called *The Narrow House* in reference to the stifling aura of convention that surrounds some of the characters and the sexual pathology that entraps others; Faulkner's early work, too, depicts a number of narcissistic figures and others who are constricted by their conscious obeisance to custom or their unconscious confinement by neuroses. Narcissus and the confining house were evocative symbols for Faulkner as well as for Scott, and he may well have first encountered them in her trilogy.

Among the work Scott published after her essay on Faulkner were three large and ambitious novels—*The Wave, A Calendar of Sin,* and *Eva Gay.* None of them seems to have particularly influenced Faulkner except in their broad outlines and a few specific details, but all revealed an intelligent author of inclusive vision making efforts to dramatize American political and social history and to vary her fictional method. *The Wave,* published in 1929, was her first popular work, a long novel whose central focus is the Civil War and which includes an enormous array of characters and episodes, both historically "real" and fictional; it is clearly her effort to recast *War and Peace,* for she alternates between domestic and battlefield settings, but her work seems more daring than Tolstoy's in one respect, because nearly all of the characters appear only in a single scene. Her incursions into the consciousness of a wide array of individuals were conceivably responsible for Faulkner's similar, but more narrowly focused, experiment in *As I Lay Dying;* certainly one of the characters, writing from the insane asylum where he is undergoing a personal "Calvary,"[41] might be seen as a forerunner of Darl Bundren. *A Calendar of Sin,* published in 1931, was in some ways even more ambitious than *The Wave,* a treatment of several families over many years that filled almost 1,400 pages, but it is

Faulknerian only in its treatment of the haunting effect of the past upon the present. Scott's 1933 novel, *Eva Gay*, the portrait of a strong, rebellious woman who has an unusual and complicated relationship with two men, may be a crucial predecessor of the "Wild Palms" portion of Faulkner's 1939 novel. Eva is rather like Charlotte Rittenmeyer, determined, idealistic about love, and unwilling to accept the limited range of possibilities available to women of the middle class. She is also like Charlotte in leaving a first man for a second but maintaining her ties with him in times of crisis; their relationship is only slightly more bizarre than that between Charlotte, Harry, and Rittenmeyer. Scott tells the story from each person's point of view and in so doing provides a model of interleaved narratives that might possibly have contributed to Faulkner's decision to use a contrapuntal structure in *The Wild Palms*.

If Elizabeth Madox Roberts and Evelyn Scott were significant in offering Faulkner differing examples of how to present regional materials and how to continue breaking new ground technically, Ellen Glasgow was valuable in providing Faulkner with a thoroughly Southern model that was both sectional and to some degree innovative. Called by one of her biographers, in a judgment few would dispute, the "first realist in Southern letters,"[42] Ellen Glasgow was significant for her declaration of artistic independence from the moonlight and magnolia tradition and her call for "blood and irony" to replace it. We know that Faulkner was aware of Glasgow, for he cited her in his 1957 list of women writers whom he esteemed, and he actually met her years before, at the Southern Writers Conference of 1931.

That meeting bears recounting, not only because it amusingly confronted the aging and genteel grande dame from Old Virginia with the young and raw northern Mississippian who was both notorious from the recent publication of *Sanctuary* and visibly drunk during much of the conference, but also because it showed that they had an important kinship that transcended some of the striking divergences. Glasgow had been largely responsible for arranging the gathering at Charlottesville, which brought together a good-sized group of Southern writers in what proved to be a relatively rare instance of collegiality. Although Faulkner declared himself reluctant to go to Charlottesville, comparing himself in one of his more charming such metaphors to a hound dog hiding under a wagon come into town from the country—"that hound never gets very far from that wagon. He might be cajoled or scared out for a short distance, but first thing you know he has scuttled back under the wagon; maybe he growls at you a little"[43]—and although once there he was, according to Sherwood Anderson, constantly appearing, getting drunk immediately, and then disappearing, when Ellen Glasgow gave the one formal speech of the conference, Faulkner earnestly murmured agreement.[44] That he made gestures of approval is not surprising, for Glasgow's speech was about the difference between historical and fictional truth, a theme which Faulkner later discussed in similar terms in some of his public statements. Nonetheless, by the end of the conference, Faulkner was completely disaffected, perhaps partly because of guilt about some of his outrageous behavior, which included getting sick in the foyer of the Farmington Country Club, and he declared that "he didn't give a damn about Ellen Glasgow or any of [the other writers there]."[45] Glasgow's subsequent comments about Faulkner were even more hostile; she referred to him as a member of the "school of Raw-Head-and-Bloody-Bones" and expressed disapproval of his "sodden futilitarianism" and "corn-cob cavaliers."[46] Glasgow's condemnation, like Faulkner's, probably had an unacknowledged source, for by 1931 she was well aware that she was no longer the literary force she perhaps had been in the recent past, while Faulkner was one of the important new talents changing American literature.

Personal jealousies and petty criticisms notwithstanding, the connections between the work of Ellen Glasgow and William Faulkner merit serious consideration, for she was among his most influential female predecessors in American fiction, conceivably offering him inspiration at a number of levels. Like Roberts, Glasgow showed him how to transmute a specific region into a fictional cosmos and how to treat simple people fairly and unsentimentally; at the same time, the uncompromising realism of her best work, her irony, and her indictment of the "evasive idealism" that she saw as imprisoning Southerners in a mythic past all provided Faulkner with positive antecedents for his own efforts in the same direction.

Ellen Glasgow published nearly two score novels between the year Faulkner was born and 1941, and many of them sold well while receiving favorable comments from reviewers. It is unclear which of them Faulkner read, because there is no record of his having owned or commented on specific novels. Still, because a number of them were dominated by male protagonists and some of those centered on women were sufficiently tough-minded to perhaps appeal to a male reader, and because her depiction of the South was innovative, conjectures about influence seem reasonable. One of Glasgow's biographers suggests that Faulkner's 1938 story, "An Odor of Verbena," constitutes a "remarkable parallel" to her early novel, *The Deliverance*, both being about men pressured by the felt need to revenge the family honor that they manage to transcend in a moment of ethical reconsideration.[47] The likeness certainly exists, but something the biographer doesn't mention that is related to some fundamental discrepancies apparent to anyone comparing women writers to Faulkner is the fact that in Glasgow's novel a woman serves as the man's means to redemption, while in Faulkner's story she is the reverse, a destructive temptress.

One finds potential antecedents to elements of Faulkner's work in many of Glasgow's novels. A disturbing figure like Cyrus Treadwell of *Virginia,* a tycoon contemptuous of women who has a black mistress and mulatto son whom he refuses to recognize, seems in many ways to be a forerunner of Faulkner's Sutpen. In fact, Glasgow's readiness to boldly confront the issue of miscegenation involving upper middle class Southerners and their black servants in works such as *Virginia, Barren Ground,* and *The Sheltered Life* could have encouraged Faulkner when he prepared to consider the topic in novels like *Absalom, Absalom!*

286 JUDITH BRYANT WITTENBERG

and *Go Down, Moses*. Other aspects of Glasgow's fiction that may have influenced Faulkner include a passage in *The Builders* about good women—"all the bad women on earth could never do as much harm as some good ones—the sort of good ones that destroy everything human and natural that comes near them"[48]—that has its parallel in the lines in *Light in August* about the "good women" who "smell out sin" and about the ways in which "men have suffered from good women"[49]—and embodies the sort of thinking that lay behind Faulkner's portrayal of the "good" but heartless townswomen of *Sanctuary*; Glasgow's treatment of a character's struggle against "the tyranny of the past" and determination not only to endure but to prevail in one of her central works, *Barren Ground*;[50] and her use of the symbolic "bad smell" of the chemical plant in *The Sheltered Life* to represent all transience and decay, an idea Faulkner would reuse effectively in *The Wild Palms*.

The work generally considered Glasgow's finest, *The Sheltered Life*, published in 1932, contains several elements besides the treatment of miscegenation and the device of the bad smell that may have either induced or reinforced Faulkner's interest in comparable issues. It is unfortunate that we do not know whether he saw it; their disastrous encounter the year before might well have motivated him to avoid it entirely. Still, its use of two points of view, that of the old general and the young Jenny Blair, with their differing attitude toward love, offers an intriguing antecedent to *The Wild Palms*. And one finds vestiges of the portrait of the general himself, perhaps the most effective of Glasgow's characterizations, in Faulkner's subsequent fiction. When the general is "oppressed by the burden of tragic remembrance," as Glasgow described it in her preface to the novel, or laments the fact that "the heroic mould had been broken,"[51] he sounds like Mr. Compson of *Absalom, Absalom!*; when he remembers the traumatic masculine ritual of blooding by his grandfather or confronts thoughts of "The Deep Past" he is similar to Ike McCaslin of *Go Down, Moses*.

One thing that becomes strikingly apparent when one thinks

about Glasgow's work in relation to that of Faulkner—and this is true of the other women writers as well—is how little she seems to have taught him about women. Some aspects of her technique, attitudes about the South, and crucial themes and symbols all reappear in Faulkner's fiction, but few of the young women with will "of iron," to use Glasgow's recurrent phrase, do. Except for figures such as Drusilla Sartoris of *The Unvanquished* or Linda Snopes Kohl of *The Mansion,* one is hard pressed to find Faulknerian parallels to the feisty Molly Merryweather of *The Miller of Old Church,* the independent Susan Treadwell of *Virginia,* or the forceful Dorinda Oakley of *Barren Ground.* The same might be said about what Faulkner learned, and failed to learn, from Willa Cather, the American woman writer who probably influenced him the most and who perhaps deserves to be included in that hitherto all-male pantheon that Michael Millgate calls "Faulkner's Masters."

Cather is the woman writer Faulkner mentions most frequently and most respectfully, and, of the writers being discussed here, she is the one most highly regarded critically, both at the time Faulkner was beginning to write and today. One of the first American novelists to experiment with narrative structure, Cather is also notable for her evocative treatment of the landscapes of Nebraska and New Mexico and for her limpid prose style. It is little surprising that Faulkner repeatedly paid tribute to her in his letters and public statements over the years, starting with the 1926 declaration that she was an exception to his personal observation that women were deficient in the realm of intelligence.[52] In the fall of 1931 he probably met Cather in a situation only slightly less auspicious than his encounter with Ellen Glasgow, with him again playing the role of drunken visitant to a relatively restrained gathering. After a day of heavy drinking with Dashiell Hammett, Faulkner and the mystery writer invited themselves to a formal dinner at Alfred Knopf's home, where Cather was one of the honored guests. They arrived in an intoxicated state, and both soon collapsed on the floor and had to be helped out.[53] We don't kinow whether Cather and

Faulkner talked together that evening, but it is unlikely in any event that conversation would have been productive.

Whatever the circumstances of their meeting, Faulkner had a high opinion of Cather's work and on several occasions he named her to his list of established contemporaries. In 1947 he called her one of the five most important Americans writing at the time, though a few minutes later he deleted her from the group, perhaps because, as one onlooker suggested, he had meant to say "Caldwell" instead of "Cather."[54] About three years later, in a letter to Saxe Commins about current writers, Faulkner cited Cather as one of "the real ones before us who have not yet got the recog. they deserve: Anderson, and the clumsy giant Dreiser for instance, and Cather."[55] At Nagano, asked to choose the five greatest American novelists up to the end of the nineteenth century, in an answer that showed an amusing disregard for chronology (Cather published her first novel in 1912), Faulkner listed, among "the ones that I was impressed with and that probably influenced me to an extent that I still like to read . . . one woman, Willa Cather—I think she is known in Japan."[56] Cather was also on the brief 1957 list of women writers he admitted having a high esteem for.[57] In all of these comments, despite a tendency to add her name as an afterthought or to unnecessarily stress her gender, Faulkner showed a consistent admiration for her artistry.

It is difficult to ascertain which works of Cather's Faulkner actually read, since at the time of his death he owned only one volume of hers, the collection of stories published posthumously in 1948 and entitled *The Old Beauty and Others*. In 1922, however, Phil Stone ordered a copy of *My Antonia* which he may well have passed on to Faulkner.[58] I think it is also safe to assume that Faulkner saw a number of Cather's major novels, since his repeated and laudatory invocation of her suggests that he was relatively familiar with the canon. Moreover, there is much in Cather's fiction, particularly in that published before Faulkner began his first novel, which seems likely to have influenced him in both profound and specific ways.

What Faulkner might have gotten from Cather's first important novel, the 1913 *O Pioneers!*—if indeed he read it—is unclear, because it is dominated by a strong female character, the
capable and confident Alexandra Bergson, and reveals none of
the interest in experimenting with narrative structure that would
mark other of Cather's finest fiction. Still, some of the minor
elements of *O Pioneers!* are telling, such as a comment about a
character "do[ing] the best she can,"[59] the problems created by
pigs on the rampage on a neighbor's property, and a paranoid
and violent character who seems a forerunner of Mink Snopes.
And many of the novel's conceptual aspects—for example, the
use of a woman who is the focal sibling in a family that includes
three brothers, to one of whom she serves as a sort of mother
figure, like Caddy Compson, and who has a hard-headed and
Sutpenesque grand design, albeit a benign one, or the theme of
inevitable change, which is alternately lamented and praised, or
the techniques of juxtaposing death and regeneration and of
depicting the eruption of violence into daily rural life—could
have had an impact on Faulkner, if he was familiar with the work.

In Cather's 1918 novel, *My Antonia*, the work many regard as
her finest, she ignores the advice of her mentor, Sarah Orne
Jewett, to avoid using the male point of view; in so doing, she
may have betrayed the implicit feminism of her previous two
works, but she created a fiction that was artistically more complex and also more likely to appeal to the young Faulkner. So
many elements of this effective and powerful novel seem potentially to have influenced Faulkner that it is possible to mention
only a few of them. Perhaps the most significant aspect of *My
Antonia* in this respect is its narrative method, the relatively
complex presentation of its material that makes it a work as much
about the relation of teller to tale and about the process of
discovering and communicating meaning as about one woman
struggling to survive on the frontier. Antonia Shimerda is a
central figure of many facets, like Faulkner's Caddy Compson,
Addie Bundren, or Thomas Sutpen, whom her observers are
trying to "possess" in some ineffable way, even as they attempt to

know and understand her. Antonia is not as elusive or as Protean as Faulkner's comparable characters, but in evolving from lively child to quasi-masculine young farm worker to sexually active and potentially tragic woman, she invokes varying responses in those who watch her progress. The observer most focused on Antonia is also the central narrator—though Cather uses an additional frame narrator and, in the body of the story, a third person who relates a crucial portion of the tale—and in significant ways it is also *his* story, as in a Faulkner novel. In a revealing moment, Jim Burden admits changing the title of his work from *Antonia* to *My Antonia,* and one could imagine Faulkner calling his 1936 novel *My Sutpen.* Moreover, when Jim says, "I can see them now,"[60] or makes his mid-life trips to Nebraska and thus into the past in quest of more information about Antonia, he anticipates the various narrators of *Absalom, Absalom!;* one also realizes by the end of Cather's novel how much Jim's own complex psychology has affected his recounting of the story, causing him, for example, to view the nubile women with a mixture of fascination and distaste. This projective aspect of narration is one Faulkner would exploit to its fullest potential in his 1936 masterpiece.

Faulkner was often accused in the early years, particularly after the publication of *Sanctuary,* of making excessive use of violence in his fiction, but if Cather taught him something about narrative method in *My Antonia,* she may also have shown him how to incorporate large quantities of brutality and grotesquerie. From the killing of the snake, the suicide of Mr. Shimerda, and the tale of the bride thrown to her death at the jaws of ferocious wolves in the early portions of the novel to the description of the man killed horribly in the thrasher, the attempted rape of Jim, disguised as Antonia, and the murder-suicide committed by Wick Cutter, Cather shows in disturbing ways how such events are part of life on the prairie, even among the so-called respectable townspeople. In addition, Cather created some memorable minor characters whom Faulkner could have had in mind as he came to write his own fiction, including an indomitable grandmother, "a strong woman, of unusual endurance,"[61] a rigidly Protestant grandfather, an indolent and sensual young woman named Lena, and an effete intellectual.

Cather's next three novels offer somewhat less fertile ground for the harvesting of Faulknerian antecedents, but they evince qualities worthy of brief mention. *One of Ours*, her 1922 Pulitzer Prize-winning novel, has a male protagonist who finds his fulfillment and doom in World War I; when Claude Wheeler is fascinated by a glamorous young aviator with a scar, he seems like Faulkner's Julian Lowe, and when, after an accident, he spends his convalescence talking about his unhappiness to the young woman who visits him faithfully and whom he eventually marries, he anticipates young Bayard Sartoris of *Flags in the Dust*. In 1923 Cather published *A Lost Lady*, which seems in some respects a crucial predecessor of Faulkner's *The Sound and the Fury*, for the central female character is much like Caddy Compson in being an object of male covetousness and lust. At once admirably independent and distressingly vulnerable, Marian Forrester fascinates the men around her, but there is something elusive and mysterious about her to the young man through whose sensibility much of the story is filtered and who is in some ways like a brother to her; she is also, like Caddy, repeatedly invoked in olfactory images, including that of honeysuckle. If Faulkner was unaware of *A Lost Lady* when he began *The Sound and the Fury* four years later, then his thinking was certainly moving in directions parallel to Cather's. Her 1925 novel, *The Professor's House*, though less distinctly related to a key Faulkner work, still makes use of some devices that might well have influenced him. These include the use of the empty center, a character with whom others are preoccupied, but who is absent or inaccessible, a technique Faulkner began employing in the novel he published the very next year; the contrapuntal juxtaposition of two contrasting stories, the professor's and Tom Outland's, like that of the opposing narratives in *The Wild Palms;* and the use of Outland's diary, which constitutes for its interpreter both an evocative description of the past and the revelation of some unsettling truths, like the McCaslin ledgers in *Go Down, Moses*. By the end of *The Professor's House*, its protagonist seems like Ike McCaslin at the close of Faulkner's 1942 novel, defeated, disillusioned, and all too ready for death.

Willa Cather was the American woman writer who undoubtedly had the most to teach the young William Faulkner, for her work was not only structurally innovative and stylistically effective, but offered him striking depictions of characters, events, and landscapes which he could put into that "lumber room" of the imagination about which he often spoke and from which he perpetually drew in differing ways. But these other, admittedly lesser, female figures may also have been tutelary in significant ways, showing him how to respond to a regional past with both sympathy and ironic detachment, how to depict simple folk with fairness and compassion, how to carry on technical experiments over the course of a long career, how to write poetic prose, or even just how to create one comically terrifying character. What seems unfortunate is that Faulkner apparently resisted some of the other important lessons to be found in fiction by women, which is, even in those long-ago prefeminist days, rich with female characters attempting to be socially and economically autonomous, refusing to accept proscriptions on their behavior or sexual activity, running farms and making love and often criticizing the males who try to dominate them. These writers did, however, expose Faulkner to the full range of female sensibility, creating large galleries of memorable women characters whom he could invoke during the writing process. That he did less of it than he might is in some respects a loss, for the splendor of his genius might have created Isabel Archers and Molly Blooms as well as Quentin Compsons and Ike McCaslins. Nevertheless, the all-important ghosts and vestiges of his female predecessors are there to be seen, and the Faulknerian metatext is inhabited visibly and irrefutably by his American foremothers. If all of an individual writer's literary ancestors potentially influence what we might call, in a paraphrase of Shelley, that writer's Great Work continually in progress, we must recognize, despite

Faulkner's reluctance to acknowledge the crucial female dimension of his own heritage, the potent, though tantalizingly incomplete, contributions of American women novelists to his
artistic development.

NOTES

1. Sandra M. Gilbert and Susan Gubar, *The Madwoman in the Attic* (New Haven: Yale University Press, 1979), 46.

2. Quoted in ibid., 46.

3. Michael Millgate, "Faulkner's Masters," *Tulane Studies in English*, 23 (1978), 143–55.

4. Judith Bryant Wittenberg, "Faulkner and Eugene O'Neill," *Mississippi Quarterly*, 23 (Summer 1980), 327–41.

5. *Lion in the Garden: Interviews with William Faulkner, 1926–1962*, ed. James B. Meriwether and Michael Millgate (New York: Random House, 1968), 58.

6. Harold Bloom, *The Anxiety of Influence* (New York: Oxford University Press, 1973), 11, 26.

7. John T. Irwin, *Doubling and Incest/Repetition and Revenge* (Baltimore: Johns Hopkins University Press, 1975), 159, 163.

8. Gilbert and Gubar, *Madwoman in the Attic*, 9, 50, and passim.

9. Nancy Chodorow, *The Reproduction of Mothering* (Berkeley: University of California Press, 1978), 82, 174, 181.

10. Anne Robinson Taylor, *Male Novelists and Their Female Voices* (Troy, N.Y.: Whitston, 1981), 5.

11. Ellen Douglas, "Faulkner's Women," in *"A Cosmos of My Own,"* ed. Doreen Fowler and Ann J. Abadie (Jackson: University Press of Mississippi, 1981), 159.

12. Bertram Wyatt-Brown, *Southern Honor: Ethics and Behavior in the Old South* (New York: Oxford University Press, 1982), chaps. 6, 7, and passim.

13. Judith L. Sensibar, *The Origins of Faulkner's Art* (Austin: University of Texas Press, 1984), 42.

14. Ellen Glasgow, *The Sheltered Life* (New York: Hill and Wang, 1979), 102.

15. Lewis Baker, *The Percys of Mississippi* (Baton Rouge: Louisiana State University Press, 1983), chap. 4 and passim.

16. Louis D. Rubin, "William Faulkner: The Discovery of a Man's Vocation," in *Faulkner: Fifty Years After the Marble Faun*, ed. George H. Wolfe (University, Ala.: University of Alabama Press, 1976), 61.

17. *William Faulkner: Early Prose and Poetry*, comp. Carvel Collins (Boston: Little, Brown, 1962), 117.

18. Michael Grimwood, "The Femininity of Faulkner's Literary Vocation," Talk at Modern Language Association, December 1985.

19. Darden Asbury Pyron, *Recasting: "Gone with the Wind" in American Culture* (Miami: University Presses of Florida, 1983), 8.

20. *Selected Letters of William Faulkner*, ed. Joseph Blotner (New York: Random House, 1977), 32.

21. *Lion in the Garden*, 49.

22. *Faulkner in the University*, ed. Frederick L. Gwynn and Joseph L. Blotner (Charlottesville: University of Virginia Press, 1959), 202.

23. Letter from Joan Williams to Judith Bryant Wittenberg, June 25, 1985.

24. *William Faulkner's Library—A Catalogue*, comp. Joseph Blotner (Charlottesville: University Press of Virginia, 1964), 60, 61, 66, 71.

25. Joseph Blotner, *Faulkner: A Biography* (New York: Random House, 1974), 463; Anita Brookner, introduction to Margaret Kennedy, *The Constant Nymph* (Garden City, N.Y.: Doubleday and Co., 1984), xi.

26. Kennedy, *The Constant Nymph*, 24, 67, 158.

27. Millgate, "Faulkner's Masters," 145–46.

28. *William Faulkner's Library—A Catalogue*, 124.

29. Ibid., 127, 59.

30. William Faulkner, *Intruder in the Dust* (New York: Random House, 1948), 195; William Faulkner, *The Town* (New York: Random House, 1957), 317; *Faulkner in the University*, 201.

31. *Selected Letters of William Faulkner*, 32.

32. *Faulkner in the University*, 193.

33. Robert Penn Warren and William H. Slavick, introductions to Elizabeth Madox Roberts, *The Time of Man* (Lexington: University Press of Kentucky, 1982), xxxii, xviii; Millgate, "Faulkner's Masters," 149; Frederick W. P. McDowell, preface to *Elizabeth Madox Roberts* (New York: Twayne, 1963), n.p.

34. *William Faulkner's Library—A Catalogue*, 49.

35. McDowell, *Elizabeth Madox Roberts*, 26.

36. Faulkner in the University, 74.

37. Elizabeth Madox Roberts, *The Time of Man* (New York: Viking, 1926), 5, 381.

38. Evelyn Scott, "On William Faulkner's *The Sound and the Fury*," reprinted in *Twentieth-Century Interpretations* of "*The Sound and the Fury*," ed. Michael H. Cowan (Englewood Cliffs, N.J.: Prentice-Hall, 1968), 25, 26.

39. Ibid., 29; William Faulkner, Appendix to *The Sound and the Fury* (New York: Random House, 1946), 16.

40. Scott, "On William Faulkner's *The Sound and the Fury*," 26.

41. See Evelyn Scott, *The Wave* (New York: Jonathan Cape and Harrison Smith, 1929), 48–50.

42. E. Stanly Godbold, Jr., *Ellen Glasgow and the Woman Within* (Baton Rouge: Louisiana State University Press, 1972), 66.

43. *Selected Letters of William Faulkner*, 51.

44. Blotner, *Faulkner: A Biography*, 714, 711.

45. Ibid., 713.

46. Godbold, *Ellen Glasgow and the Woman Within*, 224, 226.

47. Ibid., 68–69.

48. Ellen Glasgow, *The Builders* (Garden City, N.Y.: Doubleday, Page, 1919), 212.

49. William Faulkner, *Light in August* (New York: Harrison Smith and Robert Haas, 1932), 61, 299.

50. Ellen Glasgow, *Barren Ground* [1925] (New York: Modern Library, 1933), 369.

51. Glasgow, *The Sheltered Life*, xviii, 279.

52. *Selected Letters of William Faulkner*, 32.

53. Blotner, *Faulkner: A Biography*, 742.

54. *Lion in the Garden*, 53.

55. *Faulkner: A Comprehensive Guide to the Brodsky Collection*, vol. 2: *The Letters*, ed. Louis Daniel Brodsky and Robert W. Hamblin (Jackson: University Press of Mississippi, 1984), 57.

56. *Lion in the Garden*, 168.

57. *Faulkner in the University*, 202.

58. *William Faulkner's Library—A Catalogue*, 22, 124.

59. Willa Cather, *O Pioneers!* (Boston: Houghton Mifflin, 1913), 140.

60. Willa Cather, *My Antonia* (Boston: Houghton Mifflin, 1954), 83.

61. Ibid., 11.

Faulkner and Women

Toni Morrison

I'm ambivalent about what I'm about to do. On the one hand, I want to do what every writer wants to do, which is to explain everything to the reader first so that, when you read it, there will be no problems. My other inclination is to run out here and read it; then run off so that there would be no necessity to frame it. I have read from this manuscript three or four times before, and each time I learned something in the process of reading it, which was never true with any other book that I wrote. And so when I was invited to come to Oxford and speak to this conference about some aspect of "Faulkner and Women," I declined, saying that I really couldn't concentrate enough to collect remarks on "Faulkner and Women" because I was deeply involved in writing a book myself and I didn't want any distractions whatsoever. And then very nicely the conference directors invited me to read from this manuscript that had me so obsessed, so that I could both attend the conference and associate myself in some real way with the Center for the Study of Southern Culture and also visit Mississippi and "spend the night," as they say. So, on the one hand, I apologize for reading something that is not finished but is in process; but this was a way to satisfy my eagerness to visit the campus of the University of Mississippi; and I hope there will be some satisfaction rippling through the audience once I have finished. My other hesitation is simply because some of what I read may not appear in print, as a developing manuscript is constantly changing. Before reading to a group gathered to discuss "Faulkner and Women," I would also like to add that in 1956 I spent a great deal of time thinking about Mr. Faulkner because he was the subject of a thesis that I wrote at Cornell. Such an exhaustive treatment of an author makes it impossible for a writer to go back to that author for sometime afterwards until the energy has dissipated itself in some other form. But I have to say, even before I begin to read, that there was for me not only an academic interest in Faulkner, but in a very, very personal way, in a very personal way as a reader, William Faulkner had an enormous effect on me, an enormous effect.

The title of the book is *Beloved*, and this is the way it begins:. . . .

(The author read from her work-in-progress and then answered questions from the audience.)

MORRISON: I am interested in answering questions from those of you who may have them. And if you'll stand up and let me identify you before you ask a question, I'll do the best I can.

QUESTION: Ms. Morrison, you mentioned that you wrote a thesis on Faulkner. What effect did Faulkner have on your literary career?

MORRISON: Well, I'm not sure that he had any effect on my work. I am typical, I think, of all writers who are convinced that they are wholly original and that if they recognized an influence they would abandon it as quickly as possible. But as a reader in the '50s and later, of course (I said 1956 because that's when I was working on a thesis that had to do with him), I was concentrating on Faulkner. I don't think that my response was any different from any other student at that time, inasmuch as there was in Faulkner this power and courage—the courage of a writer, a special kind of courage. My reasons, I think, for being interested and deeply moved by all his subjects had something to do with my desire to find out something about this country and that artistic articulation of its past that was not available in history, which is what art and fiction can do but sometimes history refuses to do. I suppose history can humanize the past also, but it frequently refuses to do so for perfectly logically good reasons.

But there was an articulate investigation of an era that one or two authors provided and Faulkner was certainly at the apex of that investigation. And there was something else about Faulkner which I can only call "gaze." He had a gaze that was different. It appeared, at that time, to be similar to a look, even a sort of staring, a refusal-to-look-away approach in his writing that I found admirable. At that time, in the '50s or the '60s, it never crossed my mind to write books. But then I did it, and I was very surprised myself that I was doing it, and I knew that I was doing it for some reasons that are not writerly ones. I don't really find strong connections between my work and Faulkner's. In an extraordinary kind of memorable way there are literary watersheds in one's life. In mine, there are four or five, and I hope they are all ones that meet everybody's criteria of who should be read, but some of them don't. Some books are just awful in terms of technique but nevertheless they are terrific: they are too good to be correct. With Faulkner there was always something to surface. Besides, he could infuriate you in such wonderful ways. It wasn't just complete delight—there was also that other quality that is just as important as devotion: outrage. The point is that with Faulkner one was never indifferent.

QUESTION: Ms. Morrison, would you talk a little bit about the creation of your character Sula?
MORRISON: She came as many characters do—all of them don't— rather full-fleshed and complete almost immediately, including her name. I felt this enormous intimacy. I mean, I knew exactly who she was, but I had trouble trying to make her. I mean, I felt troubled trying to make her into the kind of person that would upset everybody, the kind of person that sets your teeth on edge; and yet not to make her so repulsive that you could not find her attractive at the same time—a nature that was seductive but offputting. And playing back and forth with that was difficult for me because I wanted to describe the qualities of certain personalities that can be exploited by conventional people. The outlaw and the adventuress, not in the sense of somebody going out to

find a fortune, but in the way a woman is an adventuress: which has to do with her imagination. And people such as those are always memorable and generally attractive. But she's troublesome. And, by the time I finished the book, *Sula*, I missed her. I know the feeling of missing characters who are in fact, by that time, much more real than real people.

QUESTION: Ms. Morrison, you said earlier that reading a work-in-progress is helpful to you as a writer. Could you explain how reading helps you?

MORRISON: This whole business of reading my own manuscript for information is quite new for me. As I write I don't imagine a reader or listener, ever. I am the reader and the listener myself, and I think I am an excellent reader. I read very well. I mean I really know what's going on. The problem in the beginning was to be as good a writer as I was a reader. But I have to assume that I not only write books, I read them. And I don't mean I look to see what I have written; I mean I can maintain the distance between myself the writer and what is on the page. Some people have it, and some people have to learn it. And some people don't have it; you can tell because if they had read their work, they never would have written it that way. The process is revision. It's a long sort of reading process, and I have to assume that I am also this very critical, very fastidious and not-easily-taken-in-reader who is smart enough to participate in the text a lot. I don't like to read books when all the work is done and there's no place for me there. So the effort is to write so that there is something that's going on between myself and myself—myself as writer and myself as reader. Now, in some instances, I feel content in doing certain kinds of books without reading them to an audience. But there are others where I have felt—this one in particular because it's different—that what I, as a reader, am feeling is not enough, and I needed a wider slice, so to speak, because the possibilities are infinite. I'm not interested in anybody's help in writing technique—not that. I'm just talking about shades of meaning, not the score but the emphasis here and there. It's that kind of thing that I want to discover, whether or not my ear on this book is as reliable as I have always believed it to be with the others. Therefore, I agree quickly to reading portions of this manuscript. Every other book I wrote I didn't even negotiate a contract until it was almost finished because I didn't want the feeling that it belonged to somebody else. For this book I negotiated a contract at a very early stage. So, I think, probably some of the business of reading is a sort of repossession from the publisher. It has to be mine, and I have to be willing to not do it or burn it, or do it, as the case might be. But I do assume that I am the reader, and, in the past, when I was in doubt, if I had some problems, the people I would call on to help me to verify some phrase or some word or something would be the people in the book. I mean I would just conjure them up and ask them, you know, about one thing or another. And they are usually very cooperative if they are fully realized and if you know their name. And if you don't know their names, they don't talk much.

QUESTION: Ms. Morrison, could you discuss the use of myth and folklore in your fiction?

MORRISON: This is not going to sound right, but I have to say it anyway. There is infinitely more past than there is future. Maybe not in chronological time, but in terms of data there certainly is. So in each step back there is another world, and another world. The past in infinite. I don't know if the future is, but I know the past is. The legends—so many of them—are not just about the past. They also indicate how to function in contemporary times and they hint about the future. So that for me they were not ever simple, never simple. I try to incorporate those mythic charac-teristics which for me are very strong characteristics of black art everywhere, whether it was in music or stories or paintings or what have you. It just seemed to me that those characteristics ought to be incorporated into black literature if it was to remain that. It wasn't enough just to write about black people, because anybody can do that. But it was important to me as a writer to try to make the work irrevocably black. It required me to use the folklore as points of departure—as, for example in this book, *Beloved,* which started with a story about a slave, Margaret Garner, who had been caught with her children shortly after she escaped from a farm. And rather than subject them to what was an unlivable and unbearable life, she killed them or tried to. She didn't succeed, and abolitionists made a great deal out of her case. That story, with some other things, had been nagging me for a long, long time. Can you imagine a slave woman who does not own her children? Who cares enough to kill them? Can you imagine the daring and also the recriminations and the self-punishment and the sabotage, self-sabotage, in which one loves so much that you cannot bear to have the thing you love sullied? It is better for it to die than to be sullied. Because that is you. That's the best part of you, and that was the best part of her. So it was such a serious matter that she would rather they not exist. And she was the one to make that reclamation. That's a very small part of what this is about, but that's what was in my brain pan—as they say—when I got started. So that in this instance, I began with historical fact and incorporated it into myth instead of the other way around.

QUESTION: Ms. Morrison, earlier you said you had no intention of becoming a writer when you started to write. Could you explain what you meant by this?

MORRISON: I was in a place where I didn't belong, and I wasn't going to be there very long so I didn't want to make it any nicer than it was. And I didn't want to meet anybody, and I didn't like anybody and they didn't like me either; and that was fine with me; and I was lonely. I was miserable. My children were small, and so I wrote this story. I had written a little story before, in the time I could spare to work it up in the evening. (You know children go to bed, if you train them, at seven. Wake up at four but go to bed at seven.) And so after I put them to bed, I would write, and I liked it. I liked thinking about it. I liked making that kind of order out of something that was disorderly in my mind.

And also I sensed that there was an enormous indifference to these people, to me, to you, to black girls. It was as if these people had no life, no existence in anybody's mind at all except peripherally. And when I got into it, it just seemed like writing was absolutely the most important thing in the world. I took forever to write that first book: almost five years for just a little book. Because I liked doing it so much, I would just do a little bit, you know, and think about that. I was a textbook editor at that time. I was not even trying to be a writer, and I didn't let anybody know that I was writing this book because I thought they would fire me, which they would have. Maybe not right away, but they didn't want me to do that. They felt betrayed anyway. If you're an editor, what you're supposed to do is acquire books, not produce them. There is a light adversarial relationship between publishers and authors which I think probably works effectively. But that's why I was very quiet about writing. I don't know what made me write it. I think I just wanted to finish the story so that I could have a good time reading it. But the process was what made me think that I should do it again, and I knew that that was the way I wanted to live. I felt very coherent when I was writing that book. But I still didn't call myself a writer. And it was only with my third book, *Song of Solomon*, that I finally said—not at my own initiative I'm embarrassed to tell you but at somebody else's initiative—"this is what I do." I had written three books. It was only after I finished *Song of Solomon* that I thought, "maybe this is what I do *only*." Because before that I always said that I was an editor *who* also wrote books or a teacher *who* also wrote. I never said I was a writer. Never. And it's not only because of all the things you might think. It's also because most writers really and truly have to give themselves permission to win. That's very difficult, particularly for women. You have to give yourself permission, even when you're doing it. Writing everyday, sending books off, you still have to give yourself permission. I know writers whose mothers are writers, who still had to go through a long process with somebody else—a man or editor or friend or something—to

finally reach a point where they could say "it's all right. It's okay."
The community says it's okay. Your husband says it's okay. Your
children say it's okay. Your mother says it's okay. Eventually
everybody says it's okay, and then you have all the okays. It
happened to me: even I found a moment after I'd written the
third book when I could actually say it. So you go through
passport and customs and somebody asks, "what do you do?"
And you print it out:

W R I T E.

Contributors

André Bleikasten is Professor of English at the University of Strasbourg, France. He has published numerous works on Faulkner in French and in English. Among the latter are *Faulkner's "As I Lay Dying," "The Most Splendid Failure": Faulkner's "The Sound and the Fury," William Faulkner's "The Sound and the Fury": A Critical Casebook*, and an essay in *Faulkner and Idealism: Perspectives from Paris*. Professor Bleikasten is, along with François Pitavy, in charge of the continuation of the French edition of Faulkner in the Gallimard Pléiade series.

Joseph Blotner, Professor of English at the University of Michigan, has lectured extensively in the United States and Europe on American literature and particularly on the work of William Faulkner. Among his books are *Faulkner in the University*, edited with F. L. Gwynn; *William Faulkner's Library: A Catalogue; Faulkner: A Biography*, published in two volumes in 1974 and in a revised, one-volume edition in 1984; *Selected Letters of William Faulkner;* and *Uncollected Stories of William Faulkner*. Professor Blotner is a member of the editorial board for *The Faulkner Journal*, serves as consulting editor for Faulkner studies published by University Microfilms International Research Press, and is editing Faulkner works for Random House, Garland Publishers, and the Library of America.

Sergei Chakovsky is a research fellow at the A. M. Gorky Institute of World Literature in Moscow. He specializes in Faulkner studies as well as literary theory and the depiction of blacks in American literature. As part of a joint USA–USSR project on William Faulkner, he has lectured at three Faulkner and Yoknapatawpha Conferences and presented a paper at a Faulkner symposium held in Moscow.

Myriam Díaz-Diocaretz is a Chilean poet, translator, and critic. A researcher at the University of Utrecht since 1983, she was Fulbright Scholar-in-Residence at the University of Mississippi in the spring of 1985. Her work on North American literature, black poetry, women's writing, semiotics, and translation theory has been published in Latin America, the United States, and Europe. Her books include *Que no se pueden decir* (poetry), *The Transforming Power of Language: The Poetry of Adrienne Rich* (criticism), *Adrienne Rich: Antología poética* (translation), *Translating Poetic Discourse: Questions on Feminist Strategies in Adrienne Rich* (theory), and *Women, Feminist Identity, and Society in the 1980s* (anthology).

John N. Duvall is completing a Ph.D. degree in English and Certification in Interpretive Theory at the University of Illinois at Urbana-Champaign. He chaired the section "Faulkner's Use of the Past: Myth and Memory" at the Tenth Annual Conference on Twentieth-Century Literature and presented "A Semiotic Approach to Faulkner's Ideology" at the Ninth Annual Meeting of the Semiotic Society of America. His publications include an essay on Faulkner's "The Old People" in *College Literature* and a collaborative article in *Women's Studies International Forum*.

Doreen Fowler is an associate professor of English at the University of Mississippi. She has coedited six volumes of proceedings of the Faulkner and Yoknapatawpha Conference and has published articles on Faulkner and other writers in such journals as *American Literature, Journal of Modern Literature, Critique, Studies in the Novel, Arizona Quarterly, Renascence,* the *Explicator, Tennessee Studies in Literature,* and others. Her book, *Faulkner's Changing Vision: From Outrage to Affirmation,* was published in 1983 by University Microfilms International Research Press.

Winifred L. Frazer received the Ph.D. degree from the University of Florida, where she taught for twenty-six years. During this time she participated in discussions and presented papers at meetings of the Modern Language Association and other professional organizations, wrote the analytical "Drama" section for *American Literary Scholarship* from 1976 through 1980, and was president of the Eugene O'Neill Society from 1979 to 1981. Now Professor Emeritus, she is the author of *The Theme of Loneliness in Modern American Drama*, two monographs on *The Iceman Cometh*, the critical biography *Mable Dodge Luhan*, and numerous articles, including studies of William Faulkner, Eudora Welty, and Tennessee Williams.

Mimi R. Gladstein received the Ph.D. degree from the University of New Mexico in 1973 and is now Associate Professor of English at the University of Texas at El Paso. She is the author of *The Ayn Rand Companion; The Indestructible Woman in the Works of Faulkner, Hemingway, and Steinbeck;* and numerous essays, articles, and book reviews. Her work has appeared in *College English, Steinbeck Quarterly, Steinbeck's Women: Essays in Criticism, American Women Writers: A Critical Reference Guide*, and many other journals and collections.

Ilse Dusoir Lind is Professor of English at New York University. She has chaired special sessions on Faulkner at national meetings of the Modern Language Association, presented papers on his works at symposia in the Soviet Union and Japan, and lectured at four Faulkner and Yoknapatawpha Conferences. Her publications include "The Teachable Faulkner," "The Design and Meaning of *Absalom, Absalom!*," "Faulkner and Racism," and "Faulkner's *Mosquitoes:* A New Reading."

Robert R. Moore holds M.A. and Ph.D. degrees from the University of Virginia. Since 1978 he has taught at the State University of New York at Oswego, where he directs the composition program and teaches a variety of courses, including "Women and Men: Images and Reality." At regional meetings of the Modern Language Association he has presented papers on "Faulkner's *Sanctuary:* Radical Evil and Religious Vision" and "The Consequences of Belief: Faulkner and Southern Protestantism."

Toni Morrison taught at Texas Southern University and at

Howard University, her alma mater, before becoming an editor at Random House in 1965. During her two decades there she helped stimulate a cultural awakening in America by publishing Toni Cade Bambara, Gayl Jones, Angela Davis, and numerous other black writers, male as well as female. While at Random House Ms. Morrison also taught, first at Yale University and then at Bard College, gave numerous public lectures, was an active member of the National Council on the Arts, and established herself as a major writer with her novels *The Bluest Eye, Sula, Song of Solomon,* and *Tar Baby.* Ms. Morrison has also published a number of articles, including "What Black Woman Thinks About Women's Lib," "Behind the Making of the Black Book," and "Rediscovering Black History." She currently holds the Schweitzer Chair at the State University of New York at Albany.

Alice Hall Petry is the author of approximately sixty essays, notes, book chapters, reference-work entries, and reviews. Her work appears in *American Literature, Journal of Modern Literature, Southern Literary Journal, Southern Quarterly, Studies in Short Fiction,* and numerous other journals. She has taught at the Rhode Island School of Design since receiving her Ph.D. from Brown University in 1979. As a Fulbright scholar for 1985–86, she taught at the Federal University of Paraná at Curitiba, Brazil.

Noel Polk is Professor of English at the University of Southern Mississippi. He was Fulbright Lecturer at the University of Strasbourg in 1982–83 and has presented papers at Faulkner meetings in the United States, France, Japan, and the Soviet Union. His publications include *Faulkner's "Requiem for a Nun": A Critical Study, William Faulkner: "The Marionettes," "Requiem for a Nun": A Concordance to the Novel, "Sanctuary": The Original Text,* and *An Editorial Handbook to Faulkner's "The Sound and the Fury."* Professor Polk recently prepared new editions of *Sanctuary* and *The Sound and the Fury* for Random House and is coediting four Faulkner novels for the Library of America. He is also series editor of the Garland Faulkner Casebooks, a member of the editorial team for Garland's William Faulkner Manuscripts project, and on the editorial board of *The Faulkner Journal*.

Alexandre Vashchenko, a research fellow at the A. M. Gorky Institute of World Literature in Moscow, has published works examining the literature of the American West and the mythology of North American Indians. As a participant in a project sponsored by the American Council of Learned Societies-USSR Academy of Sciences Commission on the Humanities and Social Sciences, he lectured at the 1982 and 1985 Faulkner and Yoknapatawpha Conferences and delivered a paper at the 1984 Soviet symposium on "Faulkner and the American South."

Philip M. Weinstein is Professor and Chair of English at Swarthmore College. He is the author of *Henry James and the Requirements of the Imagination, The Semantics of Desire: Changing Models of Identity from Dickens to Joyce,* and several journal articles, among them "Caddy Disparue: Exploring the Episode Common to Proust and Faulkner" and "Precarious Sanctuaries: Protection and Exposure in Faulkner's Fiction." Professor Weinstein has received fellowships from the Woodrow Wilson Foundation, the National Endowment for the Humanities, and other agencies.

Judith Bryant Wittenberg is Associate Professor of English at Simmons College in Boston. Her publications include *Faulkner: The Transfiguration of Biography,* numerous journal articles and book reviews, and "William Faulkner: A Feminist Consideration" in the 1982 collection *American Novelists Revisited: Essays in Feminist Criticism.* In April 1985 at Ito, Japan, Professor Wittenberg discussed *The Reivers* during an international symposium on "Faulkner After the Nobel Prize."

Index